Citizenship and Education in Twenty-eight Countries

International Coordinating Center
Rainer Lehmann, International Coordinator
Wolfram Schulz, Associate International Coordinator
Humboldt University of Berlin, Germany

International Steering Committee
Judith Torney-Purta, Chair
University of Maryland at College Park, USA

Barbara Fratczak-Rudnicka, *Warsaw University, Poland*
Georgia Kontogiannopoulou-Polydorides, *University of Athens, Greece*
Bruno Losito, *National Institute for the Evaluation of the Education System, Italy*
Barbara Malak-Minkiewicz, *IEA Secretariat, The Netherlands.*
Ingrid Munck, *Swedish National Agency for Administrative Development, Sweden*
Hans Oswald, *Potsdam University, Germany*
John Schwille, *Michigan State University, USA*
Gita Steiner-Khamsi, *Teachers College, Columbia University, New York, USA*
Lee Wing On, *Hong Kong Institute of Education, Hong Kong (SAR)*
Ray Adams *(ex-officio), IEA Technical Executive Group*

Heinrich Mintrop, *Consultant to the Steering Committee*

Citizenship and Education in Twenty-eight Countries

Civic Knowledge and Engagement at Age Fourteen

Judith Torney-Purta, Rainer Lehmann,
Hans Oswald and Wolfram Schulz

With a chapter by Bruno Losito and
Heinrich Mintrop

The International Association for the
Evaluation of Educational Achievement

ISBN 90 5166 834 1

Copies of *Citizenship and education in twenty-eight countries* can be obtained from:
IEA Secretariat
Herengracht 487
1017 BT, Amsterdam, The Netherlands
Telephone + 31 20 625 3625
Fax + 31 20 420 7136
Email: Department@IEA.nl

Funding for the international coordination of the IEA Civic Education Study was provided by IEA, participating countries and the Deutsche Forschungsgemeinschaft (DFG or German Science Association) in a grant to the Humboldt University of Berlin. Funding for portions of the international analysis was provided by the William T. Grant Foundation of New York in a grant to the Department of Human Development at the University of Maryland in College Park. Other international funding sources are listed in the Acknowledgments. Each participating country was responsible for funding national project costs and for implementing the study in accord with international procedures and national requirements.

Produced by Eburon Publishers, Delft, Netherlands
Edited by Paula Wagemaker Editorial Services, Christchurch, New Zealand
Designed by Becky Bliss Design and Production, Wellington, New Zealand

TABLE OF CONTENTS

The International Association for the Evaluation of Educational Achievement, known as IEA, is an independent, international consortium of national research institutions and governmental research agencies, with headquarters in Amsterdam. Its primary purpose is to conduct large-scale comparative studies of educational achievement with the aim of gaining more in-depth understanding of the effects of policies and practices within and across systems of education.

FOREWORD

In 1994 the General Assembly of IEA decided to undertake a study on civic education. It was not the first time that IEA had focused on this issue. As early as 1971 it had taken its first look at civic education, in the context of the so-called Six Subject Study. But the decision, in 1994, to look again at the subject was a sound one given the huge changes by then facing many countries as a result of the events of the late 1980s and early 1990s. The considerable task of establishing or re-establishing democratic governments in a number of countries highlighted even more the need to develop citizenship and the role that educational systems could play in meeting that aim. Assessing civic education was important not only for those countries, however, but also for societies with long-established democratic traditions. In general, it could be said that changes in the political, social and educational scenes of many countries suggested the timeliness of this new study, particularly in terms of its potential to make a substantial contribution to an understanding of these changes.

The International Association for the Evaluation of Educational Achievement (IEA) was, and is, in an excellent position to make such contribution. It was founded in 1959 for the purpose of conducting comparative studies focusing on educational policies and practices in various countries and educational systems around the world. Since that time, it has completed a significant number of studies in different subjects, as varied as reading literacy, mathematics, science, pre-primary education, and information and communication technologies in education or languages, among others. With its nearly 60 member countries, its Secretariat located in Amsterdam and a number of interconnected research centres in all continents, IEA is in a very sound situation to produce cross-country comparative studies that are based on rigorously collected and analysed data.

In 1994, the IEA General Assembly approved the Civic Education Study as a two-phased project. The aim of Phase 1 was to collect extensive information describing the circumstances, content and process of civic education in participating countries. In doing this, IEA summarised what country experts considered 14-year-old students should know about a number of topics related to democratic institutions and citizenship, including elections, individual rights, national identity, political participation and respect for ethnic and political diversity.

The results of Phase 1 were presented in *Civic education across countries: Twenty-four national case studies from the IEA Civic Education Project*, a book that received wide recognition among researchers, practitioners and policy-makers. Its 24 national case studies were written mostly by National Research Coordinators, and also took into account opinions expressed by National Expert Panels.

The information collected in Phase 1 was also used for preparing Phase 2. This second part of the project consisted of a test (keyed cognitive items) and a survey (un-keyed attitudinal and behavioural items) administered in each participating country to representative samples of about 3,000 students in the modal grade for 14-year-olds. A questionnaire was also administered to civic-related teachers and to school principals. Data were collected in spring 1999 in most of the participating countries.

This current publication, *Citizenship and education in twenty-eight countries*, presents the first results of Phase 2 of the study. It follows a style similar to that traditionally used by IEA, and it complements the more qualitative approach of the first volume by reporting quantitative information from the tests, surveys and questionnaires. Together, the two publications provide a complete and remarkable picture of civic education policies, practices and results across countries in the late 1990s.

Having identified and discussed the outcomes of our respective countries in an international context, we know that the time has arrived to pay special attention to the factors that merit consideration and possible action. Wise action requires a deep knowledge of the field. The comparative view helps us set our reflections in a context that allows us to interpret and to explain. In this manner, the value of an international approach can be truly realised. It is this realisation that is exactly the kind of contribution IEA can make to the development of education and educational systems. In the end, our activities can only be justified if they contribute to the advancement of societies made up of better-developed individuals.

IEA is particularly grateful to the following organisations, which are the major contributors to the international overhead of Phase 2 of the study: the Deutsche Forschungsgemeinschaft (DFG or German Science Association) and the William T. Grant Foundation of New York. As in all IEA studies, individual participating countries also provided funding.

Citizenship and education in twenty-eight countries represents the results of initiatives developed by the International Steering Committee of the study and by the National Research Coordinators and National Experts. Special thanks should necessarily go to the International Steering Committee and the International Coordinators, Professor Judith Torney-Purta (University of Maryland) and Professor Rainer Lehmann (Humboldt Universität zu Berlin). As the leaders of this study, they have provided its special spirit, and so deserve our recognition and thanks.

Alejandro Tiana
CHAIR OF IEA

CHAPTER 1

Introduction to the IEA Civic Education Study

During a single decade, beginning in the late 1980s, initiatives toward democratic reform took place across the world. New constitutional regimes came into being. In countries that were establishing or re-establishing democracies after a period of non-democratic rule, the general public as well as leaders realized that major changes in formal and informal civic education were required to prepare young people for this new social, political and economic order. What those changes should be and how they should be initiated was not clear, however.

During the same period, many well-established democracies recognized that their own methods of preparing young people for citizenship were far from ideal. In some countries, young adults were unlikely to vote or participate in other conventional political activities. Youth demonstrated gaps both in their understanding of the pivotal ideas of democracy and in their knowledge of existing political structures. Few seemed to have the skills to analyze political issues presented in the newspaper or on television news (if they paid attention to these media at all). In some countries, 'civil society', the web of community groups and private associations that operates independently from government and market sectors, seemed to be drawing in few youth.

These issues called for a rethinking of civic education, a challenge that many countries began to face during the 1990s. The home, school, community, peer group and mass media remained important considerations, but there were also new factors. A global youth culture was intensifying in its importance and nurturing common aspirations for freedom along with shared consumer tastes. Environmental organizations and human rights groups often involved youth on an equal footing with adults and seemed poised to replace more hierarchically organized political groups such as political parties. An enhanced emphasis on individual choice challenged long-standing views of youth as passive recipients of lessons from their elders. Young people could be seen as active constructors of their own ideas, as people whose everyday experiences in their homes, schools and communities influenced their sense of citizenship.

In light of these factors, questions were asked regarding the direction that should be taken in order to enhance the contribution of schools to citizenship. Should the emphasis be on teaching factual information about the country and its structure of government? Should it be instead on making young people aware of political issues or interested in news provided by the mass media? Should they be encouraged to join explicitly political organizations, such as parties? Or should the emphasis be on providing opportunities for involvement in environmental organizations, or groups providing assistance to the community, or school councils? And how could community support be gained for programs that would provide more rigorous study of citizenship within schools and more opportunities for the practice of civic education outside schools? These questions were faced by countries where schools offered courses labeled civic education as well as by countries where civic-relevant material was embedded in history courses or spread throughout the curriculum.

No single piece of research could be expected to fully answer questions such as these. However, it was clear that rigorous cross-national research in civic education could play a role in providing an empirical foundation for policy-makers, those who design curricula and those who prepare educators, as well as for teachers or youth workers and the public.

Educational policy-makers in this area often operate with many aspirations but little up-to-date information about civic knowledge, attitudes and behavior in their own countries. On a cross-national basis, where the experience of other countries might provide a rich set of possibilities and comparisons, data were even more limited. The International Association for the Evaluation of Educational Achievement (IEA) Civic Education Study was designed to address this gap and to create the possibility of a rigorous data-based approach to a number of questions with implications for policy and educational practice. IEA has served as a coordinating organization for comparative research in various school subject areas since the 1960s. The best-known IEA study is TIMSS (the Third International Mathematics and Science Study), but over the years, other areas, including reading literacy and civic education, have been surveyed.

Specifically, what can a cross-national study contribute to the educational debate? It can document similarities and differences in student outcomes, and also in the organization and content of programs and practices across the world. Another contribution of well-designed cross-national research is that it can show connections between practices or policies and the achievement of certain goals for civic education in different nations. It can also foster awareness of the importance of education for citizenship in its many forms.

The goal of the IEA Civic Education Study is to identify and examine in a comparative framework the ways in which young people are prepared to undertake their role as citizens in democracies. One focus of the study is the school. This is not limited to the formal curriculum in any particular school course, but includes several subject areas across the curriculum. Opportunities for discussion in the classroom and participation in the school are important, as are textbooks and curriculum. A second focus is on opportunities for civic participation outside the school, especially in the community.

A primary purpose is to obtain a picture of how young people are initiated into the political communities of which they are members, including in- and out-of-school experience. The study concentrates on political processes and institutions. But the concept 'political' is used in a fairly broad sense and is not limited to formal political organizations or legislative structures.

The remainder of this chapter sets the IEA Civic Education Study within several frameworks:

1. the history and structure of IEA (the sponsoring organization) and the participating countries;

2. the context of its two-phased design;

3. the context of existing theoretical and research frameworks; and

4. the structure of a set of policy questions.

THE STUDY WITHIN THE CONTEXT OF IEA AND THE PARTICIPATING COUNTRIES

The Organization of the Study by IEA

Responding to the expressed need of many countries for empirical data as they began to rethink their civic education programs in the early 1990s, the International Association for the Evaluation of Educational Achievement decided to mount a cross-national study of civic education. A two-phase study was designed. The first phase would consist of qualitative case studies that would examine the contexts and meaning of civic education in different countries and provide background for the development of the instruments to be administered to students and teachers. The second phase would consist of a test of civic knowledge and a survey of civic engagement for statistical analysis. It was expected that the project would complete its testing of the 'standard population' of 14-year-olds before the end of the 20th century and release an international report early in the 21st. It was also expected that the testing of an older population would be completed in 2000 in a smaller number of countries and that the findings would be reported approximately one year after the report on the standard population.

In 1971, the IEA conducted a civic education survey that employed nationally representative samples of three age groups in the Federal Republic of Germany, Finland, Ireland, Israel, Italy, the Netherlands, New Zealand, Sweden and the United States (Torney, Oppenheim & Farnen, 1975). About 30,000 students responded to instruments measuring knowledge and attitudes, while 5,000 teachers and 1,300 principals and headmasters described pedagogy and the characteristics of schools. The instrument included a test of civic knowledge, measures of support for democratic values (including tolerance and support for women's political rights), support for the national and local government, and participation in political activities. No country's 14-year-olds achieved high scores on all of these factors. There were substantial gender differences, with males scoring higher on civic knowledge and on participation in political discussion, and females scoring higher on support for democratic values. Another major finding from this study was that stress on rote learning and on patriotic ritual in the classroom tended to be negatively related to civic knowledge and democratic attitudes, while the opportunity to express an opinion in class had a positive impact. The socioeconomic status of the family and the type of school were statistically controlled in these analyses, and the predictors of success were similar within each of the nine countries. As interesting as these findings were, the intervening 20 years had seen many changes in schools and political systems, thereby raising new issues and intensifying concern about old ones.

In 1994, the governing body of IEA, its General Assembly, voted to undertake the current Civic Education Study because of interest among its diverse member countries, many of which were experiencing political, economic and social transitions. An International Steering Committee to guide the research and an International Coordinating Center to coordinate its day-to-day operations were appointed. The international oversight and coordination of this study has been funded by agencies and foundations in Germany and the

United States, by the IEA organization, and by contributions from participating countries. The two senior authors of the current volume have been, respectively, the Chair of the International Steering Committee (at the University of Maryland in College Park, USA) and the International Coordinator (at the Humboldt University of Berlin, Germany). National Research Coordinators were appointed in each participating country. Their work, including data collection, has been funded by governments and foundations within each country.

Participating Countries

Twenty-eight countries accepted IEA's invitation, sent to all 51 member-countries, to participate in the test and survey reported in this volume. (Figure 1.1 lists the 28 countries.) Approximately two-thirds of the participating countries collaborated in the research from the beginning. They:

- completed case studies for Phase 1 (thus influencing the framework and item development);
- sent representatives to National Research Coordinators' meetings beginning in 1995;
- contributed items or critiqued instruments as they were being developed; and
- pre-piloted and pilot-tested the preliminary forms of the test and survey and examined the results.

The other one-third of the countries joined the study later; the last in November 1998.

The study was a massive one both in the breadth of its coverage relating to the material identified in Phase 1 and in the number of respondents (nearly 90,000).

Three aspects of the participating countries are important in terms of understanding the data collected: national demographics, characteristics of the educational system, and characteristics of the political system.

Table 1.1 presents selected demographic data from the participating countries. Both large and small countries participated in the study. On the United Nations Human Development Index, about three-quarters of the countries fall into the highly developed category and about one-quarter into the medium developed category. Population, GNP per capita and unemployment rates are also found in the table.

Table 1.2 presents some educational characteristics of participating countries. Adult literacy levels are generally high in participating countries. The table also shows that there is a great deal of variation in the number of Internet hosts per country (although these figures are changing rapidly), and it provides information about expenditures for public education.

Table 1.3 presents political characteristics of participating countries. These include the number of political parties represented in the lower house (ranging from two to 11), voter turnout at the last election for the lower house (ranging from 36 to 95 percent), and percentage of seats in the national legislature held by women (ranging from 5.6 to 42.7 percent). All participating countries can

Figure 1.1 Countries Participating in the IEA Civic Education (CivEd) Study

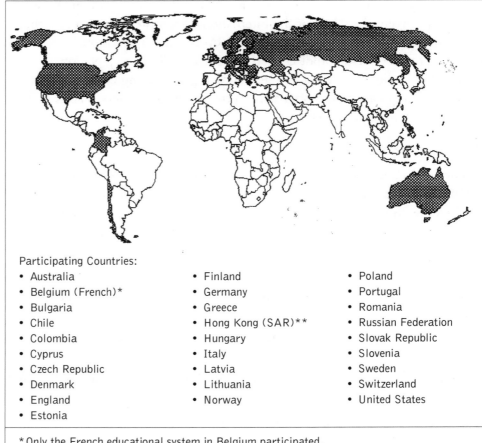

Participating Countries:

- Australia
- Belgium (French)*
- Bulgaria
- Chile
- Colombia
- Cyprus
- Czech Republic
- Denmark
- England
- Estonia

- Finland
- Germany
- Greece
- Hong Kong (SAR)**
- Hungary
- Italy
- Latvia
- Lithuania
- Norway

- Poland
- Portugal
- Romania
- Russian Federation
- Slovak Republic
- Slovenia
- Sweden
- Switzerland
- United States

*Only the French educational system in Belgium participated.
**Special Administrative Region of China.

be classified as liberal or electoral democracies, according to Diamond (1999). The age at which people can cast their first vote is 18 in all the countries in the study.

THE TWO PHASES OF THE IEA CIVIC EDUCATION STUDY

When IEA first discussed undertaking a study in this area, relatively little was known about what civic education meant in many countries. For this reason, as already mentioned, the study was designed to begin with a more qualitative case study phase and to follow it with a second phase including a test and survey more typical of IEA studies.

In Phase 1, each participating country completed a national case study of civic education, submitting four documents to an international document base:

1. A plan for Phase 1, including a summary of the current status of civic education.

2. A review of empirical literature concerning civic education and the social and political attitudes and behavior of youth.

3. Information regarding current policies, practices and issues concerning preparation for citizenship organized around a set of 18 case study framing questions.

Table 1.1 Selected Demographic Characteristics of Participating Countries

Country	Population (in millions) (1998)	Human Development Index[b] (value, rank & category) (1998)	GNP per capita (in US $)[c] (1998)	Unemployment Rate (% of labor force) (1998)
Australia	18.5	0.93 (4) High	20,640	7.6 [d]
Belgium (French)[a]	10.1	0.93 (7) High	25,380	8.8
Bulgaria	8.3	0.77 (60) Medium	1,220	12.2 [e]
Chile	14.8	0.83 (38) High	4,990	N/A
Colombia	40.8	0.76 (68) Medium	2,470	N/A
Cyprus	0.8	0.89 (22) High	11,920	N/A
Czech Republic	10.3	0.84 (34) High	5,150	6.5
Denmark	5.3	0.91 (15) High	33,040	5.1
England[a]	58.6	0.92 (10) High	21,410	6.3
Estonia	1.4	0.80 (46) High	3,360	5.1 [e]
Finland	5.2	0.92 (11) High	24,280	11.4
Germany	82.1	0.91 (14) High	26,570	9.4
Greece	10.6	0.88 (25) High	11,740	9.6 [f]
Hong Kong (SAR)	6.7	0.87 (26) High	23,660	N/A
Hungary	10.1	0.82 (43) High	4,510	8.0
Italy	57.4	0.90 (19) High	20,090	12.2
Latvia	2.4	0.77 (63) Medium	2,420	9.2 [e]
Lithuania	3.7	0.79 (52) Medium	2,540	6.9 [e]
Norway	4.4	0.93 (2) High	34,310	3.3
Poland	38.7	0.81 (44) High	3,910	10.6
Portugal	9.9	0.86 (28) High	10,670	4.9
Romania	22.5	0.77 (64) Medium	1,360	10.3 [e]
Russian Federation	147.4	0.77 (62) Medium	2,260	13.3 [e]
Slovak Republic	5.4	0.83 (40) High	3,700	15.6 [e]
Slovenia	2.0	0.86 (29) High	9,780	14.6 [e]
Sweden	8.9	0.93 (6) High	25,580	8.2
Switzerland	7.3	0.92 (13) High	39,980	4.2 [f]
United States	274.0	0.93 (3) High	29,240	4.5

a Figures for all of Belgium used for Belgium (French); figures for United Kingdom used for England.

b The Human Development Index (HDI) is a composite index that reflects three basic dimensions: (a) longevity (life expectancy at birth); (b) knowledge (adult literacy and combined gross primary, secondary and tertiary enrollment ratio); and (c) standard of living (adjusted per capita income in PPP US$). The HDI value ranges from 0 to 1. Countries are divided into categories of high, medium and low human development, and are ranked.

c Data refer to GNP calculated using the World Bank Atlas method, in current US dollars.

d Data refer to 1998-99. Source: W. McLennan, *Year book Australia*, No. 82, p. 123, Canberra, Australian Bureau of Statistics.

e Data are estimates by the UN Economic Commission for Europe, based on national statistics. They refer to registered unemployment, which is likely to bias unemployment figures downward.

f Data refer to 1997.

Sources:
All column sources are from the *Human development report 2000*, Oxford/New York, Oxford University Press (published for the United Nations Development Programme), unless noted otherwise.
Population (pp.223-26).
Human Development Index (pp.157-60).
Gross National Product per capita (GNP) (pp.202-04).
Unemployment rate (pp.241-42).

Table 1.2 Selected Educational Characteristics of Participating Countries

Country	Adult Literacy Rate (in %) (1998)	Public Education Expenditure (as % of GNP)[c] (1995-1997)	Internet Hosts (per 1000 people) (1998)
Australia	99.0 [b]	4.4 [d]	40.1
Belgium (French)[a]	99.0 [b]	3.2 [e]	20.6
Bulgaria	98.2	3.2	1.2
Chile	95.4	3.3	2.0
Colombia	91.2	4.4 [f]	0.4
Cyprus	96.6	4.5	7.9
Czech Republic	99.0 [b]	5.1	8.4
Denmark	99.0 [b]	8.1	56.3
England[a]	99.0 [b]	5.3	24.6
Estonia	99.0 [b]	7.2	16.6
Finland	99.0 [b]	7.5	89.2
Germany	99.0 [b]	4.8	17.7
Greece	96.9	3.1	4.7
Hong Kong (SAR)	92.9	2.9	12.4
Hungary	99.3	4.6	9.4
Italy	98.3	4.9	6.7
Latvia	99.8	6.3	5.8
Lithuania	99.5	5.5	2.7
Norway	99.0 [b]	7.4	71.8
Poland	99.7	4.6 [g]	3.4
Portugal	91.4	5.8	5.6
Romania	97.9	3.6	1.1
Russian Federation	99.5	3.5	1.2
Slovak Republic	99.0 [b]	5.0	4.1
Slovenia	99.6	5.7	11.5
Sweden	99.0 [b]	8.3	42.9
Switzerland	99.0 [b]	5.4	34.5
United States	99.0 [b]	5.4 [e]	112.8

a Figures for all of Belgium used for Belgium (French); figures for United Kingdom used for England.

b Human Development Report Office estimate.

c Data refer to the most recent year available during the period 1995-97.

d Source: W. McLennan, *Year book Australia*, No. 82, p.285, Canberra, Australian Bureau of Statistics.

e Data refer to a year other than those encompassed by 1995-97. Belgian data are from *Human development report 1999* and refer to years 1993-96.

f Data refer to expenditures by Ministry of Education only.

g Source: K. Konarzewski (2000) *Educational infrastructure in the first year of educational system reform in Poland*, Poland, Institute for Public Issues.

Source:

All column sources are from the *Human development report 2000*, Oxford/New York, Oxford University Press (published for the United Nations Development Programme), unless noted otherwise.

Literacy rate (pp.157-60).

Public education expenditures (pp.194-97).

Internet hosts (pp.194-97).

Table 1.3 Selected Political Characteristics of Participating Countries

Country	Seats in Parliament Held by Women as of February 2000 (% of total)	Voter Turn-out at Latest Elections[b] (%)	Political Parties Represented in Lower or Single House
Australia	25.1	95	5 [c]
Belgium (French)[a]	24.9	91	11
Bulgaria	10.8	68	5
Chile	8.9	86	7 [d]
Colombia	12.2	45	2 [d]
Cyprus	7.1	93	5
Czech Republic	13.9	74	5
Denmark	37.4	86	10
England[a]	17.1	72	10 [d]
Estonia	17.8	57	7
Finland	36.5	65	7 [d]
Germany	33.6	82	5
Greece	6.3	76	5
Hong Kong (SAR)	N/A	N/A	N/A
Hungary	8.3	56	6 [d]
Italy	10.0	83	9 [e]
Latvia	17.0	72	6
Lithuania	17.5	53	6 [d]
Norway	36.4	78	7 [d]
Poland	12.7	48	6
Portugal	18.7	62	5
Romania	5.6	76	7
Russian Federation	5.7	62	7 [d]
Slovak Republic	14.0	84	6
Slovenia	10.0	74	8
Sweden	42.7	81	7
Switzerland	22.4	43	8 [d]
United States	12.5	36	2 [d]

a Figures for all of Belgium used for Belgium (French); figures for United Kingdom used for England.

b Voter turn-out for lower or single house.

c Source: W McLennan, *Year book Australia*, No. 82, Canberra, Australian Bureau of Statistics.

d There are also independent and other parties not sufficiently represented to constitute a parliamentary group.

e Source: Italian Parliament web site.

The age of first vote for all countries is 18 years. (Source: The International Institute for Democracy and Electoral Assistance (IDEA) web site. Http://www.idea.int/turnout/>)

Source:

All column sources are from the *Human development report 2000*, Oxford/New York, Oxford University Press (published for the United Nations Development Programme), unless noted otherwise.

Seats in parliament held by women (pp.165-68).

Voter turn-out (pp.243-46)

Political parties (pp.243-46).

4. An in-depth analysis of core issues in democracy, citizenship, national identity and diversity, including an examination of textbook treatment of these issues and teaching methods.

Many countries collected data from focus groups or interviews in addition to examining printed materials as they prepared these documents. All of this material provided a view of the participating countries' intended curricula in civic education as well as extensive contextual material.

Each National Research Coordinator also prepared a chapter for *Civic education across countries: Twenty-four national case studies from the IEA Civic Education Project* (Torney-Purta, Schwille & Amadeo, 1999), the first volume arising out of Phase 1 of the study. The documents used as the basis for this publication have also been used in the preparation of the second volume from Phase 1 (Steiner-Khamsi, Torney-Purta & Schwille, forthcoming), which reports the findings of cross-national analysis of the case study material. The themes identified during the first phase are reviewed under the section on the policy questions in this chapter and in the next chapter. Chapter 2 also describes the development of the test and survey used in the second phase.

This second phase of the study, reported in this present volume, tested and surveyed nationally representative samples of 14-year-olds in 28 countries regarding their knowledge of civic-related content, their skills in understanding political communication, their concepts of and attitudes toward civics, and their participation or practices in this area. The instrument drew from material submitted during Phase 1 and benefited from the input of members of the International Steering Committee, IEA's Technical Executive Group, National Research Coordinators and National Advisory Committees throughout the five-year process of framework development, item writing, pre-piloting and piloting and final item choice.

THEORETICAL FRAMEWORKS GUIDING THE DESIGN

The National Research Coordinators at their first meeting took on the task of developing an overall model for the study. This model, described as the Octagon, graphically represents a framework for organizing the information being collected in both phases (Figure 1.2). It is a visualization of ways in which the everyday lives of young people in homes, with peers and at school serve as a 'nested' context for young people's thinking and action in the social and political environment. Learning about citizenship involves engagement in a community and development of an identity within that group. These 'communities of discourse and practice' provide the situation in which young people develop progressively more complex concepts and ways of behaving. The model has its roots in two contemporary psychological theories— ecological development (Bronfenbrenner, 1988) and situated cognition (Lave & Wenger, 1991; Wenger, 1998). At the center of this model is the individual student. The public discourse and practices of the society have an impact on the student through contacts with family (parents, siblings and sometimes extended family), school (teachers, implemented curriculum and participation opportunities), peer group (both in and out of class), and neighbors (including

Figure 1.2 Model for IEA Civic Education Study

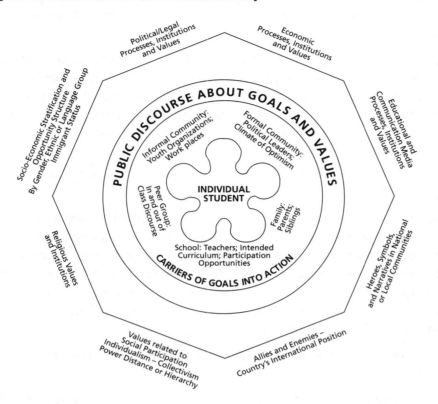

people in out-of-school youth organizations). Earlier work in political socialization usually referred to these groups of people as 'agents' of socialization.

In addition to these face-to-face relationships, there is also a broader society that has an impact through its institutions and the mass media. The outer octagon in Figure 1.2, which circumscribes these processes, includes institutions, processes and values in domains such as politics, economics, education and religion. It also includes the country's position internationally, the symbols or narratives important at the national or local level, and the social stratification system, including ethnic and gender-group opportunities.

Other models have also influenced the study. Sociologists and political scientists see the IEA study in relation to studies of political socialization—a sub-field of political science research that was popular 20 to 25 years ago and seems currently to be experiencing renewed interest (Niemi & Hepburn, 1995; Flanagan & Sherrod, 1998). Social scientists link studies in this area to recent surveys of adults concerned with social capital (Van Deth, Maraffi, Newton & Whiteley, 1999), democratic transitions (Diamond, 1999; Dalton, 2000), post-materialist values (Inglehart, 1997; Inglehart & Baker, 2000) and political culture and citizenship (Norris, 1999).

These models from the social sciences suggest that young people move from peripheral to central participation in a variety of overlapping communities (at the school or neighborhood level, as well as potentially at the national level). Learning about citizenship is not limited to teachers explicitly instructing young people about their rights and duties. The political community itself (and its everyday practices) surrounds and provides a context for developing political understanding (Wenger, 1998; Torney-Purta, Hahn & Amadeo, 2001).

For young people, the peer group plays a vital role. The reactions of peers to ideas and choices are essential parts of the context for civic development. The extent to which students are able to incorporate what they are learning into meaningful identities is also important. Schools as well as neighborhoods are important sites for peer interaction and identity development.

POLICY AND RESEARCH ISSUES IN THE IEA CIVIC EDUCATION STUDY

In addition to these models, a list of policy-relevant questions was developed to focus the study and make it useful to those who teach, make education policy, educate teachers, prepare curriculum materials, provide guidance to student associations and conduct research. The original list of 18 questions has been merged into 12 questions. Information from Phase 1 (reported in Torney-Purta *et al.*, 1999) and Phase 2 (reported in this volume) is referenced in treating each policy question in the following section.

Some of these policy-relevant questions deal with the *organization of educational programs*:

1. *What is the status of citizenship education as an explicit goal for schools?* There is considerable diversity among countries in the extent to which the preparation of future citizens is thought of as an important responsibility for schools. Phase 1 indicated that all the participating countries have courses under a variety of titles with specific responsibilities to prepare students for citizenship. The aims of civic education are also addressed throughout the curriculum and the entire school day, as well as through the climate for interaction in the classroom. In many countries, civic education courses and programs do not have a high status, however. Analysis relating to school experience from Phase 2 is relevant to this question (found in Chapters 7 through 9).

2. *To what extent is there agreement among nations about priorities within formal civic education?* Knowledge of domestic political institutions and traditions is a focus in most of the participating countries. Lowering levels of youth alienation or raising levels of interest in political participation is also important in many. During Phase 1 a high level of unanimity was identified across participating countries about the major content domains of civic education. These domains encompass democracy and democratic institutions, citizenship, national identity, international or regional organizations and social cohesion and diversity. Items relating to these topics form the core of the Phase 2 test and survey (reported in Chapters 3 through 9).

3. *Around what instructional principles and through what courses are formal programs of civic education organized?* There is considerable diversity in the extent to which citizenship education is addressed through subjects such as history, through more interdisciplinary programs such as social studies or social

science, through courses focused on conduct such as moral education, and
through specific courses in civic education or government. There is also
variation in the extent to which the community or the school is
of as an arena in which the student should practice citizensh
studies prepared for Phase 1 showed agreement among
civics-related courses *should be* participative, interacti
school and community, conducted in a non-auth
cognizant of diversity and co-constructed w
community. Many countries, however, sa
this kind of civic education because i
Most countries thought that the
it, however. The Phase 2 res
opportunities for interacti   y in
classroom discussion   e school,
reported in Chapt   methods,
reported in Ch

4. *To what ex*   *entity development in*
    student   e independent, national
    id   ent of citizenship. Civic
                             s relating to the ideal values of
                        rrent structure. Phase 1 of the Civic
                    complexity of this issue in many countries.
              al with positive feelings about one's nation, with
           the good citizen, and with groups that shape
        Chapters 4 and 5).

        s civic education intended to contribute to the resolution of conflicts
        between societal groups? Many societies are experiencing such
      s. The information collected during Phase 1 indicated that this was
    area of widespread concern but did not suggest clear-cut directions for
    program development. Some countries experience diversity primarily in
    terms of race or ethnicity; others in terms of immigration (often related to
    diversity in language or religion). Phase 2 assessed attitudes relating to
    support for opportunities for immigrants (reported in Chapter 5).

Some policy-relevant questions are focused on *students:*

6. *How do students define and understand the concept of citizenship and related issues?*
    Students have developed their own ideas about their political system and
    society, and about what citizenship means within it. The Phase 1 process
    identified major concepts that experts in all the participating countries
    agreed were important. Many country representatives also pointed to
    substantial gaps between the concepts that schools were trying to foster
    and what students actually believed. The Phase 2 data provide descriptive
    information on how students understand citizenship, democracy and
    government. They also allow an analysis of the extent to which
    knowledge of civics relates to expected civic engagement. These data are
    reported in Chapters 3, 4, 6 and 8.

7. *For what rights and responsibilities of participation are students being prepared in their own political system or society?* In democratic societies, participation in the community and political system is vital, although the nature of that participation may vary. Information from Phase 1 indicated that educators often seek to make students aware of the excitement of politics and the importance of participation. Students, however, often show a general disdain for politics. Some countries are responding by using student-generated projects, while others are encouraging students to assist others in the community. Such programs do not yet exist on a widespread basis across countries. The Phase 2 data describe students' current civic participation and their future expectations of participation (reported in Chapters 6 through 8).

8. *Do male and female students develop different conceptions of citizenship, and do they develop different potential roles in the political process?* Beliefs about the role of women in politics still vary across countries, even though there have been rapid changes in the past decade. Phase 1 indicated that most countries did not see gender issues as central in preparation for citizenship, although some did refer to the small proportion of women holding political office as an issue. Phase 2 data indicate the extent to which male and female students see the civic culture and citizenship similarly or differently. A set of items relating to support for women's political rights was included in the instrument. These data are reported in Chapters 3 through 8.

9. *Are there socioeconomic differences in students' understanding of or attitudes to civic-related topics or in the way their civic education is structured?* Research in political socialization and civic education suggests that there are important differences in civic knowledge between students from homes with ample educational and economic resources and those from homes that are less well endowed. The Phase 1 case studies in a few countries dealt with this concern. The Phase 2 analyses presented in this volume address this question by looking at the relation of civic education outcomes to a measure of home literacy resources (in Chapters 3 and 8).

Some policy-relevant questions focus on *teachers and teaching* and on *schools:*

10. *How do teachers deal with civic education in their teaching, and what is the influence of different types of classroom practices?* Research suggests that different pedagogies make a difference, particularly in terms of whether discussion is encouraged and how controversy and conflicting beliefs are handled. The Phase 1 material across countries confirmed that teachers are expected to balance cognitive, attitudinal and behavioral goals in preparing students for citizenship. The relevant Phase 2 data are discussed in the chapters where students report about their schools and in the chapter about teachers (Chapters 7 and 9).

11. *How well does the education of teachers prepare them to deal with the different facets of civic education?* Teacher education or training programs often do not address civic education issues explicitly. The Phase 1 documents showed that, in some countries, teachers who have prepared to teach another subject have been asked to serve as teachers of civic education.

This Phase 2 volume provides data on the extent to which the teachers themselves believe that their training has prepared them adequately to teach topics relevant to civic education (reported in Chapter 9).

12. *How does the way in which schools are organized influence students' civic education?* The opportunities schools provide for meaningful participation, self-government and respect for rights are among the factors potentially influencing students' attitudes and behaviors. Most countries' Phase 1 submissions highlighted aspirations to provide students with such experiences but few reported successful concrete initiatives. The idea that schools should be models of democracy is often stated but difficult to put into practice. Participation in the school as a community is covered in Phase 2 (Chapters 7 and 8).

SUMMARY OF AIMS OF THE STUDY AND INFLUENCES ON IT

This two-phased research study is intended to inform and stimulate discussion among policy-makers, curriculum developers, teachers, teacher educators, researchers and the general public. The study does not, however, try to identify a single best definition of citizenship or advocate a particular approach to civic education. Rather it tries to deepen the understanding of possibilities and practices in civic education as it takes place in different contexts.

Although our conceptual model has focused the study's attention on school-based, family, community and peer-group factors, the study is not an effort to refine theory. It has not been a curriculum development effort, although the test framework and the findings have implications for others who will develop curriculum, programs and materials in the future.

Three major sources of influence have shaped this study. The first relates to the IEA organization and the member countries that chose to participate in it. Rigor and collaboration are the hallmarks of IEA studies. The rigorous standards for research developed by IEA over the past decades therefore have served as our standard. At several points we chose to narrow the focus of the study to ensure that we could meet the standards of rigor in instrumentation, sampling and analysis set by recent IEA studies, including TIMSS. The participating countries were collaborators in the design of the Civic Education Study, providing the International Coordinators and the International Steering Committee with advice about models, items and interpretations throughout the process.

The second source of influence includes the theoretical frameworks and research literature not only in civic education but also in sociology, political science and developmental psychology. Some aspects of these frameworks are discussed in the sections of this chapter on the model (Figure 1.2), and others will become evident as the construction of particular scales is described in subsequent chapters.

The policy questions guiding and linking both phases of the study are the third source of influence. Although formulated by the International Steering Committee five years ago, these questions remain important. We have collected data to address all of them.

It has not been possible in this volume to explore many questions interesting to policy-makers, educators and researchers. IEA will release the full set of data in 2002 for use by the research community, which will be able to conduct many additional analyses. To give only a few examples, those researchers who focus on a subset of countries may formulate scales using items that were left out of this volume because they could not be scaled to IEA standards across the full range of countries. Other researchers may form a broader measure of attitudes toward democratic values that includes opportunities for immigrants, women and ethnic minorities (dimensions that we separated or could not include). Still others may choose different methods for analyzing socioeconomic differences or school practices.

The remainder of this volume provides analysis that is closely related to the original aims of the study, and suggests many directions that future analysis might take.

2

Instrument Development, Sampling, Testing and Quality Control

HIGHLIGHTS RELATING TO METHODOLOGY

- A review of documents submitted by countries during the first phase of the civic education study, together with extensive item writing, pre-pilot and pilot testing, and input from country representatives resulted in the development of an instrument requiring two class-hours to administer. This instrument meets IEA's standards for psychometric quality.

- During 1999 nearly 90,000 students enrolled in the modal grade for 14-year-olds from 28 countries took the test of civic knowledge and skills, and the survey assessing concepts, attitudes and participatory actions.

International assessment in civic education has been much less frequent than testing in other content areas in comparative education. More detailed information about instrument development is therefore contained in this report than would be required in frequently tested areas.

In the first section of this chapter, we review the two-year process of identifying a common core of topics to form a content framework relating to citizenship and democracy valid across the 28 countries that participated in the civic education study. We also detail the three-year process of developing a fair and valid test (items designed with keys for correct answers) and survey (items assessing attitudes or beliefs for which there are no correct answers) to meet IEA standards.

In the next section, we describe the study's sampling. We chose the modal grade for 14-year-olds as the target population for two reasons. First, it is the standard IEA population, and it was the target population sampled in the 1971 study of civic education (Torney, Oppenheim & Farnen, 1975). Secondly, and more importantly, some National Research Coordinators noted during the development of the 1999 plans that testing an older group meant facing substantial student drop-out.

We devote the remainder of the chapter to a description of the international translation verification, testing, quality control and scaling. We present some characteristics of the achieved sample in a table, and summarize the modes of analysis and presentation. (For more detail, see the technical report of the study, Lehmann *et al.*, forthcoming.)

FRAMEWORK DEVELOPMENT DURING PHASE 1

The Phase 1 national case studies were the basis for Phase 2 of the study, in particular providing the material from which the testing framework was developed. This framework is similar to the intended curriculum on which tests in other IEA studies have been based.

The *data collected during Phase 1* included summaries of what panels of experts in participating countries believed that 14-year-olds should know about 18 topics relating to democratic institutions. These topics included elections, individual rights, national identity, political participation, the role of the police and the military, organizations that characterize civil society, relation of economics to politics, and respect for ethnic and political diversity (Torney-Purta, Schwille & Amadeo, 1999).

Early in the study it was clear that there was a common core of topics and concepts that experts in these countries believed 14-year-olds should understand. Following examination of Phase 1 material and a vote on these topics by the National Research Coordinators, the International Steering Committee chose three domains of clustered topics as 'core international domains'. These were:

Domain I: Democracy
What does democracy mean, and what are its associated institutions and practices? The three sub-domains were:
A) Democracy and its defining characteristics
B) Institutions and practices in democracy
C) Citizenship—rights and duties.

Domain II: National Identity, Regional and International Relationships
How can the sense of national identity or national loyalty among young people be described, and how does it relate to their orientation to other countries and to regional and international organizations? The two sub-domains were:
A) National identity
B) International/regional relations.

Domain III: Social Cohesion and Diversity
What do issues of social cohesion and diversity mean to young people, and how do they view discrimination?

We also identified three other issues as important—the media, economics and local problems (including the environment)—but these were explored less systematically during Phase 2.

As a next step in developing a content framework, personnel at the Phase 1 Coordinating Center read the case study documents. They developed statements about what young people might be expected to know and believe about the three domains, and they elaborated on and illustrated these with quotations from the national case studies. This material formed the *Content Guidelines for the International Test and Survey*, which served as a concise statement of content elements in the three domains that were important across countries. The guidelines also provided a focus for those writing the test items. It was clear from the case study material that the greatest emphasis in the test should be on Domain I: Democracy, Democratic Institutions and Citizenship.

In addition to giving input on content domains to be covered, the National Research Coordinators were involved in defining the types of items to include in the instrument:

- Type 1 items: assessing *knowledge of content.*
- Type 2 items: assessing *skills in interpretation* of material with civic or political content (including short text passages and cartoons).

Types 1 and 2 items formed the *test.* These items had keyed correct answers.

Because civic education is an area where students' content knowledge and skills are important but not the sole focus, the National Research Coordinators suggested three other item types:

- Type 3 items: assessing how students understand *concepts* such as democracy and citizenship.
- Type 4 items: assessing students' *attitudes* (for example, feelings of trust in the government).
- Type 5 items: assessing students' current and expected participatory *actions* relating to politics.

Types 3, 4 and 5 items formed the survey. These items did not have correct answers.

Intersecting these five item types with the three study domains produced the following matrix, which served as the basis for the test and survey design.

Item Type:	1	2	3	4	5
Domain I Democracy/ Citizenship					
Domain II National Identity/ International Relations					
Domain III Social Cohesion/ Diversity					

A little less than half of the testing time was devoted to a test including cognitive items that could be 'keyed' with correct and incorrect answers. A little less than half of the remaining testing time was devoted to a survey including non-keyed items that assessed concepts, attitudes and actions. The rest of the instrument asked about students' perceptions of classroom climate and their confidence in participation at school, and obtained background information (including home literacy resources and the associations or organizations to which students belonged). A short period at the end of the second testing session was reserved for countries to administer nationally developed items.

THE PROCESS OF TEST AND SURVEY DEVELOPMENT DURING PHASE 2

Because there were no large existing sets of items that were likely to yield the number of items needed to fill in the matrix, extensive item writing was required. We began by reviewing materials in the Content Guidelines, other summaries of Phase 1 documents, and messages exchanged during an on-line conference on civic issues conducted with secondary school students in seven countries. We next invited all National Research Coordinators to submit items.

Our third task was to review the 1971 IEA Civic Education instrument, released items from United States and Canadian assessments, and the published research literature. Members of the International Steering Committee then wrote items, which were subsequently entered into an item database keyed to the content guidelines. Our fifth step involved asking groups of test specialists and content experts to review items in the database and their relation to the content framework.

The result of this activity was the development of 140 knowledge and skills items (Types 1 and 2), each with one correct answer and four distracters, each of which was entered into the database for the 14-year-old population. All the items were suitable for administration in the participating countries.

The items focused on principles, pivotal ideas and general examples, and not on the details of the political arrangements in any one country. For example, Type 1/Domain I items covered the principles of democracy and its associated institutions across the countries participating in the study. The test did not include items about specific mechanisms of the electoral process or government structure in any particular country. The Type 1/ Domains II and III items likewise dealt with internationally relevant or generalized matters shared across countries. This emphasis differs from that in many national tests where items about each country's political structure predominate. The IEA Civic Education Study Phase 2 items are congruent with information gathered during Phase 1 about what students are expected to know, and with recent expert statements such as that issued under the auspices of the Council of Europe about the role of history knowledge in civic education (Slater, 1995, 146–48).

Some of the Type 2 items (skills) asked students to distinguish between statements of fact and opinion. Others were based on a leaflet of the type issued during an election campaign, on the interpretation of a short article from a mock newspaper, or on a political cartoon. The general ideas for cartoons came from those published in newspapers. They were redrawn to communicate a single message that a 14-year-old across countries could be expected to understand.

Pre-Piloting of Item Types 1 and 2 (Knowledge and Skills)

Convenience samples of 14-year-olds in 20 countries were tested with 80 items of Types 1 and 2. The National Research Coordinators discussed the content of the pre-pilot items and the test statistics at a meeting held in March 1998. They agreed to retain 62 items, and prepared six items to fill gaps.

Piloting of Item Types 1 and 2 (Knowledge and Skills) and the Resulting Final Test

Between April and October 1998, 25 countries conducted pilot studies on Forms A and B of the test (Types 1 and 2 items described above) and survey (Types 3 through 5 items described below). In each country, judgement samples of about 200 students were tested (two class periods per student). The pilot countries included Australia, Belgium (French), Bulgaria, Chile, Chinese Taipei, Colombia, Cyprus, the Czech Republic, Estonia, Finland, Germany,

Greece, Hong Kong Special Administrative Region (SAR), Hungary, Italy, Latvia, Lithuania, Norway, Poland, Portugal, Romania, the Russian Federation, Slovenia, Switzerland and the United States. In addition to these countries, Denmark, England, the Slovak Republic and Sweden participated in the final testing of 14-year-olds. (Chinese Taipei was unable to obtain funding to continue past the pilot testing.)

The National Research Coordinators were provided with item statistics for their countries, and they discussed each item within its content category at a November 1998 meeting. The small number of items that was unacceptable to one-fifth of the countries was dropped, in accordance with the rule used by IEA to promote test fairness across countries. Through a process of negotiation, the research coordinators chose, by consensus, 38 items of Types 1 and 2 (knowledge and skills) from the 68 that had been piloted. The discrimination indices were greater than .30 for most items; coverage of the content framework and the research coordinators' preferences were the decisive factors.

The ratios of 'number of items written' to 'number piloted' to 'number accepted' were similar to IEA tests in other subject areas. Confirmatory factor analysis and IRT modeling, presented in Chapter 3, indicate a high-quality test across countries. These modern scaling methods (Frederiksen, Mislevy & Bejar, 1993) were our primary guide as we developed the test. Classical scaling methods also indicate a test of high quality. The alpha reliabilities for the final 38-item civic education test exceed .85 in each of the countries (see Chapter 3 and associated appendices for details).

With respect to content coverage, within Domain I there are items covering all three sub-domains (definitions of democracy 6, democratic institutions 12, citizenship in democracy 12); within Domain II there are items covering the two sub-domains (national identification 2, international relations 3); within Domain III there are three items. Appendix Table A.1 contains short descriptions of the 38 items and of the content categories in which they were classified, along with the percentage of students answering them correctly in the final test and the respective item parameters (discussed further in Chapter 3).

Piloting of Item Types 3, 4 and 5 (Concepts, Attitudes and Actions) and the Resulting Final Surveys

The National Research Coordinators reviewed lists of suggested topics for Types 3 to 5 items and some prototype items at the March 1998 meeting. Most item sets for piloting were suggested by the research literature. Some revisions were necessary to adapt items originally designed for administration to adults in an interview, and 'don't know' options were added.

In mid-1998 the research coordinators piloted the survey items along with two forms of the knowledge and skills test. Items for the survey were chosen through a process of negotiation similar to that described in the previous section. The final survey included 52 items of Type 3 (concepts), 62 items of Type 4 (attitudes) and 22 items of Type 5 (actions). Items assessing student background, school experience, organizational membership and peer group involvement were also included. Policy in some of the participating countries prohibited questions about families' social or political values, and no such items were included. The final test and survey were designed so that they could be administered in two class periods. The texts of all of the Types 3, 4 and 5 items and of about half of the Types 1 and 2 items will be released for use by other researchers.

Chapters 4 through 7 of this publication describe the rationale for items and scales included in the student survey, along with relevant research literature.

The development of short survey instruments for teachers and for school heads (principals) began at the March 1998 meeting and covered the same content domains as the student instrument, along with questions about the school context and instruction. These instruments were piloted in the same countries and at the same time as the student instruments. The questions included and the results for the teacher survey are discussed in Chapter 9. The school questionnaire has been left for future international analysis and for national analysis.

SAMPLING, TESTING AND SCALING DURING PHASE 2

Sampling from an Internationally Defined Population

The internationally desired population was defined as follows:

> The population includes all students enrolled on a full time basis in that grade in which most students aged 14:00 to 14:11 [years; months] are found at the time of testing. Time of testing is the first week of the 8th month of the school year.

In most cases testing took place between March and June 1999 in the Northern Hemisphere and between August and October 1999 in the Southern Hemisphere. In England and Sweden, testing was conducted in the second or third month of the school year because of the countries' late entry into the study. In the United States the testing was done in the second month of the school year because of uncertainty as to the age distribution of students in the eighth month of the year (resulting from the varying school entry dates set by districts).

In the majority of countries, Grade 8 was selected. In nine countries, Grade 9 was chosen. In Switzerland, differences between regions led to the selection of Grades 8 or 9, depending on the structure of the educational system. In Portugal, Grade 8 was selected even though the proportion of 14-year-olds in this country tends to be slightly higher in the adjacent Grade 9. The average age of respondents in the selected Grade 8 was 14:5, which was similar to the average age in most other countries in this study. If Grade 9 had been used in Portugal, the average age would have been 15:4.

In two countries (Hong Kong/SAR and the Russian Federation), the average age was above 15:00 and therefore did not meet the study's age/grade specifications. In two countries (Belgium/French and Chile), the average age was between 14:00 and 14:11, but the proportion of 13-year-old students in the tested grade ended up being slightly higher than the proportion of 14-year-old students.

In Germany, three federal states ('Bundesländer') refused to participate in this study, and one federal state did not permit testing in high schools ('Gymnasium'). Therefore, the sample was not representative for the population of *all* 14-year-old students in this country but only for those in the participating federal states.

A two-stage stratified cluster design for sampling was employed in consultation with IEA sampling experts. At the first stage, schools were sampled using a probability proportional to size (PPS).[1] At the second stage the sample consisted of one intact classroom per school from the target grade. The chosen class was not to be tracked by ability and was, where possible, to be in a civic-related subject (for example, history, social studies).

Table 2.1 shows the participation rates of the 28 countries. National Research Centers made every attempt to meet the sampling requirements, but in some countries there was resistance from teachers and schools. Ten countries failed to reach a 75 percent overall participation rate before replacement as specified

Table 2.1 Participation Rates and Sample Sizes

Country	School Participation Before Replacement (Weighted Percentage)	School Participation After Replacement (Weighted Percentage)	Total Number of Schools That Participated	Student Participation Rate	Total Number of Students Assessed	Overall Participation Rate Before Replacement	Overall Participation Rate After Replacement
Australia	75	94	142	92	3331	69	86
Belgium (French)	57	75	112	93	2076	53	70
Bulgaria	86	86	148	93	2884	80	80
Chile	98	100	180	97	5688	94	97
Colombia	66	94	144	96	4926	64	90
Cyprus*	100	100	61	96	3106	96	96
Czech Republic	91	99	148	95	3607	86	94
Denmark	71	71	178	93	3208	66	66
England	54	85	128	93	3043	50	79
Estonia	84	85	145	90	3434	76	77
Finland	93	98	146	93	2782	86	91
Germany	63	94	169	89	3700	56	84
Greece	88	93	142	97	3460	85	90
Hong Kong (SAR)	90	100	150	99	4997	89	99
Hungary	99	99	146	95	3167	94	94
Italy	93	100	172	96	3808	89	96
Latvia	89	91	130	91	2572	81	82
Lithuania	93	97	169	90	3494	84	87
Norway	75	77	154	93	3321	70	71
Poland	83	90	179	94	3376	78	84
Portugal	98	99	149	95	3261	93	95
Romania	97	97	146	99	2993	96	96
Russian Federation	96	98	185	97	2129	94	95
Slovak Republic	79	97	145	94	3463	74	91
Slovenia	93	99	149	96	3068	89	95
Sweden	93	94	138	94	3073	88	88
Switzerland	71	87	157	97	3104	69	84
United States	65	83	124	93	2811	61	77

* In Cyprus two classes per school were sampled.

Source: *IEA Civic Education Study*, Standard Population of 14-year-olds tested in 1999.

in the sampling guidelines. In Belgium (French), Denmark and Norway, the overall participation rate, even after replacement of schools, was lower than 75 percent.[2] Student participation rates were at least 89 percent in all participating countries, however.

Sample sizes of schools per country varied between 112 and 185. In Cyprus, all 61 schools in the country were tested, and from each school two classes were sampled. Student sample sizes ranged between 2,076 and 5,688. In some countries, disproportional samples were drawn (for example, to include larger sub-samples of specific school types). Sampling weights were applied.

Table 2.2 summarizes three basic characteristics of the sample by country: mean and standard deviation of the age of students tested, the percentage of females, and the percentage of students who answered that they had not been born in the country. The age distribution is discussed in Chapter 3. The most serious gender disparity was in Colombia, where 58 percent of the student

Table 2.2 Sample Characteristics

Country	Age			Percentage of Females	Percentage of Students Not Born in Country
	Mean	Standard Deviation	Percentage of 14-year-olds		
Australia	14.6	0.5	67	55	10
Belgium (French)	14.1	0.7	34	49	10
Bulgaria	14.9	0.6	59	52	4
Chile	14.3	0.8	40	49	2
Colombia	14.6	1.2	35	58	3
Cyprus	14.8	0.4	75	51	9
Czech Republic	14.4	0.4	70	51	2
Denmark	14.8	0.4	66	49	7
England	14.7	0.3	79	50	6
Estonia	14.7	0.6	67	52	6
Finland	14.8	0.3	67	52	3
Germany[1]	n.a	n.a	n.a	51	19
Greece	14.7	0.5	83	52	6
Hong Kong (SAR)	15.3	0.8	38	49	20
Hungary	14.4	0.5	70	50	3
Italy	15.0	0.7	58	52	2
Latvia	14.5	0.6	62	52	5
Lithuania	14.8	0.6	67	51	3
Norway	14.8	0.3	71	51	6
Poland	15.0	0.4	54	52	1
Portugal	14.5	1.0	35	52	5
Romania	14.8	0.5	65	48	1
Russian Federation	15.1	0.5	48	53	14
Slovak Republic	14.3	0.4	69	53	2
Slovenia	14.8	0.4	74	50	4
Sweden	14.3	0.4	79	52	8
Switzerland	15.0	0.7	55	51	17
United States	14.7	0.6	74	51	11
International Sample	14.7	0.7	62	51	7

1 Information on age is not available for Germany. International sample figures based on 27 countries.

Source: IEA Civic Education Study, Standard Population of 14-year-olds tested in 1999.

respondents were female. The proportion of students not born in the country ranged from 1 percent (in Poland and Romania) to 19 and 20 percent in Germany and Hong Kong (SAR), respectively. This matter is discussed further in Chapter 5.

Instrument Translation

The pilot and final instruments were prepared in English and distributed by the International Coordinating Center (ICC). The National Research Centers then translated them into 22 languages. The ICC developed guidelines and detailed translation notes indicating alternative wordings adapted to the country's specific context.

Translated instruments for the final testing had to be submitted to the ICC for verification. Native speakers with a very good command of English and no working relationship with the National Research Centers verified the translations of school, teacher and student instruments according to guidelines issued by the ICC. The results of this verification were returned to the National Research Coordinators. In most countries, suggestions for improvement were taken into account in the final translations. In only three countries were translations not submitted in time for this process to take place. However, in these cases, the verifications did give some after-the-fact control over deviations (which were, in fact, few in number).

This process together with the translation verification of the pilot instruments in 1998 provided a high degree of quality control in this area. For 24 of the 28 countries the instruments were verified twice. For the four countries that entered the study after the pilot, there was only one verification. Instruments from English-speaking countries did not require translations but were reviewed for modifications necessary to adapt them to each country's political and cultural context.

Data Collection and Quality Control for Testing

Each participating country was responsible for data collection. Manuals for field operations, the school coordinators and the test administrators, together with tracking forms were adapted by the IEA Data Processing Center from those developed for TIMSS. The distribution of this material to the National Research Centers was carried out with the cooperation of the ICC. Where necessary, the manuals were translated into the country's language. Data collection at the schools followed strict guidelines for test administration and timing to safeguard comparability across countries. Full confidentiality of responses was guaranteed. Data entry was conducted by the National Research Centers.

The National Research Coordinators were asked to make follow-up calls on the day after testing to a 25 percent random sample of the tested schools. They were instructed to ask about deviations from testing procedures (using guidelines provided by the ICC). In a few countries, organizational problems made this task impossible, but every effort was made to examine these data with special care. In some countries, the national centers set up additional control monitoring.

After completion of the testing, the National Research Centers responded to a questionnaire on quality control that could be used as an additional check. Most centers completed this questionnaire within one month of testing.

Data Processing and Weighting

After collection, the data sets were submitted in a standard format to the IEA Data Processing Center (DPC) in Hamburg, which created the international database for the study. The DPC compared the database to the school, classroom, teacher and student tracking forms completed during data collection. They also checked and double-checked the data for inconsistencies. All deviations were documented and sent to the National Research Centers for clarification. The data-cleaning process consisted of several steps designed to guarantee high quality. The DPC also computed the weights to be applied to the sample according to the previously approved sampling design in each country (in line with IEA guidelines).

Confirmatory Factor Analysis and IRT Scaling

Structural equation modeling (SEM), including confirmatory factor analysis (CFA), was used to confirm theoretically expected dimensions or to re-specify the dimensional structure of the instruments. These procedures take into account the measurement error associated with indicators, providing more reliable estimates for latent variables and scales than classical psychometric methods.[3]

For both multiple-choice and categorical items, item response theory (IRT) scaling methods were used. For the cognitive test, a one-parameter Rasch model was fitted to the data; for attitudinal items the partial credit model was applied. The mean Rasch score for the scores derived from the test was set at 100, with a standard deviation of 20. The mean Rasch score for the scales derived from the survey (measuring concepts, attitudes and actions) was set at 10, with a standard deviation of 2.

There were several reasons for using IRT scaling. In this study all students were administered exactly the same 38-item test, so IRT scaling was not absolutely necessary (as it would have been if there had been a larger set of items from which several test forms had been constructed). In the case of the test items, however, the Rasch method provided a common scale for all countries, allowing the exclusion of items that did not fit the model in a few countries and without jeopardizing the comparability of the international scale. This method is prescribed in IEA studies.

Attitudinal items that had missing values, resulting from students who answered 'don't know' or who left items out, was a potential problem. Here, IRT scaling provided an elegant way of computing estimates for latent dimensions, even those with missing information.

SUMMARY OF ANALYSIS

The analysis of the international data consisted of several steps:

- Computation of item statistics for all test and survey items.
- Exploratory factor analysis and computation of classical scale reliabilities for the theoretically expected scales for each country.
- Confirmatory factor analysis with structural equation modeling on an international random sample of 200 students from each country, followed by the checking of models for each country.
- Selection of scales based on theoretical and empirical grounds.
- Estimation of Rasch models for the selected scales on an international random sample of 200 students per country.
- Item adjudication to examine scales by country and to make further refinements.

The final scaling used a calibration sample of 500 students selected randomly from weighted country data. Item parameters were estimated for the calibration sample and used as anchors for subsequent scaling of country data sets.

Complex sampling (such as the multi-stage sampling used here) makes simple random sampling formulas for estimating standard errors inadequate. In order to estimate correct sampling errors for each statistic in this report, we applied the 'jack-knife' procedure. The overall estimate of a sample statistic plus or minus two standard errors gives a 95 percent probability of inferring the correct mean in the population based on the student sample.

GUIDE TO THE PRESENTATION OF DATA FOUND IN CHAPTERS 3–7

Many of the scales and items in the test and the survey were derived from previous research and, in some cases, had been the subject of extensive debate and empirical study by political or educational researchers, sociologists and psychologists. An attempt has been made in the panels in Chapters 3–7 to briefly review the methods and a selection of the findings of previous cross-national research, especially that conducted in countries participating in this study.

The 38 multiple choice items in the *test of knowledge and skills have correct answers*. The IRT scaling process for these items is covered in Chapter 3. The Rasch scores presented in this chapter were normed to have an international mean of 100 and a standard deviation of 20. The scores based on these items are presented in the same format as in many other IEA studies, with the countries in rank order by score.

The items in the *survey of concepts, attitudes and actions do not have correct answers*. These results are presented in Chapters 4–7. The large majority of items were statements to which the student was to respond on a four-point scale with an additional 'don't know' option. The labeling of scale points differed. For many scales they were 'strongly agree', 'agree', 'disagree', 'strongly disagree'. Other response formats asked about how important something was or how frequently something happened.

The examination of confirmatory factor analyses by the International Steering Committee led to the choice of 11 sets of survey items for scaling. An IRT scaling procedure was applied at the International Coordinating Center to each set of items, and the resulting Rasch scales were normed to have an international mean of 10 and a standard deviation of 2. These scores allow statistically sound comparisons between countries' means and the international mean, as well as between one country's mean and that of another. Appendix B includes an item-by-score map for each concept, attitude or action scale in Chapters 4–7, allowing the reader to ascertain the response on the four-point scale that corresponds to Rasch scores from 4 to 16. Although country means were in the range from 8 to 12, there were student respondents in each country with scores well below 8, and others that were well above 12. The Appendix B material also includes the percentage distribution of responses to each scaled item based on the entire group of countries.

The figures in Chapters 4–7 present country means on these scaled scores. All countries appear in alphabetical order, with a confidence bound for each mean of two standard errors. An upward or downward arrow also appears to indicate whether a country's mean is significantly higher or lower than the international mean. Chapter 10 summarizes these differences across all scales and countries.

A figure comparing country means is included for each of the Rasch scores in Chapters 4–7. An additional figure is included to illustrate gender differences only for those scales where half or more countries show a significant gender difference ($p < .05$ with a Dunn-Bonferroni correction for multiple comparisons). If fewer than half of the countries show a significant difference, the text lists the gender differences that are statistically significant at the .05 level, but no separate figure is included.

SUMMARY OF METHODS

The following were used to develop the two class-hours of the 1999 IEA Civic Education Study test and survey:

- an iterative process of review of Phase 1 documents submitted by countries;
- references to the research and theoretical literature;
- extensive item writing;
- review by experts internationally and within participating countries;
- pre-pilot and pilot testing;
- item choice by participating countries.

The test and survey was administered to nationally representative samples totaling nearly 90,000 14-year-old students in 28 countries. Confirmatory factor analysis and Rasch scaling were used to develop scales. Much of the data is presented in this volume in figures that allow an analysis of countries' positions significantly above, not significantly different from, or significantly below the international mean.

A similar process was undertaken for the development of the Teacher Questionnaire and a very short School Questionnaire (covered in Chapter 9).

Quality control procedures were undertaken, including the review of samples by sampling experts, two translation verifications by independent experts, and other measures prescribed by the IEA technical standards. Panel 2.1 presents a listing of these quality control procedures.

PANEL 2.1 Quality Control Processes

Control Processes Anchored in the Study's Conceptualization

The study's design, instruments and reports have been:

- Connected to 15 policy questions formulated to guide Phases 1 and 2.
- Referenced to 18 case study framing questions in Phase 1.
- Framed by the 'octagon model' and 'situated cognition perspective' in Phases 1 and 2.
- Anchored in Phase 1 country case study data (leading to definition of the three domains for Phase 2).
- Scaffolded by content guidelines (including quotations from Phase 1 documents).
- Organized under three domains forming the test and survey framework.
- Referenced to the research literature on political attitudes in youth and adults and to theories of democracy.
- Built using five item types matched to country expectations identified during Phase 1.

Control Processes Relating to IEA Standards and Participating Country Input

The study's design, instruments and reports have been:

- Guided and judged by IEA technical standards and procedures (for example, regarding sampling and testing).
- Influenced by participating countries' input (through National Expert Panels and National Research Coordinators forming a de-centered network for test adaptation).
- Shaped by the analysis of pre-pilot psychometric data for test items from 20 countries interpreted by National Research Coordinators.
- Shaped by the analysis of pilot psychometric data for test and survey from 25 countries and interpreted by National Research Coordinators.
- Shaped in meetings between National Research Coordinators and Data Processing Center Personnel (regarding sampling, weighting of samples and data submission).
- Reviewed periodically by the IEA Technical Executive Group.
- Informed by independent verification of test translations and of concept equivalence (of the pilot and the final test and survey).
- Monitored using National Research Coordinators' reports regarding the testing process.
- Referenced to an analysis plan guided by policy questions and IEA principles.
- Finalized through the International Steering Committee's review of Rasch scaling for test and survey items and choice of scales to be reported.

NOTES

1 The general procedure followed closely the one adopted for the Third International Mathematics and Science Study (TIMSS) as described in Foy, Rust and Schleicher (1996). In some countries, the sample for the Civic Education Study was linked to the TIMSS-R (Repeat), which was done in the same year as the Civic Education Study.

2 Originally sampled schools that refused to participate could be replaced by additionally sampled schools. In Denmark no replacement schools were sampled.

3 We have included some classical psychometric indices in appendices because some readers may be more familiar with them.

Knowledge of Content and Skills in Interpreting Civic Information

CHAPTER 3

HIGHLIGHTS RELATING TO CIVIC KNOWLEDGE

- The results show that it is possible to construct a meaningful, reliable and valid international test of student knowledge about democratic institutions, principles, processes and related topics despite differences in the political systems in different participating countries.

- The differences between countries in mean performance on this test are in general not large. Twenty-five of the 28 countries differ by less than half a standard deviation from the international average.

- Students' abilities to answer questions requiring knowledge of civic content and questions requiring skill in *interpreting* civic-related material are distinguishable empirically. Although this distinction between content knowledge and skills in interpretation has a very limited influence on the countries' rankings, it adds to the understanding of countries' specific strengths and weaknesses.

- Unlike studies of earlier decades, this study reveals no significant differences in mean performance between boys and girls in 27 of the 28 countries, when the comparison is made without controlling for other variables.

- Students reporting more home literacy resources consistently do better on the test.

- Over 75 percent of the students in most participating countries are able to answer questions dealing with the fundamental nature of laws and political rights. However, few students in the participating countries can answer more demanding questions on the test that have to do, for example, with deciding between election candidates based on their policy positions, understanding processes of political reform, and grasping the implications of economic and political choices made by policy-makers.

The IEA Civic Education Study faced considerable skepticism about the possibility of developing a valid test to measure civic knowledge across diverse political systems. Chapter 2 has described the process by which we met this challenge, namely producing a test rooted in the content domains defined collaboratively in Phase 1 of the study, meeting IEA technical standards and allowing for extensive procedures of quality control. For a review of the previous research in this area, see Panel 3.1

In this chapter, we present a summary of the results achieved on this test by nearly 90,000 students who constituted nationally representative samples from the 28 participating countries. We describe the methods applied in the scoring and scaling of student responses, and then display the distribution of test scores by country, followed by an analysis of how the test can be partitioned into two dimensions relating to knowledge of content and skills in interpreting civic-related information. Finally, we deal with the ways in which the key variables of gender and home literacy resources are related to civic knowledge. In short, the chapter provides a base for the comparative assessment of what students in participating countries know about the nature and workings of democracy and, to some extent, about the other two core content domains of the study.

PANEL 3.1 Previous Research on Students' Civic Knowledge

First, it is important to acknowledge the role of general literacy in acquiring political knowledge. For example, Chall and Henry (1991) noted that considerably more than a minimal level of literacy is required for understanding documents such as constitutions or for locating information in sources such as newspapers.

As part of a more specific look at the role of knowledge in the context of civic education, the 1971 IEA Civic Education Study used a test of 47 items for 14-year-olds (Torney, Oppenheim & Farnen, 1975). In this study, students in the Federal Republic of Germany had the second highest cognitive score. The United States ranked fourth, Finland ranked fifth, and Italy ranked seventh (out of eight countries). Among other countries that participated in the 1971 but not in the 1999 study, students from the Netherlands ranked first, those from Israel ranked third, those from New Zealand ranked sixth, and those from Ireland ranked eighth. At age 14, males performed higher on the test than females in the Federal Republic of Germany, Finland and the United States (but not in Italy) in a comparison similar to that reported in this chapter. Those from higher socioeconomic backgrounds performed at a higher level in all the countries, although the differences were especially large in the United States (Torney *et al.*, 1975, pp.138, 156). The encouragement of independent expression of opinion in the classroom was a positive predictor in all the countries (p.140).

In some countries there have also been large-scale national assessments of civic knowledge. In the United States a National Assessment of Educational Progress (NAEP) regularly tests students at Grades 4, 8 and 12 (ages approximately 9, 13 and 17) in civic-related content areas. Multiple choice items are used, along with items that require students to write a response (sometimes relating to a picture of a historical event, cartoon or newspaper article). No attempt is made to separate performance on knowledge of content and skills in interpretation (as in the current IEA study). Proficiency levels for the 'total knowledge' scores are set by experts. Most students are classified as having 'basic' rather than 'proficient' or 'advanced' understanding (Lutkus, Weiss, Campbell, Mazzeo & Lazer, 1999; Torney-Purta, 2000). There is a substantial gap between the scores of students from more and less affluent and highly and less educated home backgrounds (Niemi & Junn, 1998).

Gender differences in the NAEP have been variable. In the 1988 assessment, males tended to perform at a somewhat higher level than females. Gender differences were especially pronounced in knowledge of political parties, elections and protest activities. In the 1998 assessment, these differences were either very small or showed females to have slight superiority. The most comprehensive recent analysis of school-based predictors of achievement in NAEP, by Niemi and Junn (1998, using the 1988 data), found that frequent testing seemed to be counterproductive in students' learning of civic content. The taking of classes in which civic topics were studied and where participation in role-playing elections or mock trials was included seemed to have a positive effect.

A study in Australia with 1,000 students from Years 5 and 9 tapped political understanding by asking questions to which students wrote answers (Doig, Piper, Mellor & Masters, 1993/94). Topics included the meaning and origin of laws, the electoral process, influences on political decisions, processes of enactment and implementation of parliamentary decisions, and the meaning of democracy. Each response was scored as being at one of several levels ranging from simplistic, vague or confused to sophisticated and complex (including the ability to apply principles). The average student was found to be able to 'recognize key aspects of democracy in a generalized way'. On average, Year 9 students had higher scores than Year 5 students. Females at Year 5 had higher scores than males, but there were no significant gender differences among the older students.

For a fuller review of studies in these areas, see Torney-Purta, Hahn and Amadeo (2001).

CIVIC KNOWLEDGE IN THE 1999 IEA INSTRUMENT: HOW IT WAS MEASURED

The IEA civic knowledge test consists of 38 items, 25 of which refer to knowledge of content (Type 1) and 13 to skills in interpretation (Type 2). All items were given in a multiple-choice format, with student responses coded as correct or incorrect. The items cover a broad range of content areas selected from a much larger set of trial items after intensive piloting (see Chapter 2). In the final test version, the international average of correct answers was 64 percent, which indicates that, for the majority of students, the test was far from being too difficult. The results of Rasch scaling as well as classical item statistics (Appendix Tables C.1 and C.2) show that the test has satisfactory characteristics; for example, alpha coefficients are at least .85 in all countries. More detail will appear in the technical report (Lehmann *et al.*, forthcoming).

SAMPLE ITEMS AND THEIR RESULTS

To convey a notion of what was measured by the test, five examples are given and briefly discussed here (refer to Figures 3.1a-e).

Figure 3.1a Item Example: Identify a non-democratic government

Country	Correct Answers (in %)	Example 3 (Item #17) Type 1: Knowledge of Content
Australia	50 (1.3)	
Belgium (French)	51 (1.8)	
Bulgaria	53 (2.0)	
Chile	44 (1.3)	
Colombia	38 (1.9)	
Cyprus	59 (1.3)	**17.** Which of the following is most likely to cause a government to be called non-democratic?
Czech Republic	60 (1.6)	
Denmark	46 (1.1)	
England	45 (1.1)	A. People are prevented from criticising the government.*
Estonia	39 (1.4)	
Finland	63 (1.3)	B. The political parties criticise each other often.
Germany	56 (1.2)	
Greece	67 (1.2)	C. People must pay very high taxes.
Hong Kong (SAR)	73 (1.3)	D. Every citizen has the right to a job.
Hungary	45 (1.2)	
Italy	63 (1.5)	
Latvia	36 (1.9)	
Lithuania	44 (1.6)	
Norway	57 (1.0)	
Poland	65 (2.3)	
Portugal	55 (1.5)	
Romania	42 (1.8)	
Russian Federation	57 (2.3)	
Slovak Republic	60 (1.6)	
Slovenia	50 (1.3)	
Sweden	66 (1.6)	
Switzerland	56 (1.6)	
United States	53 (1.7)	
International Sample	53 (0.3)	

( ) Standard errors appear in parentheses.
* Correct answer.

Source: IEA Civic Education Study, Standard Population of 14-year-olds tested in 1999.

Figure 3.1b Item Example: This is the way history textbooks are sometimes written

Country	Correct Answers (in %)	Example 5 (Item #36) Type 2: Skills in Interpretation
Australia	75 (1.2)	
Belgium (French)	66 (2.1)	
Bulgaria	47 (2.3)	
Chile	49 (1.5)	
Colombia	48 (2.3)	
Cyprus	53 (1.1)	
Czech Republic	54 (1.5)	
Denmark	60 (1.0)	
England	76 (1.2)	
Estonia	39 (1.2)	
Finland	65 (1.3)	
Germany	61 (0.9)	
Greece	56 (1.3)	
Hong Kong (SAR)	76 (1.4)	
Hungary	67 (1.3)	
Italy	61 (1.3)	
Latvia	48 (1.7)	
Lithuania	48 (1.4)	
Norway	49 (1.0)	
Poland	64 (2.1)	
Portugal	49 (1.1)	
Romania	26 (1.7)	
Russian Federation	45 (2.1)	
Slovak Republic	72 (1.5)	
Slovenia	56 (1.1)	
Sweden	52 (1.2)	
Switzerland	67 (1.4)	
United States	79 (1.4)	
International Sample	57 (0.3)	

36. What is the message or main point of this cartoon? History textbooks ...

A. are sometimes changed to avoid mentioning problematic events from the past.*

B. for children must be shorter than books written for adults.

C. are full of information that is not interesting.

D. should be written using a computer and not a pencil.

( ) Standard errors appear in parentheses.

* Correct answer.

Source: IEA Civic Education Study, Standard Population of 14-year-olds tested in 1999.

The first example (Figure 3.1a; see also example 3 in Figure 3.2) is a typical Type 1 item. It requires respondents to demonstrate knowledge of content by identifying a practice that 'most likely causes a government to be called non-democratic'. Figure 3.1a displays the question and the four answers from which the students had to choose. Among these four answers, the first one (A: 'People are prevented from criticising the government') is the correct response. The percentages of correct answers range from 36 to 73 percent. The average of correct answers across all countries (equally weighted) is 53 percent. If this international mean is compared with the overall percentage of correct answers in the test (64 percent), it is clear that the item is relatively difficult, although certainly within reach for most of the students. The correct answer requires a reliable knowledge base as to the properties of democratic governments and the ability to apply that knowledge to the opposite case ('non-democratic government').

The second example (Figure 3.1b; example 5 in Figure 3.2) is a Type 2 item that is intended to measure skills in the interpretation of civic-related material. Figure 3.1b demonstrates how the item was presented. There is a cartoon showing someone erasing words from a book, presumably one on the history of a nation as suggested by a flag and the word 'history'. The students were asked about the message or main point of this cartoon and had to select the correct response (A: 'History textbooks are sometimes changed to avoid mentioning problematic events from the past'). The distribution of correct answers across countries ranges from 26 to 79 percent. The international mean of 57 percent correct answers shows that this item is less difficult for students than the previous example, although it is slightly harder than the test on average. The task relates to the domain of national identity and international relations and requires the ability to interpret or comprehend the message that the cartoonist has attempted to convey.

Figure 3.1c   Item Example: This is an election leaflet

Country	Correct Answers (in %)	Example 6 (Item #23) Type 2: Skills in Interpretation
Australia	78 (1.3)	
Belgium (French)	56 (1.8)	
Bulgaria	47 (2.4)	
Chile	54 (1.5)	
Colombia	40 (2.4)	
Cyprus	81 (0.9)	**We citizens have had enough!**
Czech Republic	66 (1.6)	A vote for the Silver Party means a vote for
Denmark	49 (1.1)	higher taxes.
England	75 (1.2)	It means an end to economic growth and a waste
Estonia	54 (1.4)	of our nation's resources.
Finland	85 (0.8)	Vote instead for economic growth and
Germany	81 (0.9)	free enterprise.
Greece	73 (1.3)	Vote for more money left in everyone's wallet!
Hong Kong (SAR)	76 (1.4)	Let's not waste another 4 years!
Hungary	78 (1.2)	VOTE FOR THE GOLD PARTY.
Italy	85 (1.2)	
Latvia	44 (1.9)	
Lithuania	55 (1.6)	23. This is an election leaflet which has probably been
Norway	57 (0.9)	issued by ...
Poland	58 (2.0)	A. the Silver Party.
Portugal	55 (1.3)	B. a party or group in opposition to the Silver Party.*
Romania	46 (2.0)	C. a group which tries to be sure elections are fair.
Russian Federation	45 (1.9)	D. the Silver Party and the Gold Party together.
Slovak Republic	66 (1.6)	
Slovenia	75 (1.0)	
Sweden	73 (1.5)	
Switzerland	77 (1.3)	
United States	83 (1.4)	
International Sample	65 (0.3)	

( ) Standard errors appear in parentheses.
* Correct answer.

Source: IEA Civic Education Study, Standard Population of 14-year-olds tested in 1999.

CITIZENSHIP AND EDUCATION IN TWENTY-EIGHT COUNTRIES

Figure 3.1d Item Example: Importance of many organisations for democracy

Country	Correct Answers (in %)	Example 7 (Item #07) Type 1: Knowledge of Content
Australia	78 (1.2)	
Belgium (French)	68 (1.6)	
Bulgaria	71 (1.9)	
Chile	69 (1.1)	
Colombia	60 (2.0)	
Cyprus	80 (1.1)	7. In a democratic country [society]
Czech Republic	76 (1.2)	having many organisations for
Denmark	75 (0.9)	people to join is important
England	79 (1.0)	because this provides ...
Estonia	61 (1.1)	A. a group to defend members who
Finland	82 (1.0)	are arrested.
Germany	67 (1.0)	B. many sources of taxes for the
Greece	76 (0.9)	government.
Hong Kong (SAR)	79 (1.1)	C. opportunities to express different
Hungary	46 (1.3)	points of view.*
Italy	71 (1.4)	D. a way for the government to tell
Latvia	55 (1.8)	people about new laws.
Lithuania	61 (1.4)	
Norway	69 (0.9)	
Poland	78 (1.6)	
Portugal	59 (1.2)	
Romania	48 (2.2)	
Russian Federation	68 (1.6)	
Slovak Republic	75 (1.1)	
Slovenia	62 (1.1)	
Sweden	70 (1.5)	
Switzerland	68 (1.3)	
United States	78 (1.4)	
International Sample	69 (0.3)	

( ) Standard errors appear in parentheses.
* Correct answer.

Source: IEA Civic Education Study, Standard Population of 14-year-olds tested in 1999.

The third example (Figure 3.1c; example 6 in Figure 3.2) is also a Type 2 item, in this case referring to institutions and practices in democracy. Here, students were asked to interpret an electoral leaflet directed against an imaginary party (presumably in power) and to indicate which political group had probably issued it. The correct answer is B ('a party or group in opposition to the Silver Party'). The lowest proportion of correct answers found in any country is 40 percent and the highest 85 percent. The international average is 65 percent. Thus, the item is slightly easier than the international average of the test as a whole. There are several clues suggesting the correct solution, although the interpretation of some of these requires quite complex inferences as to the two mentioned parties' approaches to taxation and government spending. The last line of the leaflet ('Vote for the Gold Party') is unambiguous and clearly marks its origin. As such, the interpretative task is primarily to identify the alleged negative economic consequences of the Silver Party's fiscal policies and to recognize that such arguments could come only from an opposing group.

The fourth example (Figure 3.1d; example 7 in Figure 3.2) is a Type 1 item, aiming at civic-related content knowledge, more specifically knowledge as to the rights and duties of citizens in a democratic country. The students could choose from four reasons justifying 'freedom of association', with the correct response being C ('Having many organizations for people to join is important because this provides "opportunities to express different points of view"'). National percentages of correct responses range from 46 to 82 percent. With an international mean of 69 percent correct, this item is clearly among the easier ones in the test. It calls for basic background knowledge, or perhaps some recall of politics-related experience, to rule out the incorrect responses and to select the correct one.

Figure 3.1e   Item Example: Function of having more than one political party

Country	Correct Answers (in %)	Example 8 (Item #11) Type 1: Knowledge of Content
Australia	75 (1.3)	
Belgium (French)	67 (1.7)	
Bulgaria	70 (1.6)	
Chile	60 (1.2)	
Colombia	54 (1.6)	
Cyprus	88 (0.9)	11. In democratic countries what is the function of having more than one political party?
Czech Republic	79 (1.0)	
Denmark	84 (0.8)	
England	78 (1.0)	
Estonia	62 (1.2)	A. To represent different opinions [interests] in the national legislature [e.g. Parliament, Congress].*
Finland	80 (1.0)	
Germany	84 (0.9)	
Greece	85 (0.7)	B. To limit political corruption.
Hong Kong (SAR)	76 (1.1)	C. To prevent political demonstrations.
Hungary	75 (1.2)	
Italy	86 (0.9)	D. To encourage economic competition.
Latvia	57 (1.7)	
Lithuania	68 (1.2)	
Norway	83 (0.7)	
Poland	82 (1.1)	
Portugal	84 (0.8)	
Romania	67 (1.7)	
Russian Federation	71 (1.6)	
Slovak Republic	77 (1.0)	
Slovenia	81 (0.7)	
Sweden	75 (1.5)	
Switzerland	82 (0.9)	
United States	72 (1.5)	
International Sample	75 (0.2)	

( ) Standard errors appear in parentheses.
* Correct answer.

Source: IEA Civic Education Study, Standard Population of 14-year-olds tested in 1999.

The fifth example (Figure 3.1e; example 8 in Figure 3.2) is another Type 1 item, this time relating to institutions and practices in a democracy. In this item, four potential functions of a political system with more than one party were presented to the students who had to select the correct one (A: 'to represent different opinions [interests] in the national legislature'). The task turned out to be quite easy, with an international average percentage correct of 75 and a range across countries of 54 to 88 percent. In terms of its cognitive demands, this item is quite similar to the previous example, that is, a certain amount of political background knowledge and/or politics-related experience is needed if the correct response is to be identified. Some might argue that option B ('to limit political corruption') is not entirely wrong. The students who generally did well on the test, however, shared the conviction that the function of parties to represent different opinions or interests refers to a more fundamental role and is the more appropriate choice.

Three more sample items from the IEA test are given in Appendix A (Figures A.1a–c). They are intended to illustrate further the kind of questions and cognitive demands presented in the questions. Table A.1 in Appendix A lists the domain categories and short titles for all items contained in the test, along with the percentages of correct responses (international means).

ESTIMATION OF ITEM DIFFICULTIES AND STUDENT ABILITIES

One can always rank the items of a test according to the respective percentages of correct responses, the easiest ones being those with the highest percentage of correct answers and the most difficult ones those with the lowest. These percentages, however, are not the most informative measures of difficulty, since they do not take into account the ability levels of those who answered the item correctly. Similarly, 'percent correct' (or the sum of correct responses) is not a very good measure of student ability, because it assumes implicitly that all items are equally difficult.

When certain assumptions are met, it is possible to apply modern scaling techniques to arrive at an interval scale onto which measures of both item difficulty and student ability can be projected at the same time. The most important of these conditions is that a student with an ability thus determined solves—*at a defined or reasonable level of success*—all of the items with difficulties up to his or her ability level and fails most of the harder items. Following the example of the Third International Mathematics and Science Study (TIMSS), we chose in the present study a probability of .65 to represent this defined level of success. Because the simultaneous estimation of student abilities and item difficulties is based on probability functions, such an approach is sometimes called 'probabilistic'. The more widely used term is 'Item Response Theory' or 'IRT' (see, for example, Hambleton, Swaminathan & Rogers, 1991). We used one of its models (the so-called one-parameter model that produces maximum likelihood estimates) to scale the 38 cognitive test items, once we had established that the required underlying assumptions held empirically. Because this model leaves researchers free to choose the mean and the standard deviation for the metric to be used, we set the international mean of the scale for civic knowledge (and two sub-scales, to be discussed later) to 100, with a standard deviation of 20.

Figure 3.2 International Difficulty Map for Sample Items Relating to Civic Knowledge

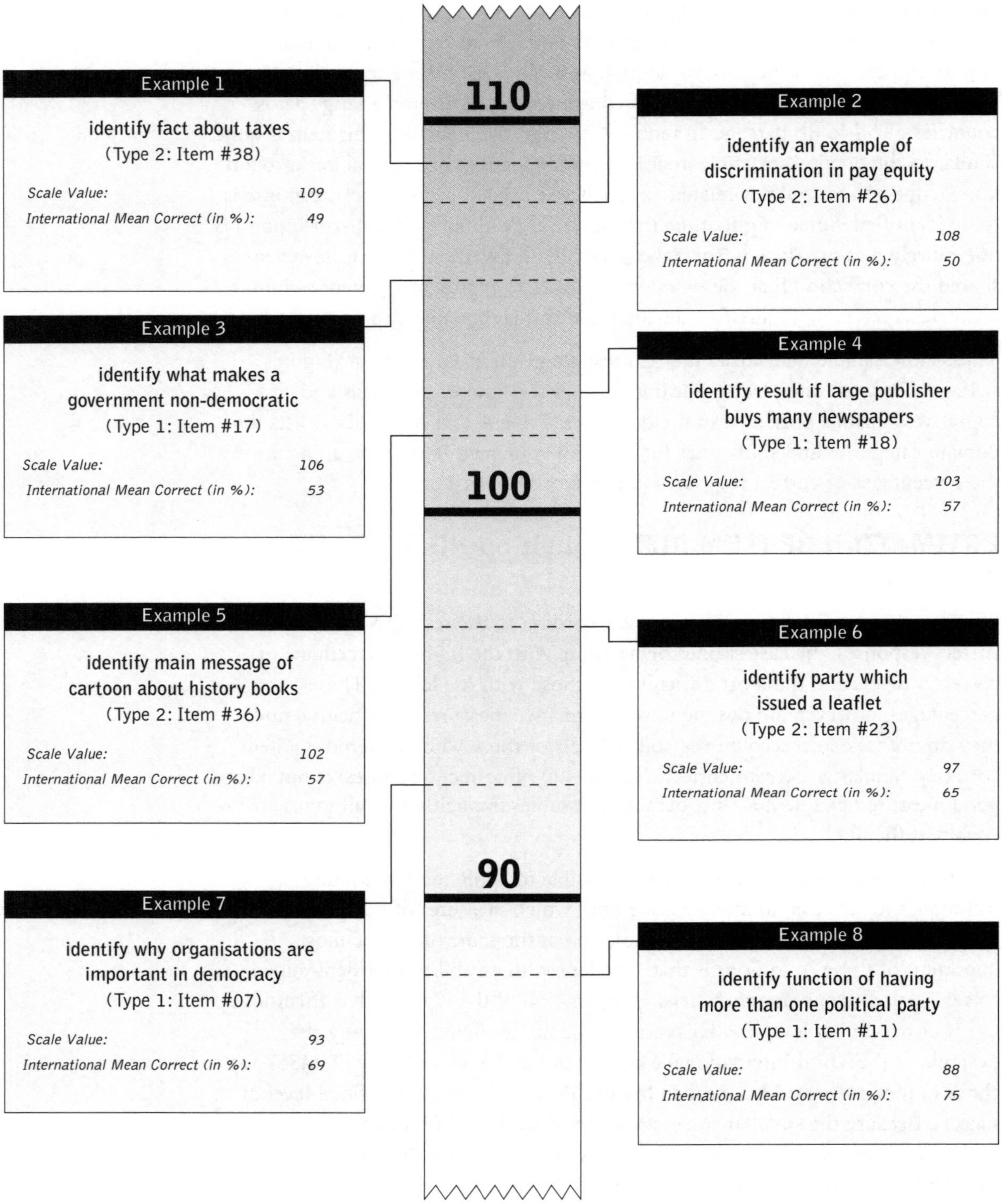

110

100

90

Example 1

identify fact about taxes
(Type 2: Item #38)

Scale Value: 109
International Mean Correct (in %): 49

Example 2

identify an example of discrimination in pay equity
(Type 2: Item #26)

Scale Value: 108
International Mean Correct (in %): 50

Example 3

identify what makes a government non-democratic
(Type 1: Item #17)

Scale Value: 106
International Mean Correct (in %): 53

Example 4

identify result if large publisher buys many newspapers
(Type 1: Item #18)

Scale Value: 103
International Mean Correct (in %): 57

Example 5

identify main message of cartoon about history books
(Type 2: Item #36)

Scale Value: 102
International Mean Correct (in %): 57

Example 6

identify party which issued a leaflet
(Type 2: Item #23)

Scale Value: 97
International Mean Correct (in %): 65

Example 7

identify why organisations are important in democracy
(Type 1: Item #07)

Scale Value: 93
International Mean Correct (in %): 69

Example 8

identify function of having more than one political party
(Type 1: Item #11)

Scale Value: 88
International Mean Correct (in %): 75

NOTE: Each item was placed onto the International Civic Knowledge Scale. Items are shown at the point on the scale where students with that level of proficiency had a 65 percent probability of providing a correct response.

Because percentages and scale values are rounded to the nearest whole number, some results may appear inconsistent.

Source: IEA Civic Education Study, Standard Population of 14-year-olds tested in 1999.

The item difficulty estimates produced by using an IRT model allowed us to demonstrate the substantive meaning of the items in the context of the test as a whole. Figure 3.2 provides an 'item difficulty map' that illustrates the relationship between the item-specific performance levels and the international knowledge test score as defined.

In this figure, the item examples (including those given in Appendix A) are placed on the scale—the gray bar in the middle—at the point where a student with the respective ability has a probability of .65 to provide the correct answer. For example, a student with a scale score of at least 106 on the civic knowledge scale has a chance of two in three or better to identify correctly what makes a government non-democratic (item example 3). Similarly, students with scale scores lower than 97 will have less than a 65 percent chance to identify correctly the origin of the imaginary electoral leaflet (item example 6).[1]

We had determined that the probability level of .65, which links item difficulties and student abilities, should be set as a formal characteristic of the metric used. Substantively, however, we considered this to be an appropriate interpretation of the somewhat vague term 'reasonable level of success'. It reflects our attempt to take into account knowledge expectations with a higher than 50 percent chance, even though this level is still below that which some might call mastery of the subject.

Figure 3.2 also displays, for each item example, the international average of correct answers. For the test as a whole, including those items not illustrated here, the percentages of correct responses range from 35 percent for the hardest item in the test to 85 percent for the easiest one. The respective difficulty parameters, or scale values, are 77 for the easiest item and 121 for the hardest. A fairly wide range of difficulties and student abilities therefore could be covered by the test. Table A.1 in Appendix A also contains the difficulty parameters for each item. Thus, it is possible to see how item difficulties are distributed across content domains.

One crucial point in the selection of items was to ensure that the item difficulties, and consequently the estimated student abilities, were truly comparable across countries. We had anticipated that this assumption would be difficult to meet, that is, 'differential item-functioning' or 'item-by-country interaction' would occur. This is the case when an item of a certain international difficulty level is relatively easier or harder for students in a country than one would expect on the basis of that country's overall mean. Different civic education curricula or differences in the historical and political context might cause such deviations in a country's response pattern from the international findings. Although there were 1,064 item-by-country pairs (38 items for each of 28 countries), only eight of these showed a clear item-by-country interaction. Because there were so few, we decided not to re-estimate ('float') the item difficulty parameters for the countries concerned, but to rely on the fact that the interaction effects within a country sum to zero.

Another potential problem was that, in a particular country, some items might not discriminate well between high- and low-achieving students. This happens when many able students in that country fail to choose the correct response, or when many weaker students do choose it ('item misfit'). Again, we found that such deviations from the international test characteristics were rare: we encountered 33 instances out of the 1,064. To ensure full international comparability, however, we deemed it appropriate to exclude the misfitting items countrywise from the final analysis of scores by treating them statistically as not having been administered. We therefore re-estimated all parameters, taking these cases into account. In no case is a country's civic knowledge score based on fewer than 35 out of the 38 available items, and in no case did we implicitly penalize a country for not being scored on the full set of 38 items. For further detail, see the technical report (Lehmann *et al.*, forthcoming).

In general, careful analysis showed us that it was possible to construct a meaningful, reliable and valid international test of student knowledge about democratic institutions, principles, processes and related topics that has a high degree of comparability across countries.

CIVIC KNOWLEDGE ACROSS COUNTRIES

Figure 3.3 presents a summary of the results of the international test on civic knowledge for all participating countries. To aid interpretation of these results, we added the date of testing, the tested grade and the average age of students to the figure. For some countries, readers should also take into account the specific information contained in the footnotes and the fuller elaboration given in Chapter 2.

On the basis of the scaling technique just explained, the table within Figure 3.3 contains the average test score and the standard error of sampling for each participating country. The international mean of the distribution (based on the 28 equally weighted national samples) and its standard error are included to give an orientation mark for each country to compare itself to the international average. Thus, the table indicates which countries differ significantly (after correction for multiple comparisons) from the international average.

Ten countries have means that are significantly higher and eight countries have means that are significantly lower than the international mean. The remaining ten countries belong to a middle group with country means that do not differ significantly from the international mean. For the most part, differences between countries within the three major groups are not significant (Figure 3.4).

Poland, the Czech Republic and the Slovak Republic, three post-communist countries from Central and Eastern Europe, belong to the top group. Other countries in this group are the Greek-speaking countries Greece and Cyprus, the United States, Italy and two Nordic countries (Finland and Norway). Students from Hong Kong (SAR) also perform significantly better than the international average.

In the group of countries with means significantly below average, only Portugal and French-speaking Belgium are in Western Europe, and both tested very young students. Romania and the three Baltic countries Estonia, Latvia and Lithuania have average scores between 92 and 94. Chile and Colombia, the two Latin American countries in this study, have the lowest means (88 and 86 respectively). Here, 75 percent of the students have scores below the international average.

Figure 3.3 Distributions of Civic Knowledge

Country	Mean Scale Score	Testing Date	Tested Grade*	Mean Age**	Cognitive Civic Competence Scale Score
Poland	▲ 111 (1.7)	5/99 - 6/99	8	15.0	
Finland	▲ 109 (0.7)	4/99	8	14.8	
Cyprus	▲ 108 (0.5)	5/99	9	14.8	
Greece	▲ 108 (0.8)	3/99 - 6/99	9	14.7	
Hong Kong (SAR)[3]	▲ 107 (1.1)	6/99 - 7/99	9	15.3	
United States[1]	▲ 106 (1.2)	10/99	9	14.7	
Italy	▲ 105 (0.8)	4/99 - 5/99	9	15.0	
Slovak Republic	▲ 105 (0.7)	5/99 - 6/99	8	14.3	
Norway[4]	▲ 103 (0.5)	4/99 - 6/99	8	14.8	
Czech Republic	▲ 103 (0.8)	4/99 - 5/99	8	14.4	
Australia	● 102 (0.8)	8/99	9	14.6	
Hungary	● 102 (0.6)	3/99	8	14.4	
Slovenia	● 101 (0.5)	4/99	8	14.8	
Denmark[4]	● 100 (0.5)	4/99	8	14.8	
Germany[2]	● 100 (0.5)	4/99 - 7/99	8	n.a.	
Russian Federation[3]	● 100 (1.3)	4/99 - 5/99	9	15.1	
England [1]	● 99 (0.6)	11/99	9	14.7	
Sweden[1]	● 99 (0.8)	10/99 - 12/99	8	14.3	
Switzerland	● 98 (0.8)	4/99 - 7/99	8/9	15.0	
Bulgaria	● 98 (1.3)	5/99 - 6/99	8	14.9	
Portugal[5]	▼ 96 (0.7)	4/99	8	14.5	
Belgium (French)[4]	▼ 95 (0.9)	3/99 - 4/99	8	14.1	
Estonia	▼ 94 (0.5)	4/99	8	14.7	
Lithuania	▼ 94 (0.7)	5/99	8	14.8	
Romania	▼ 92 (0.9)	5/99	8	14.8	
Latvia	▼ 92 (0.9)	4/99 - 5/99	8	14.5	
Chile	▼ 88 (0.7)	10/99	8	14.3	
Colombia	▼ 86 (0.9)	4/99 and 10/99	8	14.6	

Scale values: 40 60 80 100 120 140 160

( ) Standard errors appear in parentheses.

▲ Country mean significantly higher than international mean.

● No statistically significant difference between country mean and international mean.

▼ Country mean significantly lower than international mean.

1 Countries with testing date at beginning of school year.
2 National Desired Population does not cover all International Desired Population.
3 Countries did not meet age/grade specification.
4 Countries' overall participation rate after replacement less than 85 percent.
5 In Portugal, Grade 8 selected instead of Grade 9 due to average age. Mean scale score for Grade 9 was 106.

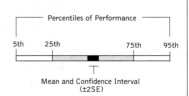

Percentiles of Performance
5th 25th 75th 95th
Mean and Confidence Interval (±2SE)

* In Switzerland, Grade 8 was tested mainly in German cantons; Grade 9 mainly in French and Italian cantons. In the Russian Federation, students in Grade 9 have eight or nine years of schooling depending on the duration of the primary school they finished. In 1999 about 70 percent of Russian students tested had eight years of schooling at the end of Grade 9.

** Information on age was not available for Germany. International mean age based on 27 countries only.

*Source: IEA Civic Education Study,*Standard Population of 14-year-olds tested in 1999.

A closer look at these averages reveals the necessity to consider mean age differences. At the country level, the national average of civic knowledge is correlated with the mean age of the sample ($r = .37$). Thus, countries with an older sample have an advantage over those that tested younger students. While it would be possible to adjust national averages of knowledge for differences in mean age (on the assumption of equal growth with age across all countries), such adjustment changes relatively little in the rank order of countries: the correlation between adjusted and unadjusted country means is $r = .92$.[2] The issue of age and growth will be explored more fully in a future report.

It is beyond the scope of the present volume to try and explain these country differences. Apart from the mean age of the sample, however, other factors can be shown to be correlated, such as the economic situation (gross national product per capita, $r = .32$, or the general level of literacy, $r = .26$; see Tables 1.1 and 1.2). But again, these findings should be taken primarily as evidence that more thorough analyses are needed, both at the international level and the country level with respect to individual and classroom-level processes.

The graphic representation on the right-hand side of Figure 3.3 shows the distribution of civic knowledge in the tested grade for each country. The cognitive score is shown for the mean as well as for the 5th, 25th, 75th and 95th percentiles. Each percentile point indicates the percentage performing below and up to the respective score. To give an example, 25 percent of the students perform below and up to the score marked by the 25th percentile. Seventy-five percent have attained a result above the corresponding score. The dark boxes in the center of each distribution stand for the country means and their 95 percent confidence interval (mean ± two standard errors of sampling). For an approach that gives substantive meaning to these percentiles, see Panel 3.2.

The variation of means between countries gives further information about the characteristics of this subject area. Twenty-five of the 28 countries differ by less than half of a standard deviation from the international average. Exceptions are Poland, with the highest national average score of 111, and Chile and Colombia, with mean scores below 90. This range can be compared to the results of other international studies on educational achievement. First, it is similar to that of the IEA Reading Literacy Study (Elley, 1994). Fifteen of the 28 countries participating in the Civic Education Study also participated in that study. The range between the highest and the lowest ranking country was .79 of an international standard deviation, compared with .70 in the present study. Secondly, 22 of the 28 countries also participated in the Third International Mathematics and Science Study (Beaton, Mullis, Martin, Gonzalez, Kelly & Smith, 1996). Among these countries, country means for mathematics achievement differed by 1.79 standard deviations between the highest and the lowest achieving country (and still by 1.10 standard deviations if the special case of Colombia was excluded). One of the reasons for this difference between the Reading Literacy Study and the Civic Education Study on the one hand and TIMSS on the other may be that reading (at the age of 14) and civic knowledge are less closely linked to curriculum and instruction than is mathematics.

It is informative to attribute substantive meaning to characteristics of the distribution, such as means and percentiles, by relating them to the item-difficulty parameters. These are indicated in the item examples given and in the item overview presented in Table A.1, Appendix A. This procedure can be done for each country separately. The following provides a demonstration of this mode of interpretation for the results for the weighted international file.

The 5th percentile in the international sample corresponds to a scale value of 71, which is lower than the item difficulty parameter of the easiest item in the test. This is Item 16, scale value 77, which pertains to the domain of national identity and international relations and which asks students to identify the major purpose of the United Nations (Table A.1, Appendix A). Thus, the probability that the lowest achieving students—internationally speaking—will respond correctly to this task is less than .65. In contrast, the probability that some students among the lowest 5 percent in a number of countries (for example, Cyprus, the Slovak Republic and Finland) will be able to identify the main purpose of the United Nations at the defined 'reasonable level of success' is .65 or higher.

Similarly, the 25th percentile in the international score distribution corresponds to a scale value of 85. This value is close to the item difficulty parameter (scale value 88) of the example given in the text (Figure 3.1e) in which students were asked to identify the function of having more than one political party in a democratic country. More than 75 percent of the students in the participating countries have a probability of .65 or higher of being able to respond correctly to this item, which refers to one of the fundamental traits of representative democracies. Twenty-five percent of the students in the international sample were found to lack such a level of civic knowledge as exemplified by this item (and others of equal difficulty). Another item of approximately this difficulty level is, for instance, Item 12, which asks who ought to govern in a democracy (Appendix Table A.1).

The international mean of 100 corresponds to an item also pertaining to the domain of democracy and its defining characteristics. This is Item 14, which calls on students to evaluate the strengths and weaknesses of democratic systems by identifying the main message of a cartoon about differences of opinion in a democracy. The typical student across participating countries has a reasonable chance (about two in three) to respond correctly to tasks of this difficulty level (Appendix A, Table A.1).

The 75th percentile, separating the top quarter from the lower 75 percent in the distribution, was found at a scale value of 112. This difficulty level exceeds the difficulty parameters of all of the examples given above. Item 22, which asks about the functions of periodic elections and which also was used by IEA in 1971, comes closest, with a difficulty level of 113. Thus, a little less than one out of four students in the participating countries was—with the defined minimal degree of likelihood—able to respond correctly to this item or others of the same level of difficulty. In some countries, most notably in Poland, the national mean is almost at the level of the international 75th percentile.

The 95th percentile, finally, indicates the lower bound of achievement for the top 5 percent in the international distribution of civic knowledge. It is found at a scale value of 135, which implies that in this international top group the probability of success is higher than .65 for all the items in the test.[3] This threshold is attained by the highest achieving students in a good

Panel 3.2 continued

number of participating countries (given here in the order of national means): the Slovak Republic, the Czech Republic, Australia, Hungary, Slovenia, Denmark, Germany, England, Sweden and Bulgaria. Another group of countries where the top 5 percent of the students were even more successful on the test includes Poland, Finland, Cyprus, Greece, Hong Kong (SAR), the United States, Italy, Norway and the Russian Federation.

The diagram in Figure 3.3 thus provides considerably more information than a simple ranking of countries by national average. The distributional properties for each country can and should be studied, preferably in close linkage with the appropriate statistics (such as the percentiles that were used here) and the item characteristics of the test.

Figure 3.4 provides a visual presentation of country averages showing those that differ significantly from each other at the 95 percent significance level. By selecting a country and reading across the table, we can see that the triangles pointing up indicate a significantly higher average performance than the country listed across the top, whereas the triangles pointing down stand for a significantly lower average. Dots indicate that the two country averages do not differ significantly from each other.[4]

The differences upon which this multiple-comparison table is based are mostly quite small between adjacent countries. For example, the country mean in Poland, where students have the highest average of all participating countries, does not significantly differ from the next seven countries. The Colombian average does not differ significantly from the Chilean one, but it does so from all other country means. Given that sampling errors are not identical across countries, it is possible that in some cases an apparently smaller difference is statistically significant while a larger one is not.

There is no obvious pattern in the distribution of national mean scores on the civic knowledge scale. Western European, North American and post-Communist countries lie in the top group of countries. The two Latin American countries and the Baltic countries as well as Romania have similar country means on the IEA civic knowledge test. We have already stated that many factors are likely to be involved in the emergence of between-country differences, even at the level of aggregate national indicators.

DISTINGUISHING BETWEEN CONTENT KNOWLEDGE AND INTERPRETATIVE SKILLS

As was shown above, the IEA test was designed to contain two different types of items: Type 1, tapping the students' knowledge of content; and Type 2, measuring their skills in interpreting civic-related material (cartoons, leaflets, descriptions of issues) and also incorporating their ability to distinguish between facts and opinions. It is also clear from the previous analysis that a one-dimensional representation of the students' response patterns is a psychometrically sound and meaningful way to present the findings. In this analysis each student is

Figure 3.4 Multiple Comparisons of Civic Knowledge

Instructions: Read *across* the row for a country to compare performance with the countries listed in the heading of the chart. The symbols indicate whether the mean achievement of the country in the row is significantly lower than that of the comparison country, significantly higher than that of the comparison country, or if there is no statistically significant difference between the two countries.

Country	Poland	Finland	Cyprus	Greece	Hong Kong (SAR)	United States	Italy	Slovak Republic	Norway	Czech Republic	Australia	Hungary	Slovenia	Denmark	Germany	Russian Federation	England	Sweden	Switzerland	Bulgaria	Portugal	Belgium (French)	Estonia	Lithuania	Romania	Latvia	Chile	Colombia
Poland		●	●	●	●	●	●	●	▲	▲	▲	▲	▲	▲	▲	▲	▲	▲	▲	▲	▲	▲	▲	▲	▲	▲	▲	▲
Finland	●		●	●	●	●	▲	▲	▲	▲	▲	▲	▲	▲	▲	▲	▲	▲	▲	▲	▲	▲	▲	▲	▲	▲	▲	▲
Cyprus	●	●		●	●	●	●	●	▲	▲	▲	▲	▲	▲	▲	▲	▲	▲	▲	▲	▲	▲	▲	▲	▲	▲	▲	▲
Greece	●	●	●		●	●	●	●	▲	▲	▲	▲	▲	▲	▲	▲	▲	▲	▲	▲	▲	▲	▲	▲	▲	▲	▲	▲
Hong Kong (SAR)[3]	●	●	●	●		●	●	●	●	●	▲	▲	▲	▲	▲	▲	▲	▲	▲	▲	▲	▲	▲	▲	▲	▲	▲	▲
United States[1]	●	●	●	●	●		●	●	●	●	▲	▲	▲	▲	▲	▲	▲	▲	▲	▲	▲	▲	▲	▲	▲	▲	▲	▲
Italy	●	▼	●	●	●	●		●	●	●	▲	▲	▲	▲	▲	▲	▲	▲	▲	▲	▲	▲	▲	▲	▲	▲	▲	▲
Slovak Republic	●	▼	●	●	●	●	●		●	●	▲	▲	▲	▲	▲	▲	▲	▲	▲	▲	▲	▲	▲	▲	▲	▲	▲	▲
Norway[4]	▼	▼	▼	▼	●	●	●	●		●	●	▲	▲	▲	▲	▲	▲	▲	▲	▲	▲	▲	▲	▲	▲	▲	▲	▲
Czech Republic	▼	▼	▼	▼	●	●	●	●	●		●	●	▲	▲	▲	▲	▲	▲	▲	▲	▲	▲	▲	▲	▲	▲	▲	▲
Australia	▼	▼	▼	▼	▼	▼	▼	▼	●	●		●	●	●	●	●	▲	▲	▲	▲	▲	▲	▲	▲	▲	▲	▲	▲
Hungary	▼	▼	▼	▼	▼	▼	▼	▼	▼	●	●		●	●	●	●	●	●	▲	▲	▲	▲	▲	▲	▲	▲	▲	▲
Slovenia	▼	▼	▼	▼	▼	▼	▼	▼	▼	▼	●	●		●	●	●	●	●	●	●	▲	▲	▲	▲	▲	▲	▲	▲
Denmark[4]	▼	▼	▼	▼	▼	▼	▼	▼	▼	▼	●	●	●		●	●	●	●	●	●	●	▲	▲	▲	▲	▲	▲	▲
Germany[2]	▼	▼	▼	▼	▼	▼	▼	▼	▼	▼	●	●	●	●		●	●	●	●	●	●	●	▲	▲	▲	▲	▲	▲
Russian Federation[3]	▼	▼	▼	▼	▼	▼	▼	▼	▼	▼	●	●	●	●	●		●	●	●	●	●	●	●	▲	▲	▲	▲	▲
England[1]	▼	▼	▼	▼	▼	▼	▼	▼	▼	▼	▼	●	●	●	●	●		●	●	●	●	●	●	●	▲	▲	▲	▲
Sweden[1]	▼	▼	▼	▼	▼	▼	▼	▼	▼	▼	▼	●	●	●	●	●	●		●	●	●	●	●	●	●	▲	▲	▲
Switzerland	▼	▼	▼	▼	▼	▼	▼	▼	▼	▼	▼	▼	●	●	●	●	●	●		●	●	●	●	●	●	●	▲	▲
Bulgaria	▼	▼	▼	▼	▼	▼	▼	▼	▼	▼	▼	▼	●	●	●	●	●	●	●		●	●	●	●	●	●	●	▲
Portugal[5]	▼	▼	▼	▼	▼	▼	▼	▼	▼	▼	▼	▼	▼	●	●	●	●	●	●	●		●	●	●	●	●	●	▲
Belgium (French)[4]	▼	▼	▼	▼	▼	▼	▼	▼	▼	▼	▼	▼	▼	▼	●	●	●	●	●	●	●		●	●	●	●	●	▲
Estonia	▼	▼	▼	▼	▼	▼	▼	▼	▼	▼	▼	▼	▼	▼	▼	●	●	●	●	●	●	●		●	●	●	●	▲
Lithuania	▼	▼	▼	▼	▼	▼	▼	▼	▼	▼	▼	▼	▼	▼	▼	▼	●	●	●	●	●	●	●		●	●	●	▲
Romania	▼	▼	▼	▼	▼	▼	▼	▼	▼	▼	▼	▼	▼	▼	▼	▼	▼	●	●	●	●	●	●	●		●	●	▲
Latvia	▼	▼	▼	▼	▼	▼	▼	▼	▼	▼	▼	▼	▼	▼	▼	▼	▼	▼	●	●	●	●	●	●	●		●	▲
Chile	▼	▼	▼	▼	▼	▼	▼	▼	▼	▼	▼	▼	▼	▼	▼	▼	▼	▼	▼	●	●	●	●	●	●	●		●
Colombia	▼	▼	▼	▼	▼	▼	▼	▼	▼	▼	▼	▼	▼	▼	▼	▼	▼	▼	▼	▼	▼	▼	▼	▼	▼	▼	●	

Countries are ordered by mean achievement across the heading and down the rows.

▲ Mean achievement significantly higher than comparison country.

● No statistically significant difference from comparison country.

▼ Mean achievement significantly lower than comparison country.

NOTE: Significance tests at .05 level, adjusted for multiple comparisons.
1 Countries with testing date at beginning of school year.
2 National Desired Population does not cover all International Desired Population.
3 Countries did not meet age/grade specification.
4 Countries' overall participation rate after replacement less than 85 percent.
5 In Portugal, Grade 8 selected instead of Grade 9 due to average age. Mean scale score for Grade 9 was 106.

Source: IEA Civic Education Study, Standard Population of 14-year-olds tested in 1999.

simply awarded one total civic knowledge score, and from these scores the reported national means and distributions presented in the last section are derived.

Even though this method is completely defensible, it was of interest to investigate whether the distinction between the two item types would map the students' response patterns even more appropriately. Might it be possible to derive a sub-score for content knowledge and for skills in interpreting civic-related material that would allow additional insights? To ascertain the dimensional structure of the IEA test under the assumption that two dimensions (corresponding to content knowledge and interpretative skills) could be distinguished, we performed confirmatory factor analyses (CFA). These were based on a calibration sample of 500 randomly selected students per country. As a contrast to the one-dimensional model with all 38 items on a single factor, we estimated a second model that allocated the 25 Type 1 items to one factor (content knowledge) and the remaining 13 items to a second factor (interpretative skills).[5]

Figure 3.5 shows a graphical display of the two-factor-structure and the results of a comparison of the model fit with the one-factor-solution. The diagram includes the factor correlation between the two latent constructs 'knowledge of content' and 'skills of interpretation', as well as the factor loading for each item and the proportion of (unexplained) error. The variance of the items explained by the latent dimensions ranges from 17 to 53 percent.

Both models show good statistical properties, but the two-factor-solution that is shown graphically has a relatively better model fit than the one-factor-solution. The difference in the chi-square statistic is 604, with one degree of freedom, which is highly significant.[6] However, the two factors are strongly correlated with each other ($r = .91$), which indicates that the two abilities—'content knowledge' and 'interpretative skills'—refer to highly similar but not identical aspects of student performance. While it is true that the students who know much about civic-related content are likely also to have highly developed skills in interpreting civic-related material, this is not always the case. It is also possible that systematic differences occur between groups of students and even countries. Based on these results, we decided to present, in addition to the total cognitive score on *civic knowledge*, findings based on the two component sub-scales *content knowledge* and *skills in interpreting civic-related information*.

In Figure 3.6, we have again ranked the participating countries in the order of average achievement in civic knowledge (total score), but we also have given the means for the sub-scales of content knowledge and interpretative skills. All three scales are one-parameter Rasch scales, and all three have been set to an international mean of 100 and an international standard deviation of 20. It is not our assumption that one of the sub-scales refers to more complex or superior abilities than the other. On the contrary: in recognition of the fact that scale properties always depend on the particular choice of items used, our underlying assumption is that there is no meaningful way of comparing directly the scores on one of the sub-scales with those on the other. Given, however, that the students who took the items from the two sub-scales were identical, it is meaningful to compare the performance of countries on the two sub-scales, *relative to the respective international means*. In a sense, this analysis amounts to investigating the differential functioning of two groups of items that can be considered as measuring two different aspects of civic knowledge.

Figure 3.5 Confirmatory Factor Analysis of Civic Knowledge Items

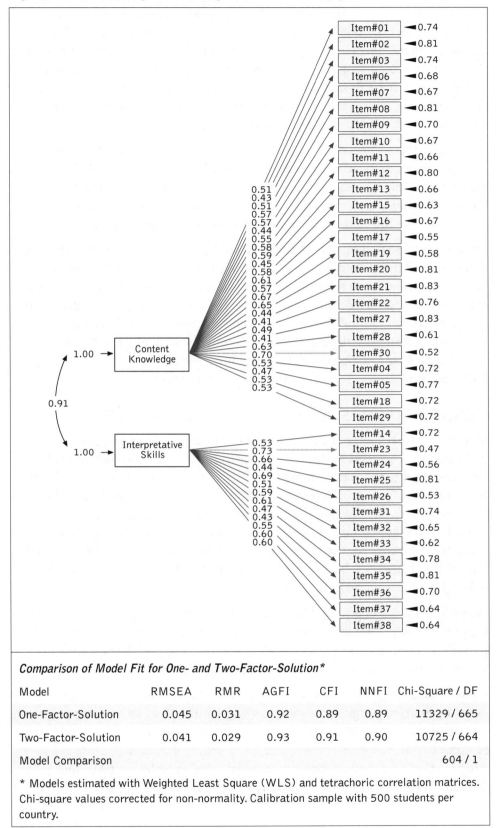

Comparison of Model Fit for One- and Two-Factor-Solution*

Model	RMSEA	RMR	AGFI	CFI	NNFI	Chi-Square / DF
One-Factor-Solution	0.045	0.031	0.92	0.89	0.89	11329 / 665
Two-Factor-Solution	0.041	0.029	0.93	0.91	0.90	10725 / 664
Model Comparison						604 / 1

* Models estimated with Weighted Least Square (WLS) and tetrachoric correlation matrices. Chi-square values corrected for non-normality. Calibration sample with 500 students per country.

Source: IEA Civic Education Study, Standard Population of 14-year-olds tested in 1999.

Figure 3.6 demonstrates that the outcomes on the two sub-scales do vary somewhat within countries. In 26 countries (the exceptions are Denmark and Germany), either the content or skills sub-score average is significantly above or below the international mean. In contrast, the total civic knowledge score reveals that 18 of the countries are above or below the international mean. This suggests that looking at two sub-scores rather than a single civic knowledge score does contribute to an understanding of relative strengths and weaknesses of civic knowledge as developed in the participating countries.

In five countries—Australia, England, Sweden, Switzerland and the United States—relative to the sub-scale means, the items pertaining to the skills dimension are more likely to be answered correctly than those from the content dimension. In two countries, Poland and the Russian Federation, relative performance on the content items is better than that on the skills items.

Once again these findings depend heavily on the specific items in the respective sub-scales and therefore can only be interpreted as pertaining to the *relative* position of countries on the two sub-scales. Nevertheless, it is interesting that, in some countries, students have acquired their content knowledge and interpretative skills differentially. In the absence of any obvious explanation, it is all the more important to systematically investigate such patterns in future analyses and to relate results to the findings from Phase 1 (Torney-Purta, Schwille & Amadeo, 1999; Steiner-Khamsi, Torney-Purta & Schwille, forthcoming).

GENDER DIFFERENCES IN CIVIC KNOWLEDGE

Most previous research has shown gender differences regarding cognitive performance of students in this area. In particular, according to studies conducted a decade or more ago, males scored higher on civic knowledge tests than females. In the first IEA Civic Education Study (1971), gender had a significant effect on cognitive achievement among the 14-year-old students in four out of eight countries, and these gender differences became more notable among older students, with males consistently outscoring females (Torney *et al.*, 1975, p.148). National studies mostly have had similar results on different tests measuring political knowledge (see Panel 3.1).

Figure 3.7 shows the gender differences in civic knowledge for all 28 countries in the present study. After correcting for multiple comparisons, we found no statistically significant differences in 27 of the 28 countries.[7] The exception is Slovenia, where females perform better than males.

These findings suggest that, at least in a simple comparison, among 14-year-olds in most countries, political content knowledge and skills in interpreting political communication are unrelated to gender and that the previously found dominance of males in this area, even at the age of 14, is greatly diminished. This interpretation needs some modification when other variables are taken into account, however. More about this topic will be said in Chapter 8.

Figure 3.6 Content Knowledge Subscore and Interpretative Skills Subscore

Country	Mean Scale Scores					
	Content Knowledge	Interpretative Skills	Total Civic Knowledge	80	100	120
Poland	▲ 112 (1.3)	▲ 106 (1.7)	▲ 111 (1.7)			
Finland	▲ 108 (0.7)	▲ 110 (0.6)	▲ 109 (0.7)			
Cyprus	▲ 108 (0.5)	▲ 108 (0.5)	▲ 108 (0.5)			
Greece	▲ 109 (0.7)	▲ 105 (0.7)	▲ 108 (0.8)			
Hong Kong (SAR)[3]	▲ 108 (1.0)	▲ 104 (1.0)	▲ 107 (1.1)			
United States[1]	● 102 (1.1)	▲ 114 (1.0)	▲ 106 (1.2)			
Italy	▲ 105 (0.8)	▲ 105 (0.7)	▲ 105 (0.8)			
Slovak Republic	▲ 107 (0.7)	▲ 103 (0.7)	▲ 105 (0.7)			
Norway[4]	▲ 103 (0.5)	▲ 103 (0.4)	▲ 103 (0.5)			
Czech Republic	▲ 103 (0.8)	● 102 (0.8)	▲ 103 (0.8)			
Australia	● 99 (0.7)	▲ 107 (0.8)	● 102 (0.8)			
Hungary	▲ 102 (0.6)	● 101 (0.7)	● 102 (0.6)			
Slovenia	▲ 102 (0.5)	● 99 (0.4)	● 101 (0.5)			
Denmark[4]	● 100 (0.5)	● 100 (0.5)	● 100 (0.5)			
Germany[2]	● 99 (0.5)	● 101 (0.5)	● 100 (0.5)			
Russian Federation	● 102 (1.3)	▼ 96 (1.3)	● 100 (1.3)			
England[1]	▼ 96 (0.6)	▲ 105 (0.7)	● 99 (0.6)			
Sweden[1]	▼ 97 (0.8)	▲ 102 (0.7)	● 99 (0.8)			
Switzerland	▼ 96 (0.8)	● 102 (0.8)	● 98 (0.8)			
Bulgaria	● 99 (1.1)	▼ 95 (1.3)	● 98 (1.3)			
Portugal[5]	▼ 97 (0.7)	▼ 95 (0.7)	▼ 96 (0.7)			
Belgium (French)[4]	▼ 94 (0.9)	▼ 96 (0.9)	▼ 95 (0.9)			
Estonia	▼ 94 (0.5)	▼ 95 (0.5)	▼ 94 (0.5)			
Lithuania	▼ 94 (0.7)	▼ 93 (0.7)	▼ 94 (0.7)			
Romania	▼ 93 (1.0)	▼ 90 (0.7)	▼ 92 (0.9)			
Latvia	▼ 92 (0.9)	▼ 92 (0.8)	▼ 92 (0.9)			
Chile	▼ 89 (0.6)	▼ 88 (0.8)	▼ 88 (0.7)			
Colombia	▼ 89 (0.8)	▼ 84 (1.2)	▼ 86 (0.9)			

( ) Standard errors appear in parentheses. Because results are rounded to the nearest whole number, some totals may appear inconsistent.

▲ Country mean significantly higher than international mean.

● No statistically significant difference between country mean and international mean.

▼ Country mean significantly lower than international mean.

⊢◇⊣ = Mean Subscore Civic Content (± 2 SE).
⊢●⊣ = Mean Subscore Civic Skills (± 2 SE).
▪ = Mean Total Civic Knowledge Score.

1 Countries with testing date at beginning of school year.
2 National Desired Population does not cover all International Desired Population.
3 Countries did not meet age/grade specification.
4 Countries' overall participation rate after replacement less than 85 percent.
5 In Portugal, Grade 8 selected instead of Grade 9 due to average age. Mean scores for Grade 9 were 108 on the Civic Content Scale, 103 on the Civic Skills Scale and 106 on the Total Civic Knowledge Scale.

Source: IEA Civic Education Study, Standard Population of 14-year-olds tested in 1999.

Figure 3.7 Gender Differences in Civic Knowledge

Country	Mean Scale Score Females	Mean Scale Score Males	Difference Absolute Value	Gender Difference
				+10 0 +10
Denmark[4]	99 (0.7)	102 (0.7)	3 (1.0)	Males Score Higher Females Score Higher
Switzerland	97 (0.8)	100 (0.9)	2 (1.2)	
Chile	88 (0.8)	89 (0.8)	2 (1.1)	
Czech Republic	102 (0.8)	104 (1.0)	2 (1.3)	
Portugal[5]	96 (0.8)	97 (0.9)	1 (1.2)	
Germany[2]	99 (0.6)	101 (0.7)	1 (0.9)	
Norway[4]	103 (0.6)	103 (0.7)	1 (0.9)	
Russian Federation[3]	99 (1.2)	100 (1.7)	0 (2.1)	
Slovak Republic	105 (0.8)	105 (0.9)	0 (1.1)	
England[1]	99 (0.8)	100 (1.0)	0 (1.3)	
Cyprus	108 (0.7)	108 (0.6)	0 (0.9)	
Colombia	87 (1.3)	86 (1.1)	0 (1.7)	
Romania	92 (1.0)	91 (0.9)	0 (1.4)	
Hungary	102 (0.7)	101 (0.8)	1 (1.0)	
Hong Kong (SAR)[3]	108 (1.1)	106 (1.4)	1 (1.8)	
Sweden[1]	100 (0.8)	99 (1.1)	1 (1.3)	
Estonia	95 (0.6)	93 (0.7)	1 (0.9)	
Finland	110 (0.9)	108 (0.8)	2 (1.2)	
United States[1]	107 (1.2)	106 (1.3)	2 (1.8)	
Greece	109 (0.8)	107 (0.9)	2 (1.2)	
Italy	106 (0.9)	104 (1.1)	2 (1.4)	
Bulgaria	99 (1.5)	97 (1.2)	2 (2.0)	
Lithuania	95 (0.8)	92 (0.8)	2 (1.1)	
Australia	103 (0.9)	101 (1.1)	2 (1.4)	
Poland	112 (2.2)	109 (1.5)	3 (2.6)	
Slovenia	102 (0.6)	99 (0.6)	4 (0.8)	
Latvia	93 (0.9)	90 (0.9)	4 (1.3)	
Belgium (French)[4]	97 (1.1)	93 (1.3)	5 (1.7)	

( ) Standard errors appear in parentheses. Because results are rounded to the nearest whole number, some totals may appear inconsistent.

■ Gender difference statistically significant at .05 level.

□ Gender difference not statistically significant.

International Means

Female	Male	Difference
100.4	99.7	0.7

(Averages of all country means)

1 Countries with testing date at beginning of school year.
2 National Desired Population does not cover all International Desired Population.
3 Countries did not meet age/grade specification.
4 Countries' overall participation rate after replacement less than 85 percent.
5 In Portugal, Grade 8 selected instead of Grade 9 due to average age.

Source: IEA Civic Education Study, Standard Population of 14-year-olds tested in 1999.

HOME LITERACY RESOURCES AND CIVIC KNOWLEDGE

Previous research has consistently shown students' social background to be important in fostering civic knowledge. Students from less affluent and less educated families have less knowledge in this area than those with more affluent and better-educated parents. In the first IEA Civic Education Study, social status was a consistently positive predictor for the cognitive test score in all participating countries (Torney *et al.*, 1975).

For international studies it is very difficult to find comparable indicators for the social background of families. Social status is defined differently across countries, and it is usually impractical to measure social status by asking 14-year-old students about their parents' occupation(s) or family income. The Student Background Questionnaire of the present study included questions to the students as to their father's and mother's educational attainment, but the validity of this indicator may not be beyond question either. Students of this age sometimes do not know the educational level of their parents: in some of the participating countries more than 20 percent of the students did not answer this question. Another serious problem is that the different structure of educational systems across countries may jeopardize the comparability of the educational levels.

We therefore decided to use the number of books in the home as the indicator for the students' social background. This variable has been used before in international studies on educational achievement and has proven to be a very consistent predictor of educational achievement (see, for example, the reports of TIMSS, Beaton *et al.*, 1996). The number of books in the home can be interpreted as a proxy for the emphasis placed on education, the resources available to acquire and support literacy and, more generally speaking, the academic support a student finds in his or her family.

Table 3.1 shows that home literary resources are quite consistently correlated with the civic knowledge score. The inspection of squared Etas—a measure of the proportion of variance in the (dependent) knowledge scores attributable to the (independent) variable 'number of books in the home'—reveals that in all but one country (Hong Kong/SAR) home literacy resources account for more than 5 percent of the variance in the test scores. The strongest effects of 12 percent and more are found in Chile, England, Germany, Hungary and the United States. In the large majority of countries, the more books that students report in their homes, the better they perform on the civic knowledge test.

It should be noted that there are substantial differences in the students' report of home literacy resources across countries. Whereas in most European countries, Australia and the United States less than 10 percent of students report no or very few books in the home, in Chile, Colombia and Hong Kong (SAR) this is true of almost one-third. In Portugal and Romania, one-fifth of the students fall into this category. In Chile, Colombia and Romania this finding coincides with the fact that the overall average test scores are considerably below the international mean. As such, the low level of home literacy resources in these countries may be one reason among others for the relatively low performance on the test, at least as compared to other countries in this study. It may be recalled that a similar effect was suggested by the statistical relationship between national literacy rates and student average performance in the civic knowledge test.

Table 3.1 Civic Knowledge and Students' Reports on Home Literacy Resources

Country	None or Very Few (0-10 books)		About One Shelf (11-50 books)		About One Bookcase (51-100 books)		About Two Bookcases (101-200 books)		Three or More Bookcases (More than 200 books)		Eta Squared
	Percent of Students	Mean Scale Score	Percent of Students	Mean Scale Score	Percent of Students	Mean Scale Score	Percent of Students	Mean Scale Score	Percent of Students	Mean Scale Score	
Australia	4 (0.4)	88 (1.4)	14 (0.8)	95 (1.2)	20 (0.9)	100 (1.0)	23 (1.0)	104 (1.1)	39 (1.3)	106 (1.0)	0.05
Belgium (French)	10 (1.1)	83 (1.1)	18 (1.1)	90 (1.2)	22 (0.9)	93 (1.1)	18 (0.9)	97 (1.0)	32 (1.5)	102 (1.6)	0.11
Bulgaria	14 (1.8)	86 (1.5)	15 (1.4)	92 (1.4)	20 (1.6)	96 (1.3)	19 (0.8)	100 (1.7)	32 (1.8)	105 (1.9)	0.11
Chile	32 (1.6)	80 (0.6)	33 (1.0)	89 (0.7)	19 (0.7)	94 (0.8)	8 (0.6)	97 (0.9)	8 (0.5)	96 (1.1)	0.13
Colombia	29 (2.5)	81 (1.1)	33 (1.2)	87 (0.9)	21 (1.4)	90 (1.3)	10 (0.9)	92 (1.3)	7 (0.7)	90 (1.5)	0.06
Cyprus	8 (0.5)	97 (1.2)	27 (0.8)	105 (0.7)	31 (0.9)	109 (0.8)	18 (0.6)	112 (0.9)	15 (0.8)	113 (1.1)	0.06
Czech Republic	2 (0.3)	93 (2.5)	12 (0.8)	93 (0.9)	29 (1.1)	99 (1.1)	31 (1.3)	105 (0.8)	27 (1.3)	110 (1.2)	0.07
Denmark	6 (0.5)	89 (1.3)	17 (0.8)	95 (1.0)	23 (0.8)	98 (0.8)	21 (0.7)	103 (0.9)	32 (0.9)	106 (0.7)	0.06
England	8 (0.7)	86 (0.9)	19 (0.8)	92 (0.7)	23 (0.9)	97 (0.9)	22 (0.9)	102 (0.8)	27 (1.3)	109 (0.9)	0.15
Estonia	1 (0.2)	83 (2.2)	7 (0.5)	89 (1.2)	17 (0.8)	89 (0.6)	27 (0.9)	93 (0.6)	49 (1.2)	98 (0.8)	0.05
Finland	5 (0.5)	96 (1.5)	24 (0.9)	105 (0.8)	30 (0.9)	109 (0.8)	22 (0.8)	112 (0.8)	20 (1.1)	116 (1.4)	0.05
Germany	6 (0.5)	86 (1.3)	21 (0.7)	93 (0.7)	24 (0.8)	97 (0.6)	19 (0.7)	103 (0.7)	30 (1.0)	108 (0.9)	0.14
Greece	8 (0.7)	95 (1.4)	34 (1.0)	104 (0.8)	27 (0.8)	109 (0.9)	15 (0.8)	113 (1.4)	15 (0.8)	116 (1.2)	0.07
Hong Kong (SAR)	31 (1.0)	103 (1.2)	35 (0.9)	111 (1.2)	16 (0.6)	107 (1.4)	8 (0.4)	109 (1.7)	9 (0.5)	104 (1.6)	0.02
Hungary	5 (0.6)	86 (1.2)	12 (0.8)	91 (0.7)	21 (1.0)	97 (0.8)	24 (0.9)	103 (0.7)	38 (1.4)	108 (0.8)	0.14
Italy	15 (0.8)	95 (0.9)	30 (1.1)	103 (0.8)	24 (0.7)	107 (0.9)	16 (0.8)	111 (1.1)	14 (0.9)	113 (1.5)	0.08
Latvia	2 (0.4)	82 (1.7)	10 (0.8)	86 (1.2)	20 (0.9)	88 (1.0)	26 (1.1)	91 (1.0)	40 (1.6)	96 (1.1)	0.05
Lithuania	8 (0.7)	85 (1.6)	23 (1.0)	90 (1.0)	26 (0.9)	93 (0.7)	18 (0.7)	96 (0.9)	24 (1.1)	100 (1.0)	0.07
Norway	3 (0.4)	88 (1.5)	15 (0.8)	96 (0.9)	21 (0.9)	100 (0.7)	26 (0.8)	104 (0.7)	35 (1.3)	109 (0.7)	0.07
Poland	6 (0.5)	94 (1.3)	20 (1.2)	103 (1.6)	24 (1.3)	109 (1.4)	19 (1.1)	113 (1.8)	31 (2.2)	119 (1.9)	0.11
Portugal	22 (1.3)	90 (0.6)	36 (1.2)	94 (0.6)	20 (0.8)	98 (1.0)	11 (0.8)	103 (1.1)	11 (1.1)	106 (2.1)	0.09
Romania	24 (1.9)	87 (1.7)	28 (1.2)	90 (0.9)	21 (1.0)	91 (0.9)	12 (0.9)	96 (1.1)	14 (1.1)	98 (1.5)	0.05
Russian Federation	6 (1.0)	84 (3.2)	17 (1.4)	94 (1.6)	26 (1.0)	98 (1.6)	21 (1.0)	102 (1.6)	30 (1.4)	106 (1.7)	0.08
Slovak Republic	4 (0.5)	90 (1.6)	21 (1.0)	100 (1.0)	30 (1.1)	104 (0.7)	24 (1.0)	108 (1.0)	21 (1.3)	113 (1.1)	0.09
Slovenia	7 (0.8)	89 (0.8)	29 (1.0)	96 (0.6)	30 (0.9)	101 (0.7)	17 (0.9)	105 (1.0)	17 (0.8)	107 (1.0)	0.08
Sweden	5 (0.5)	84 (1.3)	16 (0.9)	93 (1.2)	24 (1.2)	98 (1.1)	23 (1.2)	99 (0.9)	32 (1.9)	106 (1.1)	0.09
Switzerland	6 (0.7)	86 (1.0)	24 (1.3)	93 (0.9)	25 (0.9)	98 (0.9)	21 (0.8)	102 (1.0)	23 (1.2)	105 (1.3)	0.10
United States	9 (0.9)	91 (1.3)	22 (1.2)	99 (0.9)	22 (0.8)	105 (1.3)	20 (1.0)	112 (1.5)	28 (1.4)	115 (1.7)	0.12
International Sample	10 (0.2)	89 (0.3)	22 (0.2)	96 (0.2)	23 (0.2)	100 (0.2)	19 (0.2)	103 (0.2)	25 (0.2)	106 (0.3)	0.07

( ) Standard errors appear in parentheses. Because results are rounded to the nearest whole number, some totals may appear inconsistent.

Source: IEA Civic Education Study, Standard Population of 14-year-olds tested in 1999.

Hong Kong (SAR), however, shows a very different pattern. Civic knowledge does not increase significantly with home literacy resources: most students report a low number of books at home and the overall test score is above the international average, a pattern which is parallel to findings from TIMSS (Beaton *et al.*, 1996). Conversely, students from some countries, for example, Belgium (French) and the Baltic countries, report a relatively high number of books in their homes, but their average performance on the civic knowledge test is below the international mean. These exceptions demonstrate once more the need for more specific investigation that goes beyond the general trends appearing in this first cross-national volume.

SUMMARY

The analysis of responses to the IEA test of civic knowledge presented in this chapter shows that students do vary in their civic knowledge (and in sub-scores distinguishing content knowledge and interpretative skills). Differences between countries are smaller than in such school subjects as mathematics where the acquisition of the respective abilities is likely to depend more on the instruction received, and are relatively similar to studies in reading literacy. Most of the students in the participating countries give evidence of a fairly adequate content knowledge base when questioned about basic notions of democracy and citizenship. However, the analysis also reveals that in some countries there is a considerable group of students whose civic knowledge is below the level that might be considered 'basic'. At the same time, it should be noted that the questions in the test answered correctly by only relatively small numbers of students are part of what might be required to perform such civic tasks as deciding between candidates based on their election leaflets, understanding newspaper editorials and deciding whether to join a political organization with a particular ideology.

Gender differences in civic knowledge that were prominent in earlier research are not manifest in the present data. As more recent studies have also shown, boys no longer seem to have a clear advantage over girls in their knowledge of political content and their skills in interpreting civic-related materials. The question will be addressed again in Chapter 8, which considers the potentially moderating effects of other variables.

Knowledge differences between students that can be traced back to differences in the learning environments of the homes persist, however. In other international achievement surveys, home literacy resources have been closely related to the test results, and here, too, it remains to be seen how much of this effect stands if it is investigated in conjunction with other factors related to the emergence of civic knowledge among 14-year-olds.

NOTES

1 The relationship between the item scale value (difficulty parameter) and the percentage of correct answers is not as direct as it seems here. Thus, the idea that a student with a scale score of 106 has a .65 percent chance of scoring correctly on item example 3 appears to conflict with the fact that the United States' mean scale score is 106, with the percentage correct being 53, not 65. Likewise, on item example 5, Australia's mean scale score is 102, with a percentage correct of 75, not 65. Reasons for such discrepancies can be found in distributional properties, minor item-by-country interactions, and the fact that parameter estimates are based on the entire response matrix that includes local deviations from the model assumptions.

2 The adjustment procedure renders a gross measure of annual growth in civic knowledge that is in the order of 40 percent of an international standard deviation and thus roughly in line with the difference found between the two Portuguese samples (see Figure 3.3, footnote 5).

3 This observation is compatible with the fact that the most difficult item in the test has a scale value of only 121. If we take the case of a student who answered all the items correctly, we can see that his or her ability level is 'unknown' (and therefore set to some pragmatically plausible value), given that there were no items difficult enough to facilitate an ability estimate at the defined probability level of .65. Similarly, and with good mathematical reason, students with near-perfect test results can receive scores well above the item difficulty parameter of the most difficult item.

4 All significance tests ($p < .05$) are based on the Dunn-Bonferroni procedure for multiple comparisons, applied here to one country at a time ($df = 27$). Differences in rounding conventions used in different statistical packages may result in small inconsistencies.

5 Because all items considered are dichotomously keyed (correct vs. incorrect response), we chose a conservative approach. We estimated the two models according to the 'weighted least squares estimation' (WLE) algorithm, using a matrix of tetrachoric correlations and an asymptotic covariance weight matrix (see Jöreskog, 1990).

6 However, in view of the large sample size of 14,000 students (500 randomly selected students from each participating country), the interpretation of the chi-square statistic is generally problematic because even small differences tend to be significant.

7 Comparisons within a single country that are not corrected in this way may show a significant difference.

CHAPTER 4

Students' Concepts of Democracy, Citizenship and Government

HIGHLIGHTS RELATING TO CIVIC CONCEPTS

- Fourteen-year-olds across countries recognize the importance of some basic attributes of democracy that are highlighted by political theorists. For example, they believe that free elections and the availability of many organizations for people to join strengthen democracy. They believe democracy is weakened when wealthy people have undue influence on government, when politicians influence the courts, and when people are forbidden to express ideas critical of the government.

- Fourteen-year-olds believe that obeying the law is the most important attribute of the good adult citizen. Voting in elections is also seen as important. In many countries, young people believe that joining a political party and discussing political issues are of little importance for citizenship. Activities in the community and in relation to social movement groups have considerable importance, however.

- Fourteen-year-olds are already members of a political culture. They possess concepts of the social and economic responsibilities of government that largely correspond to those of adults in their societies. They are more likely to believe that the government should take responsibilities such as providing education or preserving order than take responsibility for activities associated with the economy, such as reducing income inequalities or controlling prices.

- Fourteen-year-old males and females possess similar concepts of democracy and government responsibility.

What does democracy mean to young people in different parts of the world? What is their implicit theory regarding what a democracy is and what is likely to strengthen or to weaken it? They are exhorted to be good citizens, but what does that concept imply? If young people read that 'the government' should (or should not) be expected to take certain responsibilities, what do they think that means?

Understanding the concepts of democracy, citizenship and government is an educational expectation that all the participating countries mentioned for young people in the Phase 1 case studies (Torney-Purta, Schwille & Amadeo, 1999). These concepts are embedded in each of the three domains of the content framework—especially *democracy, democratic institutions and citizenship*, but also in *national identity* and in *social cohesion and diversity*. Social representation has a meaning similar to the term concept as used in this study.

We have measured the attributes which students in different countries think strengthen democracy, the attributes of good citizenship for adults, and the responsibilities of the government. Because it is important to understand the content of young people's concepts, we present more detail at the item level in this chapter than we do in the chapter about attitudes, where scale scores predominate.

CONCEPTS OF DEMOCRACY

Relation of this Area to the Study's Design

'Democracy and democratic institutions' comprise the first domain identified in the country reports submitted during Phase 1 of the IEA Civic Education Study (Torney-Purta *et al.*, 1999). In countries establishing democratic governments there were especially pressing questions. For example, do young people see ways that democracy might be threatened as well as strengthened? How much consensus exists across countries about what is good or bad for democracy?

Other evidence in Phase 1 indicated that the emphasis in textbooks and curricula was on giving students a positive view of democracy. Schools generally focused on a few prominent elements such as elections, good citizenship involving responsibilities as well as rights, and government as providing essential services to citizens. Democracy and its development was often studied in history courses, as well as in classes with 'civic' or 'citizenship' in their titles.

Some questions about the principles or pivotal ideas of democracy were successfully formulated with right and wrong answers for the test. If we had been limited to questions of this type, it would have been impossible to cover the content topics emphasized in the Phase 1 material, however. We therefore designed a measure of the concept of democracy using a rating scale without designated correct and incorrect answers, and we consulted the theoretical and research literature to identify the elements that should be included (see Panel 4.1).

Development of Items on Democracy in the 1999 IEA Instrument

We laid out several contrasting models of democracy based on theories and previous research with adults and youth, and held on-line conferences to debate these models. The models include a generic or rule of law model, a liberalism model, a pluralism model, a participation model, a communitarian model, a social welfare model and an élitism model. The items that we wrote to cover these models (some items relating to more than one model) were phrased in a way that would allow us to ascertain whether respondents believe that a given situation or condition would be good or bad for democracy. An example follows:

> When many different organizations [associations] are available [exist] for people who wish to belong to them that is _____ [alternatives: very good for democracy, good for democracy, bad for democracy, very bad for democracy].

This formulation allowed the inclusion of items concerning threats to democracy (for example, political corruption) as well as positive factors (for example, free elections). Although the emphasis was on Domain I, we also included items related to the other domains. After pilot testing, we reduced the 39 items to 25.

PANEL 4.1 Previous Research on Concepts of Democracy

Political theories on concepts of democracy

Political theorists have written extensively about concepts of democracy. Held (1996) described republicanism, classical democracy, liberal democracy and direct democracy as among those with long-standing roots. Twentieth century models included competitive élitist democracy, developmental democracy and participatory democracy, among others. Dahl's often-cited work (1998) described the ideals and realities of democracy. Fuchs (1999) referred to constitutionally guaranteed rights, free elections and rule of law as 'minimal elements of democracy', adding three supplemental elements emphasizing social rights. Beetham (1994) dealt with indices of democracy covering basic freedoms, citizenship and participation, administrative codes, public notification and social rights.

Previous research on students' and adults' concepts of democracy

The 1971 IEA Civic Education Study (described in Chapter 1) required students to rate the democratic system of government. The respondents endorsed items indicating that they thought democracy gave people a chance to write or say what they think and that it helped people to make important decisions about their lives (Torney, Oppenheim & Farnen, 1975).

Some researchers have asked open-ended questions of youth to probe their concepts of democracy. Sigel and Hoskin (1981) asked (through an interview) 1,000 American Grade 12 students to imagine that they had to explain to a student from a non-democratic country what makes a country democratic. More than half gave answers that were simplistic, often little more than slogans. The most prevalent themes were individual political freedoms or people having a voice in government through elections. Menezes and Campos (1997) conducted research in Portugal on the meaning of freedom, documenting in particular the extent to which adolescents take a self-centered perspective. Sinatra, Beck and McKeown (1992) found that students' concepts relating to democracy such as representation were sometimes poorly formed. Young people knew that their country had elections or a legislature but had little grasp of their function for democracy. Ascertaining the attributes of the concept of democracy held by adolescents therefore seemed an important topic for the IEA survey.

A survey of university students in the United States who were participants in community service programs investigated their endorsement of several models of democracy, for example, participant involvement by individuals, election of strong leaders and group participation (Walt Whitman Center at Rutgers University, 1997).

In another empirical study (Moodie, Markova & Plichtova, 1995), adults in Scotland and Slovakia were presented with 30 political terms and asked to write the first word that came to mind. They also rated the extent to which each of the terms characterized an ideal democratic society. In both countries, freedom, individual rights and justice were important parts of the social representation of democracy, especially for the younger adults. The second most important cluster of terms related democracy to institutions and processes such as voting. There was considerable similarity between the two countries.

Rose, Mishler and Haerpfer (1998) used data from the New Democracies Barometer in Bulgaria, the Czech Republic, Hungary, Poland, Romania, Slovakia and Slovenia (also Belarus and the Ukraine). They identified five non-democratic attributes such as dismantling parliament and a military takeover of government, and found in 1990 that nearly half of this adult sample endorsed none of these attributes, with small numbers endorsing one or two.

Confirmatory factor analysis showed one factor with items relating to the generic or rule of law model. A second factor, participatory democracy, did not meet IEA scaling standards.

On some individual items there was great consensus across countries; on others very substantial differences between countries. One alternative, quickly discarded because of length limits on this volume, was to present country patterns on each of the 25 items. Instead, we chose to look at the international means for all countries and the overall amount of consensus or lack of consensus about democracy across countries for all the items. We did not examine individual country patterns or within-country variation (leaving that for later analysis).

Results for Concepts of Democracy

Panel 4.2 presents the items in three categories—those for which there is *a high level of consensus* across countries about an aspect of democracy, those for which there is *moderate consensus* across countries, and those for which there is *a lack of consensus* across countries. Items were classified into these three categories according to the *range from the highest to the lowest country mean*. Other methods, such as the standard deviation of the countries' means around the international mean and the amount of variance accounted for by country, gave highly similar classifications. We did not examine either the amount of variation or consensus within each country or the particular countries in which the means were low or high, leaving that for later analysis.

The international mean, averaging across all countries, for each item is also given in Panel 4.2. Within the three consensus categories, items are ranked by that mean. Means of 3.00 to 3.99 are interpreted as indicating that the average respondent believes that the attribute is 'good for democracy'. Means between 2.00 and 2.99 are classified as 'mixed' (usually meaning that some country means are in the 'good for democracy' range and some in the 'bad for democracy range'). Means between 1.00 and 1.99 are interpreted as indicating that the average respondent believes that the attribute is 'bad for democracy'.

Panel 4.2 reveals *seven items with strong consensus across countries*. Three of them refer to attributes that the respondents judge to be good for democracy (free elections, strong civil society in the form of organizations, and support for women entering politics). Four items refer to attributes that the respondents judge to be bad for democracy (limitations on speech critical of government, monopoly newspaper ownership, political influence in the judicial sphere, and special influence by the wealthy on government). It is noteworthy that 14-year-olds across countries recognize the importance of many of the same basic attributes that political theorists believe strengthen or weaken democracy.

In the previous section we reported that there was one strong dimension in the confirmatory factor analysis representing the generic or rule of law model of democracy. This factor includes the large majority of the high consensus items listed in the previous paragraph. Factors that might have emerged corresponding to other models of democracy (for example, participation, communitarianism or élitism) did not appear clearly in these students' concepts across countries. Not surprisingly, 14-year-olds do not make the subtle

PANEL 4.2 Consensus on Concepts of Democracy based on the Range of Country Means

IS IT GOOD OR BAD FOR DEMOCRACY . . .? (4 = very good, 3 = good, 2 = bad, 1 = very bad)

Items with high consensus across countries (range of country means: less than .70)

. . . When citizens have the right to elect political leaders freely? (good for democracy, 3.43)*
. . . When many different organizations exist for people who wish to belong to them? (good for democracy, 3.14)
. . . When political parties have rules that support women to become political leaders? (good for democracy, 3.07)
. . . When people who are critical of the government are forbidden from speaking at public meetings? (bad for democracy, 1.86)
. . . When one company owns all the newspapers? (bad for democracy, 1.85)
. . . When courts and judges are influenced by politicians? (bad for democracy, 1.73)
. . . When wealthy business people have more influence on the government than others? (bad for democracy, 1.62)

Items with moderate consensus across countries (range of country means: .70–1.00)

. . . When everyone has the right to express their opinions freely? (good for democracy, 3.41)
. . . When a minimum income is assured for everyone? (good for democracy, 3.03)
. . . When people peacefully protest against a law they believe to be unjust? (good for democracy, 3.07)
. . . When laws that women claim are unfair to them are changed? (mixed, 2.65)
. . . When newspapers are forbidden to publish stories that might offend ethnic groups? (mixed, 2.44)
. . . When private businesses have no restrictions from government? (mixed, 2.33)
. . . When all the television stations present the same opinion about politics? (mixed, 2.16)
. . . When people refuse to obey a law which violates human rights? (mixed, 2.08)
. . . When immigrants are expected to give up the language and customs of their former countries? (bad for democracy, 1.96)
. . . When political leaders in power give jobs in the government to members of their families? (bad for democracy 1.85)

Items with a lack of consensus across countries (range of country means: greater than 1.00)

. . . When people demand their social and political rights? (mixed, 2.97)
. . . When young people have an obligation to participate in activities to benefit the community? (mixed, 2.80)
. . . When differences in income and wealth between the rich and the poor are small? (mixed, 2.70)
. . . When political parties have different opinions on important issues? (mixed, 2.57)
. . . When people participate in political parties in order to influence government? (mixed, 2.52)
. . . When newspapers are free of all government control? (mixed, 2.50)
. . . When government leaders are trusted without question? (mixed, 2.33)
. . . When there is a separation between the church and the state? (mixed, 2.27)

Note: *International item means appear in parentheses.

distinctions that characterize the thinking of political theorists. Nevertheless, the international item means and the range of country means provide useful information regarding 14-year-olds' thinking about aspects of democracy.

There are *eight items with a lack of consensus across countries*. Many of the means are categorized as 'mixed'. In some countries these attributes are thought to be good for democracy and in others bad for democracy. Two items on which there is very little consensus deal with political parties having different opinions on important issues and people participating in political parties in order to influence government. This is the first of several examples of the ambivalent or even negative images of political parties held by adolescents in some countries, especially when parties are associated with conflict and differences of opinion. Another item with marked lack of consensus across countries asks whether it is good or bad when 'government leaders are trusted without question'.

There are *ten items with moderate consensus across countries*. A selection of these items will be discussed along with other items on the same topics in the next section.

Several items deal with the role mass media plays in democracy. Fourteen-year-olds widely agree that having one company own all the newspapers is a threat. This is the only item about the media on which there is consensus across countries. Political theorists also suggest that freedom from government control of newspapers can be important for strong democracy, but in fact young people in many countries believe that some control is a good thing. Likewise, the respondents in some countries express little concern about the situation in which television stations all present the same opinion about politics. If newspapers were forbidden to publish stories that might offend ethnic groups, this would be neither very good nor very bad for democracy, according to the average respondent across countries. It is possible that when two values are counterposed in a question, as they are here, many students focus on one value and downplay the other value.

Furthermore, although many would argue that it is bad for democracy when political leaders in power give jobs to members of their families, these 14-year-olds do not necessarily agree. Students across countries are also mixed in their opinions about whether it is advisable for government to place restrictions on private business.

There is also relatively little consensus across countries about whether it is good or bad for citizens to participate actively in support of causes promoting justice or community improvement. No item on this topic appears in the highest consensus category. There is a moderately positive view of the contribution made by peaceful protests against laws believed to be unjust (with moderate consensus across countries). There is somewhat less agreement across countries about whether it is good or bad for democracy when people demand their social and political rights. The item about whether it is good or bad when young people have an obligation to participate in activities to benefit the community is relatively low in consensus. Average responses from some countries indicate that this obligation is seen as somewhat good for democracy, while averages from other countries indicate that it is seen as somewhat bad for democracy (perhaps because of the term 'obligation').

Encouragement by political parties to women entering politics is seen as good for democracy across countries. Changing laws that women claim to be unfair, however, is viewed in a mixed way and with only moderate consensus across countries. With respect to another group often experiencing discrimination, requiring immigrants to give up their language and customs was seen on average as bad for democracy.

Summary for Concepts of Democracy

Fourteen-year-olds across the 28 participating countries seem to have a fairly strong grasp of most of the basic tenets of democracy, including factors likely to strengthen or weaken it. Their concepts of democracy include not only formal structures like elections but also civil society organizations. There are substantial differences across countries in the perceived role of political parties. Fourteen-year-olds' view of the mass media is not clear from these responses. In some countries, respect for government leaders is a hallmark of stable democracy, while in others it is viewed negatively. Likewise, participation and conflict of opinion seem to be viewed as part of the political culture of a strong democracy in some countries but not in others. Fourteen-year-olds in most countries give evidence that they can recognize the most basic attributes of democracy. More sophisticated ideas about political process seem to elude them. This large cross-national data set confirms previous research conducted with interview or open-ended questions in a few countries.

The basic ideas associated with democracy are implicitly transmitted to young people as they participate in many societal institutions, including their families and peer groups. None of the countries in this study, however, appears to believe that this implicit process is sufficient to prepare young people for citizenship (Schwille & Amadeo, forthcoming). Curricula, textbooks and teaching activities of various sorts (ranging from recitations to mock elections) are designed to provide an explicit focus on democracy, usually on core elements such as elections and lack of restrictions on citizens who wish to express political views. These emphases are among those found in the responses of the students in this IEA study.

Education about the media exists in some countries, but it is usually concerned with teaching students to read articles with a critical attitude, not with discussing the role of the news media in preserving or enhancing democracy. Economic issues are seldom linked explicitly to the study of democracy. These features of the curricula noted in Phase 1 help to interpret both some of the consensus and some of the lack of consensus about the concept of democracy in the data reported here.

Some of these topics will also be taken up in later sections dealing with concepts of citizenship and government responsibility and those dealing with attitudes toward political rights for women and immigrants.

CONCEPTS OF CITIZENSHIP

Relation of this Area to the Study's Design

The dimensions of citizenship and ways to create the qualities of the good citizen in young people were central concerns in the Phase 1 case studies. One sub-domain of the democracy and democratic institutions domain focuses on citizenship. When questions were formulated with right and wrong answers for the test, it was much easier to include citizens' rights than citizens' responsibilities. We included this concept scale in order to focus some attention on responsibilities.

Citizenship can have a very broad meaning, including, for example, national identity, legal or social entitlement, obligations such as military service, and opportunities such as political participation. In this section we are concerned with the concept of the good citizen for adults that young people actually have and how it relates to what others have found (see Panel 4.3).

Development of the Citizenship Scales in the 1999 IEA Instrument

Questions from the 1971 IEA Civic Education Study served as the basis of the item pool for the concept of citizenship. The stem was as follows: 'An adult who is a good citizen . . .'. The response options were 4 = very important, 3 = somewhat important, 2 = somewhat unimportant, 1 = not important. The pilot instrument contained 21 items; the final instrument contained 15.

Confirmatory factor analysis revealed two factors, importance of conventional citizenship (six items) and importance of social-movement-related citizenship (four items). (See Panel 4.4 for the wording of these items and Appendix Table C.1 for alpha reliabilities.) We use the term 'social movements' to refer to non-partisan mainstream groups acting in their communities or improving the environment of their schools, in order to link these data to recent research.

In this section we present both a display that describes young people's concepts of citizenship across countries (including the same information about consensus and non-consensus items across countries as in the previous section) and also comparisons between countries using the two scaled scores (conventional citizenship and social-movement-related citizenship). As in the previous section, when comparing items, we classified the international means between 3.00 and 3.99 as 'important for citizenship' and those between 2.00 and 2.99 as 'mixed'. There were no items with international means less than 2.00 (which would have been 'unimportant for citizenship').

Results for Concepts of Citizenship

Items forming the concept of citizenship

Here, we are looking again at consensus and level of rating internationally. The first thing to notice in Panel 4.4 is that there are only two items about which there is consensus across countries according to this categorization. The first item, 'an adult who is a good citizen obeys the law', is rated as very important (international mean of 3.65). The second, ' . . . engages in political discussion', is rated much lower (international mean of 2.37). Among the items rated as quite important on which students have different opinions in different

PANEL 4.3   Previous Research on Concepts of Good Citizenship

The 1971 IEA Civic Education Study used a 16-item measure of the meaning of citizenship. Two scales, active citizenship and non-political citizenship, were developed, but the items received little analysis at the student level.

There has been useful theorizing and empirical research on adults. Janoski (1998) derived models of adult citizenship relating to three models: liberal democracy, communitarian democracy and social or expansive democracy. Theiss-Morse (1993) found four concepts of citizenship among adults in the United States: representative democracy (responsibility to be an informed voter); political enthusiast (advocacy through protest and little trust in elected officials); pursued interest (joining groups to pursue issues); and indifferent (trusting leaders and placing a low priority on trying to influence them).

Anderson, Avery, Pederson, Smith and Sullivan (1997) identified citizenship concepts among a sample of teachers in the United States. Almost half believed students should be taught to be questioning citizens, about one-quarter focused on teaching from a culturally pluralistic perspective, and fewer than 15 percent stressed learning about government structures or obedience to law and patriotism. A study by Davies, Gregory and Riley (1999) of teachers in England also found that social concern and tolerance for diversity received the greatest support, with percentages comparable to those in the United States for government structure and obedience or patriotism. Prior (1999) in Australia also found that social concerns or social justice and participation in school/community affairs were important to teachers. In Hong Kong, Lee (1999) found that teachers were more likely to endorse the socially concerned citizen and the informed citizen, and less likely to endorse the obedient citizen.

Conover, Crewe and Searing (1991) found that adults in the United States saw the citizen as someone with freedom and rights, as well as responsibilities to vote. British adults placed more emphasis on identity within a community. In a second study, adolescents, parents and teachers in four communities in the United States were interviewed about citizenship practices (Conover & Searing, 2000). Obeying the law, voting in elections, being loyal to the country, performing military service during war, and taking part in activities to protect the environment were among the citizenship duties that students most highly endorsed. The students had a more highly developed sense of citizens' rights than of their responsibilities. The authors called this a minimalist version of citizenship.

Ichilov and Nave (1981) reported that Israeli youngsters conceptualized citizenship in relation to the political sphere rather than as a commitment to a broader community. They emphasized obedience and loyalty more than active political participation. Whether a student was in an academic or vocational track also had an effect that seemed to be mediated through the curriculum, interaction with a particular set of peers and prospects for future mobility (Ichilov, 1991).

Vontz, Metcalf and Patrick (2000) in a study of the effectiveness of a civic curriculum in Latvia, Lithuania and the United States found a positive impact on students' knowledge and skills but not on their sense of citizen responsibility.

Plasser, Ulram and Waldrauch (1998) found in a survey of adults in the Czech Republic, Hungary, Poland, Slovakia and Slovenia that there had been a considerable drop in citizen participation in social and political movements in the years between 1991 and 1995, especially in the Czech Republic, Poland and Slovakia.

countries are patriotism and loyalty to the country and being willing to serve in the military to defend the country. These two items were not included in either of the scales, however.

Across countries the items relating to participation in social movement groups are more likely to be endorsed as important for citizenship than are conventional citizenship activities (Panel 4.4). Three out of four of the social movement items have means above 3.0 (indicating an overall rating of important), while only one out of six of the conventional citizenship items, voting in every election, has a mean above 3.0. The least important activities are joining a party and engaging in political discussions, both from the conventional scale.

Another way to describe student responses is to examine the percentage distribution of responses of the weighted pooled sample for the ten items that appear on the two scales (see Appendix B, Figures B.2a and B2.b). Eighty percent or more of the respondents rate participating in environmental groups, in human rights groups, in activities to benefit the community, and voting in every election as 'somewhat important' or 'very important'. All these items, except voting, appear on the social movement dimension of citizenship. The next category includes items with a somewhat lower level of endorsement. Between 65 and 75 percent of the respondents rate showing respect for government representatives, knowing about political issues, knowing about history, and participating in a peaceful protest against a law believed to be unjust as 'somewhat important' or 'very important'. All these items, except the one concerning peaceful protest, appear on the conventional dimension of citizenship. Then there is a big gap in endorsement level. Between 30 and 45 percent rate joining a political party and engaging in political discussions as 'somewhat important' or 'very important'. Both appear on the conventional dimension of citizenship.

In summary, by looking at both means and percentages, we can see that these 14-year-olds are somewhat more likely to include social movement participation than more conventional political activities in their concepts of good citizenship for adults. Voting is important to these young people, but activities that imply conflict of opinions (political party membership and political discussion) are not highly rated on average. There are quite a few differences across countries, however, and we explore some of these in the next section.

Analysis of scale scores by country

Figure 4.1 shows that *conventional citizenship activities are most important to the concept of adult citizenship in Chile, Colombia, Cyprus, Greece, Poland and Romania.* Other countries whose means are significantly above the international mean are Bulgaria, Italy, Lithuania, Portugal, the Slovak Republic and the United States. The majority of these countries have experienced within the past three decades dramatic political changes that have strengthened conventional political institutions and forms of participation. These institutions are now receiving enhanced attention in schools, and young people seem to be developing a concept of citizenship that includes conventional political activities. Whether these concepts will be translated into actual participation once these young people are adults remains an open question.

AN ADULT WHO IS A GOOD CITIZEN . . . (4 = very important; 3 = somewhat important; 2 = somewhat unimportant; 1 = very unimportant)

Items with high consensus across countries (range of country means: less than .70)

. . . Obeys the law. (important, 3.65)*
. . . Engages in political discussions. (mixed, 2.37) Conv**

Items with moderate consensus across countries (range of country means: .70-1.00)

. . . Takes part in activities promoting human rights. (important, 3.24) SocMo
. . . Takes part in activities to protect the environment. (important, 3.15) SocMo
. . . Participates in activities to benefit people in the community. (important, 3.13) SocMo
. . . Votes in every election. (important, 3.12) Conv
. . . Would be willing to ignore a law that violated human rights. (mixed, 2.86)
. . . Follows political issues in the newspaper, on the radio or on TV. (mixed, 2.85) Conv
. . . Joins a political party. (mixed, 2.11) Conv

Items with a lack of consensus across countries (range of country means: greater than 1.00)

. . . Is patriotic and loyal to the country. (important, 3.20)
. . . Would be willing to serve in the military to defend the country. (important, 3.18)
. . . Works hard. (important, 3.13)
. . . Knows about the country's history. (mixed, 2.96) Conv
. . . Shows respect for government representatives. (mixed, 2.89) Conv
. . . Would participate in a peaceful protest against a law believed to be unjust. (mixed, 2.83) SocMo
NOTE:
* International item means appear in parentheses.
**Conv indicates that the item appears in the scale for conventional citizenship.
SocMo indicates that the item appears in the scale for social-movement-related citizenship.
Items without a label do not appear on either scale.

Figure 4.2 shows that *social-movement-related citizenship activities are especially important in Colombia, Cyprus and Greece.* Other countries with means significantly above the international mean are Chile, Italy, Lithuania, Norway, Portugal, Romania, the Slovak Republic and the United States.

In contrast, Figure 4.1 shows that *conventional political activity receives low ratings for importance to citizenship in Belgium (French), the Czech Republic, Denmark, England, Estonia and Finland.* Other countries whose means are also significantly below the international mean are Australia, Germany, Norway, the Russian Federation, Slovenia, Sweden and Switzerland.

Social-movement-related citizenship is rated low in importance for citizenship in Belgium (French), England, Estonia and Finland (Figure 4.2). Other countries whose means are also significantly below the international mean are Australia, the Czech Republic, Denmark, Hong Kong (SAR), Latvia, Slovenia, Sweden and Switzerland. The countries that have low ratings on both scales are a mixture of Northern European, Nordic and post-Communist countries (and also Australia). Phase 1 case studies indicated that Australia, Belgium (French),

England and Hong Kong (SAR) recently identified weaknesses in students' knowledge or engagement and instituted new policies or programs in education for citizenship. These efforts were not implemented in time to influence these student respondents in 1999, however. Several of the other countries are new democracies that have only recently begun the process of instituting democratic civic education.

Norway is the only country that is significantly below the international mean on conventional citizenship but significantly above the mean on social movement citizenship. Hungary has scores relatively near the mean on both conventional and social-movement-related citizenship.

Analysis of scale scores by gender

Figures illustrating gender differences by country are presented only for those scales where there is a significant difference between males and females in at least half of the countries. There are no significant gender differences in 25 countries on the importance of conventional citizenship scale. There are significant gender differences in Portugal, the Russian Federation and the Slovak Republic. Males are higher than females in each country.

There are no significant gender differences in 19 countries on the importance of social-movement-related citizenship scale. There are significant gender differences, with females having higher scores than males, in Denmark, Finland, Germany, Greece, Italy, Norway, Sweden, Switzerland and the United States.

Summary for Concepts of Citizenship

There is somewhat less consensus across countries about the components of the concept of adult citizenship than about the concept of democracy. Obeying the law is clearly important. Among conventional political activities, voting is most likely to be thought important. Political party membership and participation in political discussion are not important according to the 14-year-olds in most countries (although parties receive support in a few countries). In contrast, these young people believe that it is important for adult citizens to participate in environmental, human rights and community betterment organizations.

Some theorists contrast minimal and maximal aspects of citizenship, usually placing voting, party membership, media use and political discussion at the minimal level. Peaceful protests and membership in social action groups are thought of as activities that might be added on to these minimal activities. This model does not apply very well to the data from this cohort of students. The generation of young people represented by the study's 14-year-olds is gravitating to affiliation and action connected to social movement groups and not to political discussions or formal relations with political parties.

The differences between countries present another perspective. Students in some countries believe that both conventional and social movement activities are very important to citizenship for adults. Students in some other countries believe that both types of activities are unimportant. Young people in several countries that have recently experienced changes strengthening formal political institutions are likely to prescribe conventional citizenship

Figure 4.1 Importance of Conventional Citizenship

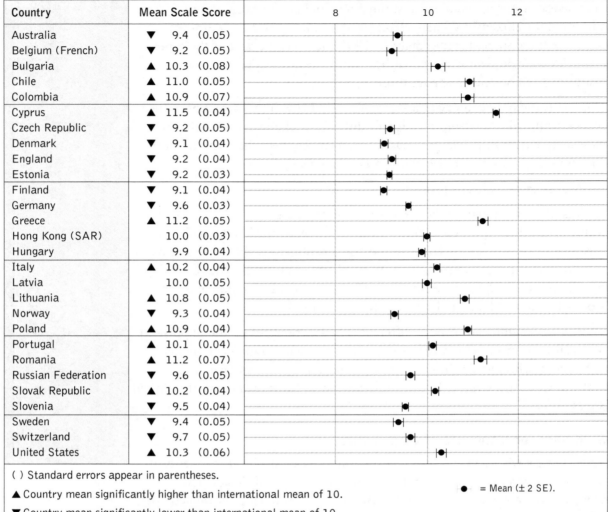

Country	Mean Scale Score	8　　　　10　　　　12
Australia	▼　9.4　(0.05)	
Belgium (French)	▼　9.2　(0.05)	
Bulgaria	▲　10.3　(0.08)	
Chile	▲　11.0　(0.05)	
Colombia	▲　10.9　(0.07)	
Cyprus	▲　11.5　(0.04)	
Czech Republic	▼　9.2　(0.05)	
Denmark	▼　9.1　(0.04)	
England	▼　9.2　(0.04)	
Estonia	▼　9.2　(0.03)	
Finland	▼　9.1　(0.04)	
Germany	▼　9.6　(0.03)	
Greece	▲　11.2　(0.05)	
Hong Kong (SAR)	10.0　(0.03)	
Hungary	9.9　(0.04)	
Italy	▲　10.2　(0.04)	
Latvia	10.0　(0.05)	
Lithuania	▲　10.8　(0.05)	
Norway	▼　9.3　(0.04)	
Poland	▲　10.9　(0.04)	
Portugal	▲　10.1　(0.04)	
Romania	▲　11.2　(0.07)	
Russian Federation	▼　9.6　(0.05)	
Slovak Republic	▲　10.2　(0.04)	
Slovenia	▼　9.5　(0.04)	
Sweden	▼　9.4　(0.05)	
Switzerland	▼　9.7　(0.05)	
United States	▲　10.3　(0.06)	

( ) Standard errors appear in parentheses.

▲ Country mean significantly higher than international mean of 10.

▼ Country mean significantly lower than international mean of 10.

●| = Mean (± 2 SE).

Source: IEA Civic Education Study, Standard Population of 14-year-olds tested in 1999.

responsibilities for adults. They may be more idealistic than some adults in those nations about the possibilities that these channels of influence present. Phase 1 case studies showed an emphasis on voting and other conventional activities when citizenship is discussed in schools. Students are urged to see competitive elections and independent political parties as resources to be used by citizens to take control of the political system. Civic education may be a major source of belief in the importance of conventional citizenship in some of these nations.

Females in about one-third of the countries are more likely than males to endorse social-movement-related citizenship. This includes all the Nordic countries, several Western European countries and the United States.

Aspects of adult political culture appear to be reinforced by what is presented in schools. At the same time, youth (of the next generation) are attracted to and sometimes are creating for themselves a set of less hierarchically organized groups to take the place of the political parties and voter-interest groups prominent in the past. Chapter 6 addresses the extent to which students believe they will participate in these activities when they are adults.

Figure 4.2 Importance of Social-Movement-related Citizenship

Country	Mean Scale Score	8	10	12
Australia	▼ 9.3 (0.04)			
Belgium (French)	▼ 9.1 (0.09)			
Bulgaria	10.0 (0.08)			
Chile	▲ 10.5 (0.04)			
Colombia	▲ 11.3 (0.07)			
Cyprus	▲ 11.0 (0.04)			
Czech Republic	▼ 9.7 (0.05)			
Denmark	▼ 9.5 (0.04)			
England	▼ 9.2 (0.04)			
Estonia	▼ 9.2 (0.03)			
Finland	▼ 8.9 (0.04)			
Germany	9.9 (0.04)			
Greece	▲ 11.4 (0.05)			
Hong Kong (SAR)	▼ 9.6 (0.03)			
Hungary	9.9 (0.04)			
Italy	▲ 10.2 (0.05)			
Latvia	▼ 9.5 (0.05)			
Lithuania	▲ 10.6 (0.04)			
Norway	▲ 10.2 (0.04)			
Poland	10.1 (0.05)			
Portugal	▲ 10.6 (0.04)			
Romania	▲ 10.7 (0.07)			
Russian Federation	9.9 (0.05)			
Slovak Republic	▲ 10.4 (0.05)			
Slovenia	▼ 9.6 (0.04)			
Sweden	▼ 9.8 (0.05)			
Switzerland	▼ 9.6 (0.04)			
United States	▲ 10.3 (0.06)			

( ) Standard errors appear in parentheses.

▲ Country mean significantly higher than international mean of 10.

▼ Country mean significantly lower than international mean of 10.

● | = Mean (± 2 SE).

Source: IEA Civic Education Study, Standard Population of 14-year-olds tested in 1999.

CONCEPTS OF THE RESPONSIBILITIES OF GOVERNMENT

Relation of this Area to the Study's Design

Democracy and citizenship are relatively abstract concepts. Government is somewhat more concrete. The areas in which government is expected to take action (or refrain from action) are important parts of the web of concepts covered in the democracy domain. In developing the measure of concepts of democracy (presented earlier in this chapter), we found it challenging to formulate the aspects dealing with economic or social welfare processes. Students had difficulty relating economic issues to the concept of democracy, which is usually taught as a political concept without much attention to its economic ramifications.

In this area there was an existing instrument dealing with government in relation to economic and social issues, namely a set of adult items in the General Social Survey and the International Social Survey Project (ISSP) that seemed simple enough to be used with 14-year-olds. These items are usually called 'role of government', 'government responsibility' or 'scope of government' items (Kaase & Newton, 1995; Robinson, Shaver & Wrightsman, 1999). Considerable research with adults has been published (see Panels 4.5 and 4.6).

Development of the Government Scales in the 1999 IEA Instrument

We started with seven basic ISSP items and added nine from other sources. In the final survey we included 12 items. The response scale was 4 = definitely should be the government's responsibility, 3 = probably should be the government's responsibility, 2 = probably should not be the government's responsibility and 1 = should not be the government's responsibility.

A confirmatory factor analysis showed two separable factors. The first was economy-related government responsibilities, (five items—guarantee a job, keep prices under control, support industries, provide for unemployed, reduce income differences). The second was society-related government responsibilities (seven items—provide health care, provide for old people, provide education, ensure political opportunities for women, control pollution, guarantee order, promote moral behavior). See Appendix Table C.1 for alpha reliabilities.

Results for Concepts of Government

Items forming the concept of government

The international percentage distributions of item responses for the weighted pooled sample and the wording of these items are given in Appendix Figures B.2c and B.2d. Adding together the two response categories for 'probably should be the government's responsibility' and 'definitely should be the government's responsibility' produced percentages about as high as or a little higher than those reported in the research literature on adults. To put this in another perspective, only about 10 percent of the students in the present study say that economy- and society-related activities definitely should not be the government's responsibility; this is similar to adults' responses.

In general, 14-year-olds are more likely to think of societal items rather than economic items as the government's responsibility. The items most frequently endorsed as definitely government responsibilities are 'to guarantee order and stability within the country', 'to provide free basic education for all', and 'to provide basic health care for everyone'. The two least endorsed items are 'to reduce differences in income and wealth among people' and 'to provide industries with the support they need to grow' (refer Appendix Figures B.2c and B.2d). This finding matches quite well with previous findings for adults. It is worth noting that school curricula and instruction described in Phase 1 emphasize the societal rather than the economic responsibilities of government.

The large majority of studies of adults have used the items from the International Social Survey Project (ISSP). Kaase and Newton (1995) argued that Western Europeans are willing to expand the extent to which government takes responsibilities for social and economic well-being. In 1990 a large majority of respondents believed that the government has a responsibility to be involved in health care, elder care, unemployment, controlling prices and reducing differences in income. Miller, Timpson and Lessnoff (1996) qualified this by showing a contrast of 90 percent support by respondents for government responsibility in health, education and housing with 70 percent support for action relating to jobs and living standards in Britain. Roller (1994) found that East Germans placed more emphasis on government responsibility than did West Germans. A number of these studies found social class position and party identification to be good predictors of concepts of the government's responsibility. Some studies found females more supportive of the government's social and economic role than males.

A few studies have focused specifically on items relating to economics, sometimes in relation to other priorities. Using ISSP data, Roller (1995) found high levels of support for government providing a job and reducing income inequities in Australia and Italy, more moderate support in Germany and Great Britain, and lower support in Switzerland. Weiss (1999) studied adults in the Czech Republic, Hungary, Poland and Slovakia, and found that a majority of respondents believed that the government should control industries and fix prices. Sapiro (1998) used Eurobarometer data, finding particular concern for poverty as a problem in Italy, Portugal and the United Kingdom, with less concern in Denmark and Germany, where environmental concerns predominated. Rasinski and Smith (1994), using 1990 ISSP data, found that Hungary, Norway and West Germany had the highest support for government spending for the environment.

Inglehart and Baker (2000) found using World Values Survey data considerable variation in the extent to which adults in different countries were concerned with economic survival values (as contrasted with values of self-expression). Russia and all other post-Communist countries were at one end of the continuum, voicing much more concern for economic survival. Belgium, Chile and Finland were in a moderate position. The other Nordic countries, along with Australia, Britain and the United States, scored toward the end of the continuum that emphasized self-expression over economic survival. Adults from countries with low GNP per capita expressed more concerns about economic survival than about self-expression. (Note that countries included in Inglehart and Baker's study that were not in the IEA study have not been included in this summary.)

The 1971 testing by IEA of civic education included ratings of social welfare agencies. These concepts were not well developed among students in some countries, but generally the respondents believed that these agencies contributed to ensuring fair shares for everyone.

Using an adolescent sample in Britain, Furnham and Gunter (1989) found that unemployment was rated as the most important problem (out of a list of nine), while reducing numbers of very rich and very poor people was the least important.

A recent study in seven countries focused on distributive justice and the interpretation of the social contract by Grades 8 and 11 students (Jonsson & Flanagan, 2000). A widening economic gap was perceived especially among respondents in Bulgaria, Hungary and Russia. The importance of government support for the unemployed, housing and health was highest in Russia and moderate in Bulgaria, the Czech Republic, Hungary and Sweden. This aspect of the government's activities received a lower rating in Australia and the lowest in the United States. Females were more likely than males to perceive an economic gap, but there were quite modest gender differences in ratings of government responsibility.

In many ways these findings paralleled the adult findings cited in Panel 4.5.

Analysis of scale scores by country

The results by country in Figure 4.3 indicate that *the concept that government has society-related responsibilities is most likely to be endorsed by students in Chile, England, Greece, Poland and Portugal.* Other countries with scores that are significantly above the international mean on the scale for society-related government responsibilities are Finland, Italy and the Slovak Republic. In contrast, *students in Belgium (French), Denmark, Germany, Latvia and Switzerland are least likely to include responsibilities for society* in their view of government. Other countries with scores that are significantly below the international mean on society-related government responsibilities are Colombia, Estonia, Hong Kong (SAR), Hungary and Lithuania.

Figure 4.4 indicates that *students in Bulgaria and the Russian Federation are the most likely to endorse concepts of government that include responsibility for economy-related activities.* Other countries with scores on economy-related government responsibilities significantly above the international mean are Cyprus, Finland, Hungary, Italy, Lithuania, Poland, Portugal, Romania, the Slovak Republic and Sweden. In contrast, *students in the United States and Denmark are least likely to believe that the government should take action in the economic sphere.* Other countries with scores on economy-related government responsibilities significantly below the international mean are Australia, Belgium (French), Germany, Greece, Hong Kong (SAR), Norway and Switzerland.

Figure 4.3 Society-related Government Responsibilities

Country	Mean Scale Score		8	10	12
Australia		10.1 (0.04)			
Belgium (French)	▼	9.5 (0.07)			
Bulgaria		9.9 (0.14)			
Chile	▲	10.5 (0.04)			
Colombia	▼	9.8 (0.05)			
Cyprus		10.1 (0.04)			
Czech Republic		10.0 (0.04)			
Denmark	▼	9.1 (0.03)			
England	▲	10.8 (0.04)			
Estonia	▼	9.7 (0.05)			
Finland	▲	10.4 (0.06)			
Germany	▼	9.4 (0.04)			
Greece	▲	10.8 (0.05)			
Hong Kong (SAR)	▼	9.8 (0.05)			
Hungary	▼	9.9 (0.04)			
Italy	▲	10.4 (0.05)			
Latvia	▼	9.5 (0.06)			
Lithuania	▼	9.6 (0.04)			
Norway		10.0 (0.04)			
Poland	▲	10.8 (0.06)			
Portugal	▲	10.5 (0.04)			
Romania		9.7 (0.09)			
Russian Federation		10.2 (0.06)			
Slovak Republic	▲	10.3 (0.06)			
Slovenia		9.9 (0.04)			
Sweden		9.9 (0.03)			
Switzerland	▼	9.5 (0.04)			
United States		10.0 (0.05)			

( ) Standard errors appear in parentheses.

▲ Country mean significantly higher than international mean of 10.

▼ Country mean significantly lower than international mean of 10.

● = Mean (± 2 SE).

Source: *IEA Civic Education Study*, Standard Population of 14-year-olds tested in 1999.

Analysis of scale scores by gender

There are no significant gender differences in 20 countries in rating society-related government responsibilities. There are significant gender differences, with females attributing more society-related responsibilities than males, in Belgium (French), England, Finland, Greece, Italy, Portugal, Slovenia and the United States.

There are no significant gender differences in 23 countries in rating economy-related government responsibilities. There are significant gender differences, with females attributing more economic responsibilities to government than males, in England, Greece, Hungary, Italy and Slovenia.

Summary for Concepts of Government

To a great extent the 14-year-olds in these countries endorse the views about government responsibilities for economics and society that have been held by adults in their countries for several generations. In particular, students from countries that were socialist in the recent past expect government activity in

Figure 4.4 Economy-related Government Responsibilities

Country	Mean Scale Score	8	10	12
Australia	▼ 9.8 (0.05)			
Belgium (French)	▼ 9.5 (0.08)			
Bulgaria	▲ 10.6 (0.14)			
Chile	10.1 (0.03)			
Colombia	9.9 (0.05)			
Cyprus	▲ 10.3 (0.03)			
Czech Republic	9.9 (0.04)			
Denmark	▼ 9.4 (0.03)			
England	10.1 (0.04)			
Estonia	10.1 (0.05)			
Finland	▲ 10.4 (0.05)			
Germany	▼ 9.5 (0.04)			
Greece	▼ 9.8 (0.04)			
Hong Kong (SAR)	▼ 9.5 (0.03)			
Hungary	▲ 10.2 (0.04)			
Italy	▲ 10.2 (0.04)			
Latvia	9.8 (0.06)			
Lithuania	▲ 10.2 (0.04)			
Norway	▼ 9.6 (0.03)			
Poland	▲ 10.4 (0.04)			
Portugal	▲ 10.3 (0.04)			
Romania	▲ 10.4 (0.06)			
Russian Federation	▲ 10.6 (0.05)			
Slovak Republic	▲ 10.4 (0.05)			
Slovenia	9.9 (0.05)			
Sweden	▲ 10.4 (0.04)			
Switzerland	▼ 9.6 (0.04)			
United States	▼ 9.2 (0.04)			

( ) Standard errors appear in parentheses.

▲ Country mean significantly higher than international mean of 10.

▼ Country mean significantly lower than international mean of 10.

● = Mean (± 2 SE).

Source: *IEA Civic Education Study*, Standard Population of 14-year-olds tested in 1999.

the economy. This is especially true if they are currently experiencing economic difficulties. Students in Sweden, where there has been a strong social democratic tradition, also include responsibilities for the economy in their concept of government. Students from countries with free-market traditions, especially Denmark and the United States, but also to some extent Belgium (French), Germany, Greece, Hong Kong (SAR) and Norway, have a concept of government responsibilities that is less likely to include economic activities in support of either individuals or industries. These concepts of government are also fostered through textbooks and instruction. However, everyday life interchanges and discussions with parents and peers, as well as media experience, can also be credited (or blamed) for the economic and social dimensions of students' concepts of government.

The finding that 14-year-olds in countries with low GNP per capita are more likely than those in countries with high GNP per capita to emphasize government's responsibilities for economic actions such as reducing the gaps between rich and poor and keeping prices under control is in line with

Inglehart and Baker's (2000) analysis of adult data. A number of the attitudinal patterns among the 14-year-olds also resemble those reported in the ISSP data for adults. A look at youth research reveals that the results of the present study correspond closely to those of Jonsson and Flanagan (2000), especially the high expectation of government involvement in the economy from Russian young people and the low expectations for this type of involvement from young people in the United States.

SUMMARY

We have dealt in this chapter with three distinct yet related concepts held by young people—democracy, citizenship and government. Although there are certainly gaps and lack of depth in their understanding, many 14-year-olds in these diverse countries are aware of both the ideal functioning of democratic political systems and what is actually happening in their societies. There is considerable consensus across countries about the most basic and core meaning of democracy, and some agreement about the responsibilities of the adult citizen. These beliefs, for the most part, correspond to the emphases in schools. They also are responsive to the current and past economic situation of the country as well as to the adult political culture.

Support for many types of conventional political participation appears to be relatively weak. Young people still believe that it is important to vote, but discussion of political issues does not seem to be important in their concepts of good citizenship. In many countries, political parties are not seen as contributing to a strong democracy or as groups with which citizens can affiliate in order to have political influence. Several factors could account for these aspects of the concept of citizenship.

Although some schools attempt to foster discussion of issues, there are constraints on teachers against making statements that might be interpreted as politically partisan. In some countries it appears that the media present an image of parties that stresses conflict in the political process, while the schools avoid discussing partisan conflict. Furthermore, political parties are hierarchically organized and usually focus on attracting adults who are eligible to vote, not youth.

Young people, however, are looking for organizations with which to affiliate. They are likely to see joining activities within the community, as well as environmental and human rights groups, as part of the citizen's role. Although the issues around which these organizations mobilize actually have political dimensions, young people often do not perceive them in this way. According to the Phase 1 case studies, most schools do not encourage young people to look at the political dimensions of these issues. (For further data about group affiliations and activities, see Chapter 6.)

Organizations that take action on these issues are usually not hierarchically organized and give young people the opportunity to see more immediate results from their actions than do conventional political organizations. Some argue that these associations are developmentally appropriate for adolescents, in part because they allow them to work with peers. Whether this kind of participation can create a sense of legitimacy for the government among citizens and input for the political system to the same extent as more conventional political participation is an open question, however.

With respect to concepts of government's responsibility for aspects of the society and the economy, 14-year-olds already appear to be members of the political culture that they share with adults. If they are growing up in societies with a legacy of socialism or a strong social democratic tradition, they believe in heavier government responsibilities for certain aspects of the economy. If they are growing up within a long-standing free-market tradition, they are less likely than those from other economic traditions to believe that the government should intervene in the economy, for example, by providing jobs, controlling prices or reducing income inequality. If they are in a country experiencing economic difficulties (for example, a low standard of living), they are especially likely to want the government to assume economic responsibilities.

Dalton (2000) has observed that 'there is not just one civic culture that is congruent with the workings of a democratic system' (p. 919) and that the current period is characterized by significant cultural change and new dynamism. Clark and Hoffmann-Martinot (1998) have found evidence of a 'new civic culture' that is characterized by less hierarchy and more individual decision-making. There is considerable evidence in the IEA data about young people's concepts of democracy, citizenship and government to support these positions. Additional analysis and further research can greatly increase our understanding of the role schools are playing and might play in civic concept development.

CHAPTER 5

Students' Attitudes toward the Nation, the Government, Immigrants and Women's Political Rights

HIGHLIGHTS RELATING TO CIVIC ATTITUDES

- Fourteen-year-olds across countries are moderately trusting of their government institutions. Courts and the police are trusted the most, followed by national and local governments. In contrast, political parties are trusted very little. Most young people also seem to have a positive sense of national identity, although less so in some countries than in others. In almost all the participating countries, however, the average young person seems to have a sense of trust or attachment either to the country as a political community or to government institutions (or to both).

- Fourteen-year olds across countries are generally positive about immigrants and especially believe they should have educational opportunities. The majority of these young people also support the right of immigrants to vote and to retain their language and culture. There are national differences, however.

- Fourteen-year-olds across countries are largely supportive of women's political and economic rights. Females are much more likely to be supportive of these rights than are males, the most substantial gender difference found in the study.

- Fourteen-year-olds overall have mostly positive attitudes toward the institutions and groups asked about in the survey. The minority of those with negative attitudes may be large enough to cause some concern, however.

Knowledge of the rights and responsibilities of citizenship and the nature of government are important to creating and sustaining democratic institutions, but they are by no means sufficient for that purpose. Democracy requires a certain degree of adherence to underlying principles, along with common values and attitudes. The IEA Civic Education Study gives as much attention to attitudes and beliefs as to knowledge. In this chapter, we focus on attitudes from each of the three major domains of the study—*democracy and democratic institutions, national identity*, and *social cohesion and diversity*—choosing those scales where special interest was expressed by participating countries:

- For the first domain, we report on trust in government, addressing the fear in some countries that young people are losing confidence in their public institutions.

- For the second domain, we also deal with issues of support or alienation, touching more specifically on national feeling and attachment to the country and its political symbols. Scales in these first two domains address both support for the political community (national pride) and support for the regime (trust and confidence in political institutions) (Dalton, 1999; Norris, 1999).

- For the third domain, social cohesion and diversity, we selected two scales. The first ascertains the extent to which students support certain rights or opportunities for immigrants, and the second scale probes the extent to which they endorse political and economic rights for women.

TRUST IN GOVERNMENT-RELATED INSTITUTIONS AND THE MEDIA

Relation of this Area to the Study's Design

Students' reactions to government-related institutions were dealt with extensively in the Phase 1 studies (Torney-Purta, Schwille & Amadeo, 1999). These revealed concern in some countries that young people do not have reasonable levels of trust in the government-related institutions and that this might lead to an erosion of legitimacy of the foundations of the nation and representative government in the next generation. Concern about the fragility of support for these institutions in countries establishing democratic government anew after a period of non-democratic rule therefore prompted special scrutiny. There was also apprehension in the older democracies of the Phase 1 studies about increasing mistrust and lack of confidence among youth. There has also been considerable research, primarily by political scientists with adult samples, studying these issues (Panel 5.1).

Development of the Trust Scale in the 1999 IEA Instrument

Six items in this four-point scale (with end points of 'always' and 'never') deal with political/civic institutions, three with media institutions, one with the United Nations, one with schools and one with people in the country. A confirmatory factor analysis revealed two factors. Only items from the trust in government-related institutions factor were Rasch-scaled and are reported in that format here. (See also Appendix Table C.1 for alpha reliabilities.) A further three items that asked about trust in the news media—television, radio and newspapers—are presented here as individual items.

Results for Trust in Government-related Institutions

Item results

The courts and police are the most trusted institutions, being trusted 'always' by 20 to 25 percent of students, and trusted 'most of the time' by 40 to 45 percent of students across countries. The national legislature, local council (or government of town or city), and the national (federal) government are in an intermediate position, being 'always' trusted by about 10 percent and trusted 'most of the time' by about 40 percent of the respondents across countries. In contrast, political parties are 'always' trusted by only 4 percent, with an additional 24 percent expressing trust 'most of the time'. See Figure B.2e of Appendix B, which presents the percentages for the sample as a whole for these items along with an item-by-score map; the next section of this chapter presents country differences.

In general, these overall levels of endorsement are moderately high, indicating neither blind trust nor extreme distrust on the part of the average student across the participating countries. In other sections of the volume we have noted that students in some countries indicate that it is of little importance for adult citizens to join political parties, and that students express the view that conflict mobilized by political parties is bad for democracy.

PANEL 5.1 Previous Research on Trust in Government-related Institutions

One item in the rating scales for national government in the 1971 IEA Civic Education Study survey (previously described) dealt directly with trust. Five items (forming a scale) also dealt with the perceived responsiveness of the government (for example, 'cares about me and my family'). These were included in the 'support for national government' factor. Scores on the scales in this factor were especially high in the United States and low in Finland (Torney, Oppenheim & Farnen, 1975).

Items asking adults about their confidence in civic and political institutions were included in the World Values Survey (WVS) in 1990/91 in order to look at comparative country differences and trends across time. The WVS items called on respondents to express their level of confidence in 14 institutions, with the set of responses ranging from 'a great deal' to 'none at all'. Another item asked 'How much do you trust the government in [seat of national government] to do what is right?' (Inglehart, 1997).

In a re-analysis of the 1990/91 World Values Survey, McAllister (1999) presented country rankings of confidence in parliament and the civil service. Thirteen of the 24 countries included in that analysis of adults are also participating in the current IEA Civic Education Study of adolescents. Poland ranks first in confidence in the WVS, although that finding may be due to the time the questionnaire was administered, namely the early 1990s when Poland experienced a flush of optimism.

When McAllister plotted scores of confidence in government against the number of years of continuous democracy in each country, groupings of countries were highlighted. In well-established democracies that had not experienced major threats to the system, confidence tended to be high, with Norway ranking third out of 24 countries, Germany sixth, Britain eighth, Sweden ninth, the United States tenth and Denmark 11th. Despite its long history of democracy, Finland ranked 18th. Other studies (for example, Newton & Norris, 2000) have documented a fall in Finnish confidence during the 1980s, perhaps because of economic difficulties. In the McAllister analysis, the following countries had lower confidence scores: Czechoslovakia (a ranking of 14), Belgium (15), Hungary (17), Portugal (22) and Italy (23). Most had experienced less than 40 years of continuous democracy at the time of the survey. McAllister and also Klingemann (1999) suggest that the process of building support for democratic institutions is cumulative and so can take considerable time to achieve.

There is debate about the extent to which trust and confidence in political institutions (especially parliamentary institutions) declined during the 1980s. Using WVS data from 1981 and 1990/91, Newton and Norris (2000) concluded that there has been a significant diminution of confidence in public institutions but not in private institutions. This conclusion contrasts with that of Fuchs and Klingemann (1995), who judged the declines as less substantial. Putnam, Pharr and Dalton (2000) have attributed declines in confidence to the poor performance of governments and not to declines in interpersonal trust or membership in voluntary organizations that build social cohesion.

A number of analyses presented in Norris (1999) suggest that those who hold more political power in society (the well-educated, those who are not minority group members, those who support the political party in power) feel more confidence in government institutions than do less powerful groups.

Plasser, Ulram and Waldrauch (1998) studied adults' institutional trust in post-Communist countries and Austria in the 1994–97 period. West and East Germany were analyzed separately. Ratings of trust in government were highest in the Czech Republic, Slovenia and West Germany; the lowest were in Hungary and Russia. Trust in the media was rated at a higher level than trust in government in every country except the Czech Republic.

There have been other studies comparing confidence in a more differentiated way. These include feelings about local members of parliament versus parliament as a whole (Norton,1997); confidence in civic institutions such as the police and political institutions such as parliament (Miller, Timpson & Lessnoff, 1996); trust of the Hong Kong government compared with the Chinese government (McIntyre, 1993; Leung, 1997); and trust in the leading party as compared with the opposition party in post-Communist countries (Hibbing & Patterson, 1994).

In a study using the 'Monitoring the Future' data collected yearly in the United States from high school seniors, Rahn and Transue (1998) found a significant association between lack of interpersonal or social trust and materialistic attitudes such as the importance of possessions. Other researchers (Kaase, 1999; Newton, 1999), however, have expressed caution about attributing causality to relationships between interpersonal trust and trust in government.

Hahn (1998) surveyed small samples of adolescents in five countries (four of which overlap with IEA countries). The items had to do with government's responsiveness to citizens. She found greatest trust in the United States in 1986 and in Denmark in 1993, and the least in Germany in both years. She commented on the relatively low trust levels; as many as 60 percent of the German students said people in government could not be trusted. Ule (1995) found very low levels of confidence in political parties among youth in Slovenia, as did Minulescu (1995) in Romania.

When gender differences have been found, they usually indicate higher trust among females (Rahn & Transue, 1998; Newton & Norris, 2000).

Analysis of scale scores by country

The *highest level of trust in government-related institutions is found in Denmark, Norway and Switzerland* (Figure 5.1). Other countries in which this trust score is significantly above the international mean are Australia, Cyprus, Greece, the Slovak Republic and the United States. The *lowest trust scores are found in Bulgaria, the Russian Federation and Slovenia*. Other countries in which this trust score is significantly below the international mean are the Czech Republic, Estonia, Latvia, Lithuania and Portugal.

These results show considerable similarity to those from the 1990/91 World Values Survey of adults (Inglehart, 1997). In that study, countries with 40 years or less of continuous democracy in 1990 had lower governmental trust levels. As Figure 5.1 shows, all of the countries whose 14-year-olds are significantly below the international mean have had less than 40 years of continuous democracy. These 14-year-olds, who have lived most of their lives under a democratic system, nevertheless have levels of mistrust of government institutions similar to those of adults. The majority of the countries whose 14-year-olds are significantly above the international mean have had more than 40 years of continuous democracy.

Figure 5.1 Trust in Government-related Institutions

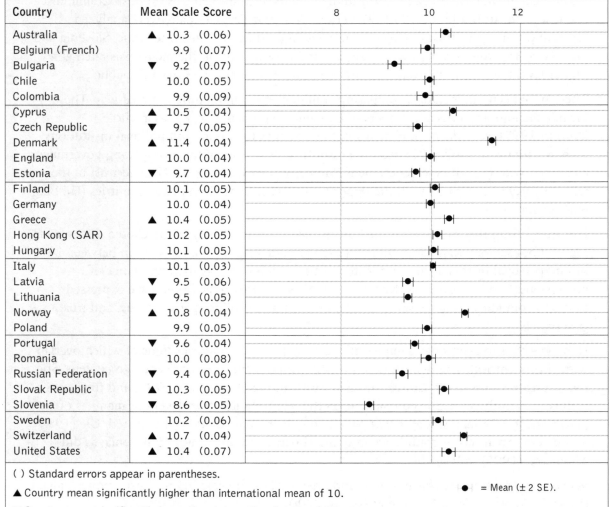

Country	Mean Scale Score			8	10	12
Australia	▲	10.3	(0.06)			
Belgium (French)		9.9	(0.07)			
Bulgaria	▼	9.2	(0.07)			
Chile		10.0	(0.05)			
Colombia		9.9	(0.09)			
Cyprus	▲	10.5	(0.04)			
Czech Republic	▼	9.7	(0.05)			
Denmark	▲	11.4	(0.04)			
England		10.0	(0.04)			
Estonia	▼	9.7	(0.04)			
Finland		10.1	(0.05)			
Germany		10.0	(0.04)			
Greece	▲	10.4	(0.05)			
Hong Kong (SAR)		10.2	(0.05)			
Hungary		10.1	(0.05)			
Italy		10.1	(0.03)			
Latvia	▼	9.5	(0.06)			
Lithuania	▼	9.5	(0.05)			
Norway	▲	10.8	(0.04)			
Poland		9.9	(0.05)			
Portugal	▼	9.6	(0.04)			
Romania		10.0	(0.08)			
Russian Federation	▼	9.4	(0.06)			
Slovak Republic	▲	10.3	(0.05)			
Slovenia	▼	8.6	(0.05)			
Sweden		10.2	(0.06)			
Switzerland	▲	10.7	(0.04)			
United States	▲	10.4	(0.07)			

( ) Standard errors appear in parentheses.

▲ Country mean significantly higher than international mean of 10.

▼ Country mean significantly lower than international mean of 10.

●── = Mean (± 2 SE).

Source: IEA Civic Education Study, Standard Population of 14-year-olds tested in 1999.

Analysis of scale scores by gender

There are no significant gender differences in 23 countries in trust in government-related institutions. In Belgium (French), Denmark and Switzerland, females express more trust than males. In Cyprus and Portugal, males express more trust than females.

Summary for Trust in Government-related Institutions

It is remarkable how closely the attitudes of 14-year-olds match those of adults in previous surveys of trust in government institutions. Substantial skepticism exists, especially in newer democracies. Will this mistrust lead to enhanced motivation to participate in, monitor or improve government, or is it likely to result in alienation from engagement?

Results for Trust in the Media

Item results

Table 5.1 presents the percentage of students who trust the three media sources 'always' or 'most of the time'. For comparison, national government (one of the government-related institutions from the scaled score) is also included in this figure. In most countries, slightly more than half of the students express trust in the media sources. Overall, news presented on television is trusted by the most respondents, followed by news on the radio, followed by news in the press (newspapers). Between-country variations exist, however, in the trustworthiness of the sources.

All three sources for news are trusted highly, with percentages significantly above the international mean percentage in the following countries: Cyprus,

Table 5.1 Trust in Media and National Government

Country	Percentage of students who trust always or most of the time in...			
	News on television	News on the radio	News in the press	The national government
Australia	▼ 50 (1.0)	▼ 49 (1.0)	50 (1.0)	▲ 59 (1.1)
Belgium (French)	58 (1.7)	▼ 53 (1.7)	54 (1.8)	45 (1.6)
Bulgaria	58 (1.6)	55 (1.4)	▼ 44 (1.4)	▼ 30 (1.3)
Chile	64 (0.9)	▼ 56 (0.8)	54 (1.0)	▼ 37 (1.4)
Colombia	60 (1.4)	57 (1.4)	▲ 58 (1.4)	44 (1.8)
Cyprus	▲ 66 (0.9)	▲ 63 (0.9)	▲ 60 (0.8)	▲ 63 (0.9)
Czech Republic	▼ 56 (1.1)	▼ 55 (1.0)	51 (1.2)	▼ 40 (1.4)
Denmark	▲ 82 (0.7)	▲ 83 (0.7)	▲ 71 (1.1)	▲ 85 (0.7)
England	▲ 66 (1.1)	61 (1.0)	▼ 28 (0.9)	▼ 44 (1.3)
Estonia	62 (1.0)	62 (0.9)	53 (1.0)	▼ 40 (1.4)
Finland	▲ 75 (1.1)	▲ 68 (1.2)	▲ 61 (1.0)	▲ 55 (1.2)
Germany	▼ 54 (0.8)	56 (1.2)	53 (0.9)	▼ 44 (1.2)
Greece	▼ 42 (1.0)	▼ 45 (0.9)	53 (0.9)	49 (1.1)
Hong Kong (SAR)	▼ 59 (0.8)	57 (0.7)	▼ 34 (1.1)	49 (1.0)
Hungary	▲ 68 (1.0)	▲ 65 (1.0)	▲ 56 (1.1)	▲ 56 (1.3)
Italy	▼ 39 (1.1)	▼ 33 (1.0)	▼ 45 (0.9)	50 (1.2)
Latvia	66 (1.2)	62 (1.4)	50 (1.3)	▼ 34 (1.4)
Lithuania	▲ 75 (0.9)	▲ 73 (1.1)	▲ 63 (1.0)	▼ 41 (1.4)
Norway	▲ 71 (1.0)	▲ 68 (0.9)	▲ 60 (1.0)	▲ 72 (1.0)
Poland	▲ 68 (1.2)	▲ 66 (1.1)	▲ 57 (1.2)	▼ 39 (1.3)
Portugal	▲ 73 (0.8)	▲ 67 (0.9)	▲ 64 (0.9)	▼ 35 (1.2)
Romania	▲ 66 (1.1)	61 (1.3)	▼ 45 (1.3)	▼ 35 (1.6)
Russian Federation	61 (1.4)	▼ 54 (1.3)	▼ 44 (1.1)	▼ 29 (1.3)
Slovak Republic	▼ 58 (1.1)	58 (1.1)	53 (1.1)	51 (1.6)
Slovenia	▼ 52 (1.1)	▼ 51 (0.9)	▼ 38 (1.0)	▼ 16 (0.8)
Sweden	▲ 70 (1.5)	▲ 68 (1.2)	▲ 56 (1.2)	▲ 53 (1.4)
Switzerland	▼ 53 (1.1)	▼ 54 (1.4)	51 (1.1)	▲ 76 (1.3)
United States	▼ 53 (1.5)	▼ 48 (1.2)	▲ 60 (1.3)	▲ 65 (1.4)
International mean percentages	62 (0.2)	59 (0.3)	52 (0.2)	48 (0.2)

( ) Standard errors appear in parentheses.

▲ Country mean significantly higher than international mean.

▼ Country mean significantly lower than international mean.

Source: IEA Civic Education Study, Standard Population of 14-year-olds tested in 1999.

Denmark, Finland, Hungary, Lithuania, Norway, Poland, Portugal and Sweden. This group includes all four Nordic countries, three post-Communist countries and two countries in Southern Europe. It is interesting to note that, among these countries, trust in government-related institutions is high in Cyprus, Denmark and Norway (see previous section). In Lithuania and Portugal, however, trust in government institutions is low while trust in the media is high. In fact, in most of the post-Communist countries, students are more likely to endorse items expressing trust in the media than an item expressing trust in the national government (Table 5.1), a finding that corresponds to previous research with adults.

In contrast, there are low levels of trust in all three media sources in Italy and Slovenia (mean percentages of endorsement significantly below the international mean percentage). In a few countries, trust in one of the media sources is higher than trust in the others. Specifically, in England and Romania the percentage who indicate that they trust television news is above the international mean percentage, while the percentage who indicate that they trust newspapers (the press) is below the international mean percentage. In the United States, in contrast, the percentage who indicate that they trust newspapers is above the international mean percentage, while the percentage who indicate that they trust television and radio news is below the international mean percentage.

Summary for Trust in the Media

Across countries, news on television tends to be the most trusted, although there are some country variations. There are countries where both media news and government institutions are trusted, countries where neither media nor government is trusted, countries where media news is trusted but the government is not, and countries where one media source is trusted more than others. Further analysis is needed to explore these patterns.

POSITIVE ATTITUDES TOWARD ONE'S NATION

Relation of this Area to the Study's Design

National identity constituted the second domain identified in the country reports of Phase 1. The content specifications for this domain were rich in implications, as were the corresponding parts of the national case study chapters. Ambivalence is sometimes expressed about positive national attitudes. They can mean many different things—political nationalism verging on arrogance or militarism, attachment to patriotic symbols, positive feelings about belonging to the national community, sense of connection to folk culture, or conviction about the existence of economic or political threat, to mention only a few. National identity has also been the subject of considerable research (see Panel 5.2).

There have been several studies of children's national attitudes. Hess and Torney (1967), in one of the first major surveys of political socialization among primary school children in the United States, found that nearly all respondents expressed a strong sense of attachment in the form of pride in the nation and flag. Connell (1972) found a similar attachment among children in Australia. Some studies by other developmental psychologists have focused on children's conceptions of the nation (Piaget & Weil, 1951, with Swiss children) and of broader alliances, such as the European Union (Barrett, 1996, with English children).

Political researchers Dalton (1999) and Norris (1999) view national pride as support for the national political community and as a vital element of healthy democracy. Their research used an item from the World Values Survey, which asked how proud adults were of their nation. Half or more of the respondents in Britain, Finland, Hungary, Norway, Sweden and the United States were very proud. Much lower percentages endorsed this item in Belgium, Germany and Italy (Inglehart, 1997).

Social psychologists Kosterman and Feshbach (1989) developed 120 items about the flag, national pride and respect. Patriotism included feelings of affection for one's country, while nationalism was the view that one's country should be dominant; these two scales had distinct patterns of correlation in the United States. Using a variation of this scale, Baughn and Yaprak (1996) separated economic nationalism from patriotism.

Weiss (1999) studied adults in the Czech Republic, Hungary, Poland and the Slovak Republic. Those over 30 years of age had a combination of nationalistic and patriotic beliefs, which contrasted with the detachment that predominated in the younger group.

Within the last decade, some researchers have concentrated on relating national identity and European identity (Chryssochoou, 1996, in France and Greece; Hilton, Erb, Dermoit & Molian, 1996, in Britain, France and Germany; Sousa, 1996, in Portugal; Cinnirella, 1997, in Britain and Italy). Italiano (1991) found in Belgium that identity with the nation is stronger than European identity (which is also important, however). Turner's (1987) social identity theory and Moscovici's (1998) paradigm of social representations have been used as frameworks. For example, Topalova (1996) studied social identities among Bulgarians and Poles using these frameworks. Muller-Peters (1998) found three factors in a survey of adults in 15 countries regarding attitudes toward the Euro: nationalism, patriotism and European patriotism. Nationalistic attitudes correlated with opposition to the Euro.

Development of the National Attitudes Scale in the 1999 IEA Instrument

The 1971 IEA Civic Education Study included several questions about the frequency with which patriotic rituals were practiced in the school, but did not include measures of attitudes toward the nation. The National Research Coordinators of the current IEA study decided to concentrate on the latter, noting that in the intervening 30 years patriotic rituals had nearly disappeared from some school systems. To the lists of items used by other researchers we added items about protecting the country against economic or political influence from outside the country, for a total of 15 items in the pilot instrument and ten in the final instrument.

A confirmatory factor analysis revealed two factors: protecting the country from outside influence and positive attitudes toward one's nation. The second is similar to the patriotism scales, such as feelings about the flag, pride in the country and disinclination to live in another country, that other reseachers have used. The positive attitudes toward one's nation scale is presented here, with the other items left for later analysis. Alpha reliabilities are found in Appendix Table C.1.

Results for Positive Attitudes toward One's Nation

Item results

In general, students have highly positive feelings about their countries. International distributions indicate that about 45 percent of students 'strongly agree' with the positively worded items about love for the country and the flag, and that another approximately 40 percent 'agree' with these items. In response to the item, 'this country should be proud of what it has achieved', 34 percent 'strongly agree' while 52 percent 'agree'. The large majority of students would not want to live permanently in another country. (See item-by-score map and distributions in Figure B.2f of Appendix B).

Analysis of scale scores by country

Figure 5.2 shows the differences by country. *Those countries showing high scores, indicating very positive attitudes toward their nation, are Chile, Cyprus, Greece and Poland.* Other countries with means significantly above the international mean are Colombia, the Czech Republic, Finland, Portugal and the Slovak Republic. In contrast, *countries with low scores, indicating relatively less positive attitudes toward their nation, are Belgium (French), Germany and Hong Kong (SAR).* Other countries with means significantly below the international mean are Denmark, England, Estonia, Italy, Latvia, Sweden and Switzerland. However, the mean of even the lowest scoring country shows that the average student does not have negative attitudes (a true negative value would correspond to a scale score of 6). Youth in some of these countries must balance identity and membership in several groups (based on language or region, for example), a situation that could lead to lower levels of positive national identity.

Analysis of scale scores by gender

There are no significant gender differences in 18 countries in positive attitudes toward one's nation. In Colombia females have more positive attitudes than males. In England, Finland, Germany, Greece, Italy, Norway, Portugal, the Russian Federation and Sweden, males have more positive attitudes than females.

Summary for Positive Attitudes toward One's Nation

A comparative look at Figure 5.1 (presenting trust in government-related institutions) and Figure 5.2 (presenting positive national feeling) reveals only two countries (Estonia and Latvia) with scores significantly below the international mean on both scales. Thus, the large majority of the adolescents in the participating countries have relatively positive feelings either to their national government institutions or to their country as a national and symbolic community.

Figure 5.2 Positive Attitudes Toward One's Nation

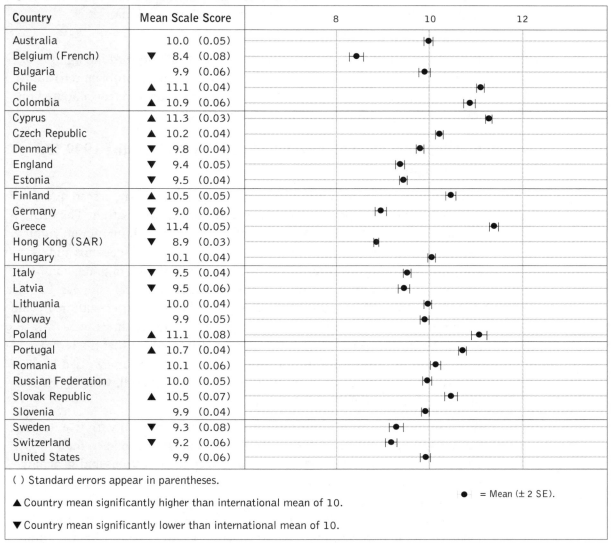

Country	Mean Scale Score	
Australia		10.0 (0.05)
Belgium (French)	▼	8.4 (0.08)
Bulgaria		9.9 (0.06)
Chile	▲	11.1 (0.04)
Colombia	▲	10.9 (0.06)
Cyprus	▲	11.3 (0.03)
Czech Republic	▲	10.2 (0.04)
Denmark	▼	9.8 (0.04)
England	▼	9.4 (0.05)
Estonia	▼	9.5 (0.04)
Finland	▲	10.5 (0.05)
Germany	▼	9.0 (0.06)
Greece	▲	11.4 (0.05)
Hong Kong (SAR)	▼	8.9 (0.03)
Hungary		10.1 (0.04)
Italy	▼	9.5 (0.04)
Latvia	▼	9.5 (0.06)
Lithuania		10.0 (0.04)
Norway		9.9 (0.05)
Poland	▲	11.1 (0.08)
Portugal	▲	10.7 (0.04)
Romania		10.1 (0.06)
Russian Federation		10.0 (0.05)
Slovak Republic	▲	10.5 (0.07)
Slovenia		9.9 (0.04)
Sweden	▼	9.3 (0.08)
Switzerland	▼	9.2 (0.06)
United States		9.9 (0.06)

( ) Standard errors appear in parentheses.

▲ Country mean significantly higher than international mean of 10.

▼ Country mean significantly lower than international mean of 10.

● = Mean (± 2 SE).

Source: IEA Civic Education Study, Standard Population of 14-year-olds tested in 1999.

The large majority of young people surveyed indicate a positive attitude toward their country and its symbols. They express little desire to live elsewhere. Together with the findings about consensus on the understanding of concepts of democracy and the findings about trust, this result suggests that youth in most of these countries are not seriously alienated.

POSITIVE ATTITUDES TOWARD IMMIGRANTS

Relation of this Area to the Study's Design

Social cohesion and diversity constitutes the third domain identified in the country reports submitted during Phase 1 of this study. Nearly all of the countries' case studies recognized problems of discrimination and disenfranchisement. It was also clear that the targets of such discrimination differed. In some countries it was a problem of racism or religious intolerance; in other places of discrimination against national minorities, immigrants or those who spoke a mother tongue different from that of the majority population. In the process of developing attitude items for the survey, we examined a number of scales relating to discrimination, most of which dealt with some form of racism or discrimination against racial minorities, immigrants or foreigners.

In many countries, discrimination directed specifically toward immigrants or foreign-born individuals was recognized as a widespread problem relevant to social cohesion and diversity. A review of previous literature concentrated on attitudes toward immigrants is presented in Panel 5.3.

Development of the Immigrant Attitudes Scale in the 1999 IEA Instrument

The items that we developed for this scale were based on the research review, and each required respondents either to agree or disagree with it. The final instrument included eight items, some of which dealt with immigrant rights, and some with opportunities for immigrants to retain their customs and language. There was one statement about the threat that immigrants might pose to having a united country and one item about political refugees. Because the items were constructed to be meaningful in both countries with many and countries with few immigrants, the items about economic threat were potentially ambiguous and not used. It must also be noted that the term 'immigrants' was translated as 'foreigners' in the German survey (used in Germany and in the German-speaking areas of Switzerland), which may have given the items a slightly different meaning.

A confirmatory factor analysis showed a one-factor solution with five items. It was comprised of affirmation of the rights of immigrants to keep their language, receive the same education, vote, keep their customs and generally have the same rights as other members of the country. Alpha reliabilities are found in Table C.1 of Appendix C. It is important to note here that although several items dealing with norms of ethnic and racial equality were also included in the pilot and the IEA instrument, they did not consistently form a scale across countries.

Results for Positive Attitudes toward Immigrants

Item results

Forty percent of the respondents 'strongly agree' and 50 percent 'agree' that immigrants should have the right to equal educational opportunity. Immigrants' rights to keep their customs, retain their language, vote and have generally the same rights are endorsed by slightly more than three-quarters of the respondents (about 25 percent 'strongly agreeing' and 50 percent 'agreeing'). Between 6 and 8 percent of the respondents 'strongly disagree' that immigrants should have the right to vote and to keep their own language, customs and lifestyle. Figure B.2g in Appendix B gives the item-by-score map and percentage distributions.

These attitudinal items give a picture similar to that provided by one of the concept items, where students on average thought that requiring immigrants to give up their customs and language would be bad for democracy. Young people in most countries do not especially restrict voting rights for immigrants, as some other studies have shown.

PANEL 5.3 Previous Research on Attitudes toward Immigrants

Miller, Timpson and Lessnoff (1996) in a study of British adults included items such as this: 'Immigrants should try harder to be like other British people.' They found that politicians were more likely to be positive about immigrants maintaining their culture than were the general public, and they also found a positive correlation between respect for women's rights and for immigrants' culture. Westin (1998) used items relating to immigrants' retention of cultural traditions and language with Swedish adults. Billiet (1995) used items regarding economic threat and the right to vote for immigrants in Flemish Belgium and found that educational level was the strongest predictor of immigrant attitudes. Knigge (1997) used Eurobarometer data from 1988 to study anti-immigrant sentiment among adults in France, Great Britain, the Netherlands and West Germany. Rights of individuals to maintain their own language and culture were assessed as well as beliefs about schooling, group threat and national pride. Negative stereotyping tended to be related to opposition to immigration primarily when there was also a perception of immigrant groups as threats.

Watts (1996) reported a study in Germany of youths' attitudes toward assimilation, award of political asylum and participation in political and electoral activities. Both his study and that of Kracke, Oepke, Wild and Noack (1998) concluded that perceptions of economic threat were important in influencing the attitudes of German youth (especially those in East Germany).

Frindte, Funke and Waldzus (1996) surveyed 14- to 18-year-olds regarding immigrants' voting rights and restrictions on asylum seekers. Flanagan (1999) formulated items for adolescents cross-nationally that dealt with immigrants as economic threats and with their possible criminal behavior. She also formulated positive statements about immigrants enriching the national culture. Angvik and von Borries (1997), in the Youth and History Study conducted in 26 countries in 1994/95, asked respondents whether immigrants should be granted the right to vote and whether immigration should be reduced. There was substantial sentiment in this study that only immigrants who accepted the host countries' language and customs should have the right to vote. Youth in post-socialist and Nordic countries appeared the least supportive of unconditional voting rights for immigrants. Most research shows the greater level of support being for limits on voting rights and the least support for limits on educational opportunity.

Sniderman, Peri, de Figueiredo and Piazza (2000) asked Italian adults to rate immigrants from North or Central Africa or from Eastern Europe on one positive adjective and seven negative adjectives and also asked them about their contact with immigrants, immigration policies and perceived problems with immigrants. When responsibility for one social problem was attributed to an immigrant group, blame tended to be ascribed to the same group for other problems. The focus of the study was on prejudice and not on immigrants' rights.

Toth (1995) found negative attitudes toward gypsies among youth in Hungary. Another recent study with similar results conducted in four post-Communist countries dealt with ethnic groups within countries, including gypsies (Weiss, 1999).

Torney-Purta (1983), using data from the Council on Learning's Survey of Global Awareness, assessed affective concern for those living in other countries. University-student respondents in the United States who themselves were immigrants expressed higher levels of positive concern, as did female respondents. A study of university students in 35 countries also found that groups who felt they had experienced collective injustice had stronger attitudes toward rights (Doise, Spini & Clemence, 1999). Other research finding that females hold more positive attitudes than males toward rights for groups such as immigrants has been conducted in Germany (Adler, 1996; Frindte, Funke & Waldzus, 1996; Watts, 1996), Hungary (Toth, 1995), Sweden (Westin, 1998) and the United States (Diaz-Veizades, Widaman, Little & Gibbs, 1995).

Many studies have asked whether respondents perceive that immigrants take jobs away from those born in the country (for example, Klein-Allermann, Kracke, Noack & Hofer, 1995; Pettigrew & Meertens, 1995; Legge, 1996). Such survey items can have different meaning in countries with many or few immigrants and in countries with strong or with weak demand for workers.

Analysis of scale scores by country

Understanding the data presented in this section is helped by knowing whether the respondents are likely to be in contact with many immigrants in their schools. Table 2.2, which describes the sample, includes information about the percentage of students who report that they had not been born in the country. Although this information does not identify students whose parents immigrated, it is a more satisfactory index of the number of immigrants with whom a student is likely to come into contact than were any we were able to obtain from other sources.

The following countries had 10 percent or more of their student sample stating that they had been born outside the country: Australia, Belgium (French), Germany, Hong Kong (SAR), the Russian Federation, Switzerland and the United States. The following countries had between 5 and 9 percent of the student sample reporting that they had been born outside the country: Cyprus, Denmark, England, Estonia, Greece, Norway, Portugal and Sweden.

Figure 5.3 shows that the following countries have *mean positive attitudes toward immigrants that are significantly above the international mean:* Chile, Colombia, Cyprus, Greece, Hong Kong (SAR), Norway, Poland, Portugal, Sweden and the United States. Some of these countries have relatively substantial numbers of students who are immigrants, but there are others whose immigrant population is quite small. Figure 5.3 also shows that the following countries have relatively more negative attitudes toward immigrants, significantly below the international mean: Bulgaria, Denmark, England, Estonia, Germany, Hungary, Italy, Latvia, Lithuania, the Slovak Republic, Slovenia and Switzerland. Again, there are some countries with substantial numbers of students who are immigrants and some countries with small numbers of students who are immigrants.

In most of the countries, respondents who are themselves immigrants are more likely to have positive attitudes about immigrant rights and opportunities than are native-born students. Even if one looks only at native-born students, however, the country differences outlined in the previous paragraphs are maintained.

Analysis of scale scores by gender

Figure 5.4 indicates significant gender differences in 23 countries. In all of these cases, females have more positive attitudes than males, supporting the findings of previous research.

This is the first concept or attitude scale examined to show substantial gender differences. Females in the Nordic countries (Denmark, Finland, Norway and Sweden) are especially likely to support opportunities for immigrants. The only countries without significant gender differences are Chile, Colombia, Hong Kong (SAR), Portugal and Romania.

Figure 5.3 Positive Attitudes Toward Immigrants

Country	Mean Scale Score		8	10	12
Australia	10.0 (0.08)				
Belgium (French)	10.0 (0.09)				
Bulgaria	▼ 9.7 (0.10)				
Chile	▲ 10.4 (0.03)				
Colombia	▲ 10.8 (0.04)				
Cyprus	▲ 10.9 (0.03)				
Czech Republic	10.0 (0.06)				
Denmark	▼ 9.6 (0.05)				
England	▼ 9.7 (0.07)				
Estonia	▼ 9.7 (0.04)				
Finland	9.8 (0.06)				
Germany*	▼ 9.2 (0.07)				
Greece	▲ 10.6 (0.05)				
Hong Kong (SAR)	▲ 10.5 (0.05)				
Hungary	▼ 9.5 (0.05)				
Italy	▼ 9.8 (0.05)				
Latvia	▼ 9.5 (0.05)				
Lithuania	▼ 9.6 (0.03)				
Norway	▲ 10.3 (0.07)				
Poland	▲ 10.6 (0.06)				
Portugal	▲ 10.3 (0.03)				
Romania	10.2 (0.06)				
Russian Federation	9.8 (0.06)				
Slovak Republic	▼ 9.8 (0.05)				
Slovenia	▼ 9.4 (0.05)				
Sweden	▲ 10.7 (0.08)				
Switzerland*	▼ 9.4 (0.07)				
United States	▲ 10.3 (0.06)				

( ) Standard errors appear in parentheses.

▲ Country mean significantly higher than international mean of 10.

▼ Country mean significantly lower than international mean of 10.

* In German, the word 'immigrants' was translated as 'foreigners'.

● = Mean (± 2 SE).

Source: IEA Civic Education Study, Standard Population of 14-year-olds tested in 1999.

Summary for Attitudes toward Immigrants

Attitudes toward immigrants are generally positive. The mean scores even in the lowest scoring countries do not indicate negative attitudes among the majority of respondents. Females have more positive attitudes than males. There is considerable potential for further analysis of these items, especially in those countries that have many immigrants. It would be possible to look also at students' perceptions of the extent to which discrimination exists (items that were included in the survey but have not yet been analyzed). It would also be interesting to examine the small group of students with especially negative attitudes.

Figure 5.4 Gender Differences in Positive Attitudes Toward Immigrants

Country	Mean Score Females	Mean Score Males	Plot (8 · 10 · 12)
Australia	10.4 (0.10)	9.6 (0.11)	
Belgium (French)	10.4 (0.08)	9.6 (0.11)	
Bulgaria	9.9 (0.13)	9.4 (0.08)	
Chile	10.5 (0.05)	10.3 (0.05)	
Colombia	10.9 (0.06)	10.7 (0.06)	
Cyprus	11.1 (0.05)	10.6 (0.05)	
Czech Republic	10.4 (0.07)	9.6 (0.08)	
Denmark	10.0 (0.05)	9.1 (0.07)	
England	10.0 (0.09)	9.5 (0.08)	
Estonia	9.9 (0.04)	9.5 (0.06)	
Finland	10.5 (0.07)	9.1 (0.07)	
Germany*	9.5 (0.08)	9.0 (0.09)	
Greece	10.8 (0.06)	10.3 (0.06)	
Hong Kong (SAR)	10.6 (0.06)	10.4 (0.07)	
Hungary	9.7 (0.05)	9.3 (0.07)	
Italy	10.1 (0.05)	9.5 (0.07)	
Latvia	9.7 (0.06)	9.3 (0.06)	
Lithuania	9.8 (0.04)	9.4 (0.05)	
Norway	10.9 (0.07)	9.7 (0.09)	
Poland	10.9 (0.06)	10.2 (0.09)	
Portugal	10.4 (0.04)	10.3 (0.04)	
Romania	10.3 (0.07)	10.0 (0.07)	
Russian Federation	10.0 (0.06)	9.7 (0.08)	
Slovak Republic	9.9 (0.05)	9.5 (0.07)	
Slovenia	9.8 (0.06)	9.1 (0.06)	
Sweden	11.3 (0.09)	10.1 (0.12)	
Switzerland*	9.8 (0.08)	9.0 (0.09)	
United States	10.7 (0.06)	10.0 (0.11)	

( ) Standard errors appear in parentheses.

▲ Gender difference statistically significant at .05 level.

* In German the word 'immigrants' was translated as 'foreigners'.

⊢●⊣ = Mean for Males (± 2 SE).

⊢◇⊣ = Mean for Females (± 2 SE).

Source: IEA Civic Education Study, Standard Population of 14-year-olds tested in 1999.

SUPPORT FOR WOMEN'S POLITICAL RIGHTS

Relation of this Area to the Study's Design

Social cohesion and diversity constitutes the third domain identified in the country reports submitted during Phase 1 of the IEA Civic Education Study. Although discrimination against minority groups or immigrants was more widely discussed in these reports, gender discrimination and the imbalance between the number of men and women holding political office also was noted in some. A review of previous literature concentrated on attitudes toward women's political rights is presented in Panel 5.4.

Development of the Women's Political Rights Scale in the 1999 IEA Instrument

Three of the 1971 IEA Civic Education Study items were used in the 1999 instrument. These were two positively stated items about women running for public office and having the same rights as men, and a negatively stated item about women staying out of politics. Eight items in the pilot instrument were reduced to six items in the final survey: the three from the 1971 study; one dealing with men having more rights to a job than women when jobs are scarce; another with equal pay; and one concerned with the suitability of men and women for political leadership.

A confirmatory factor analysis showed these items on one factor. Although two of the items deal with economic matters in the public sphere, the title of the scale is 'support for women's political rights'. Three of the items are stated negatively and reversed in scoring. For alpha reliabilities, see Table C.1, Appendix C.

Results for Support for Women's Political Rights

Item results

Nearly 60 percent of the respondents 'strongly agree' with the items about women having the same rights as men and receiving equal pay for the same job, with an additional 30 to 35 percent 'agreeing'. About 40 percent of the respondents 'strongly agree' with the positively phrased item about women running for office, and another 48 percent 'agree' (see Figure B.2h in Appendix B).

Fifty-two percent of the students 'strongly disagree' with the negatively phrased item about women staying out of politics and another 33 percent 'disagree'. A somewhat smaller percentage (35 to 40) 'strongly disagree' with the item regarding men being better qualified to be political leaders than women, and with the item about men having more right to a job than women when jobs are scarce. An additional 35 percent 'disagree' with these items.

Overall support for women's political and economic rights is strong, although there is some variation between items. It is not that young people believe that women should stay out of politics altogether, but rather that some believe they should not expect equal chances to hold elected positions. Some also believe that conditions such as high unemployment give men more rights than women to a job.

Analysis of scale scores by country

Figure 5.5 shows that students in *Australia, Denmark, England and Norway have the highest scores on support for women's political rights*. Also significantly above the international mean are Cyprus, Finland, Germany, Sweden, Switzerland and the United States. In contrast, *the lowest scores on support for women's rights are evident among students in Bulgaria, Latvia, Romania and the Russian Federation*. Other countries with means significantly below the international mean are Chile, Estonia, Hong Kong (SAR), Hungary, Lithuania and the Slovak Republic.

Table 1.1 shows that all the countries below the international mean in this analysis (with the exception of Hong Kong/SAR) have a GNP per capita of less than $5000 (US$ equivalent). A number of these countries also have unemployment rates greater than 10 percent of the labor force (Bulgaria, Romania, the Russian Federation and the Slovak Republic). The inclusion of items about men and women having rights to jobs and equal pay may have influenced students' scores on the scale in these countries. The countries with

The 1971 IEA Study of Civic Education administered four items on support for women's rights. The most supportive attitudes among 14-year-olds were found in Germany and Finland, moderately supportive attitudes were evident in Italy, and the least supportive attitudes were found in the United States. There were very large differences between the attitudes of males (less supportive of women's political rights) and females (more supportive) (analysis summarized in Torney-Purta, 1984).

Furnham and Gunter (1989), using the IEA items to which they added others about women's work opportunities and women entering politics, studied 12- to 22-years-olds from Britain in 1985. Females in this study were also substantially more supportive than males of enhanced political participation of and rights for women.

Hahn (1998) administered women's rights items in her study of adolescents in Denmark, England, Germany and the United States. In all countries except Germany there was greater support for women in politics in 1993 than in 1986. The gender difference on this scale, with females more supportive, was the largest in all the scales on her instrument. She found especially substantial differences in willingness to vote for a woman for a high political position, as did Gillespie and Spohn (1987, 1990), in studies conducted in the United States.

Angvik and von Borries (1997) reported general support for full equality for women from the Youth and History Study of 15-year-olds in 26 countries. This support was stronger in Northern, Western and Southern European countries and weaker in Eastern and Central European nations. Gender differences were substantial. The resistance of gender stereotypes to change was noted in Greece by Deliyanni-Kouimtzi and Ziogou (1995) and in Finland by Lahteenmaa (1995).

Miller, Timpson and Lessnoff (1996) in the British Rights Survey found that substantial numbers of the public favored changes in laws to encourage more female Members of Parliament.

Sapiro (1998) examined adult Eurobarometer data where adult respondents were asked which causes were 'worth the trouble of taking risks and making sacrifices for?' Achieving equality between the sexes was the lowest ranked cause in Britain, Denmark, Germany, Italy and Portugal. Poverty and the environment were among the other causes listed.

low support for women's political rights are also predominantly post-Communist countries, where there have been substantial changes during the last decade in the prevailing ideology about women's rights and in the positions of women and men in the labor market and public life.

These data also present an opportunity to compare a wide range of countries from several regions with differing representations of women in national legislatures. In Sweden and Denmark, where women hold about 40 percent of the seats in the national legislature, young people's support for women's rights is high. There are some countries, however, where adolescents show strong support for women's rights even though there are relatively few women in the national legislature (Cyprus, 7 percent, and the United States, 13 percent).

In the Russian Federation and Romania, women comprise only about 6

Figure 5.5 Support for Women's Political Rights

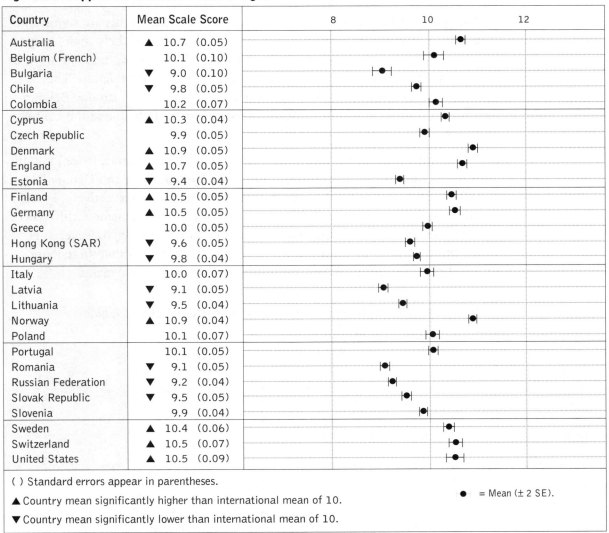

Country	Mean Scale Score			8	10	12
Australia	▲	10.7	(0.05)			
Belgium (French)		10.1	(0.10)			
Bulgaria	▼	9.0	(0.10)			
Chile	▼	9.8	(0.05)			
Colombia		10.2	(0.07)			
Cyprus	▲	10.3	(0.04)			
Czech Republic		9.9	(0.05)			
Denmark	▲	10.9	(0.05)			
England	▲	10.7	(0.05)			
Estonia	▼	9.4	(0.04)			
Finland	▲	10.5	(0.05)			
Germany	▲	10.5	(0.05)			
Greece		10.0	(0.05)			
Hong Kong (SAR)	▼	9.6	(0.05)			
Hungary	▼	9.8	(0.04)			
Italy		10.0	(0.07)			
Latvia	▼	9.1	(0.05)			
Lithuania	▼	9.5	(0.04)			
Norway	▲	10.9	(0.04)			
Poland		10.1	(0.07)			
Portugal		10.1	(0.05)			
Romania	▼	9.1	(0.05)			
Russian Federation	▼	9.2	(0.04)			
Slovak Republic	▼	9.5	(0.05)			
Slovenia		9.9	(0.04)			
Sweden	▲	10.4	(0.06)			
Switzerland	▲	10.5	(0.07)			
United States	▲	10.5	(0.09)			

( ) Standard errors appear in parentheses.

▲ Country mean significantly higher than international mean of 10.

▼ Country mean significantly lower than international mean of 10.

●━ = Mean (± 2 SE).

Source: IEA Civic Education Study, Standard Population of 14-year-olds tested in 1999.

percent of the parliament, and students' support for women's rights is low. In fact, the majority of the countries whose adolescents score significantly below the international mean on this scale have relatively few women in their national legislatures. The exceptions are Estonia, Latvia and Lithuania where women hold approximately 17 percent of the seats.

Support for women's political rights among adolescents tends to be stronger in countries where many women are in the national legislature than in countries where there are few women in these positions. One must be tentative in offering explanations because of the lack of direct evidence, but there are at least two possibilities to consider. It may be that young people see women holding political positions, view them as role models, and develop more positive attitudes toward women's political rights. Or it may be that voters who developed support for women's rights during their adolescence are more likely to vote for women candidates when they become adults. Another alternative is that a combination of these processes (and others such as a well-organized and visible women's movement) may be influential in different countries.

Analysis of scale scores by gender

The gender differences in support for women's political rights are significant and large in every country (Figure 5.6). Females are more likely than males to support women's political rights. The smallest effect is more than one-third of a standard deviation. The largest is nearly a full standard deviation. The countries that have especially large gender differences are Australia, Belgium (French), Cyprus, England, Finland, Greece, Norway, Poland and the United States.

The distributions for the two genders generally do not overlap. If we look only at male responses, the two highest means are Norway (9.9) and Denmark (10.1), just below and just above the international mean, respectively. These differences are even more striking because there are so few gender differences in the remainder of the instrument. In interpreting this scale, however, it is important to keep in mind that overall support is high and that these items may have a somewhat different meaning for males and for females.

Figure 5.6 Gender Differences in Support for Women's Political Rights

Country	Mean Score Females	Mean Score Males	8 10 12
Australia	11.5 (0.05)	9.7 (0.07)	
Belgium (French)	11.0 (0.09)	9.3 (0.13)	
Bulgaria	9.4 (0.13)	8.6 (0.08)	
Chile	10.3 (0.07)	9.3 (0.05)	
Colombia	10.5 (0.06)	9.7 (0.08)	
Cyprus	11.2 (0.05)	9.5 (0.06)	
Czech Republic	10.4 (0.07)	9.4 (0.05)	
Denmark	11.8 (0.04)	10.1 (0.07)	
England	11.6 (0.06)	9.8 (0.08)	
Estonia	9.9 (0.04)	8.9 (0.04)	
Finland	11.4 (0.05)	9.5 (0.06)	
Germany	11.3 (0.05)	9.7 (0.07)	
Greece	10.9 (0.06)	9.0 (0.07)	
Hong Kong (SAR)	10.0 (0.06)	9.2 (0.06)	
Hungary	10.4 (0.05)	9.1 (0.05)	
Italy	10.6 (0.08)	9.2 (0.06)	
Latvia	9.5 (0.07)	8.5 (0.06)	
Lithuania	10.0 (0.05)	8.9 (0.04)	
Norway	11.8 (0.05)	9.9 (0.06)	
Poland	10.9 (0.13)	9.2 (0.09)	
Portugal	10.4 (0.06)	9.8 (0.06)	
Romania	9.5 (0.07)	8.7 (0.06)	
Russian Federation	9.5 (0.05)	8.9 (0.07)	
Slovak Republic	9.9 (0.05)	9.1 (0.06)	
Slovenia	10.7 (0.06)	9.1 (0.05)	
Sweden	11.0 (0.07)	9.7 (0.09)	
Switzerland	11.3 (0.08)	9.7 (0.07)	
United States	11.4 (0.07)	9.6 (0.11)	

( ) Standard errors appear in parentheses.

▲ Gender difference statistically significant at .05 level.

⊢●⊣ = Mean for Males (± 2 SE).

⊢◇⊣ = Mean for Females (± 2 SE).

Source: IEA Civic Education Study, Standard Population of 14-year-olds tested in 1999.

Summary for Support for Women's Political Rights

There appears to be somewhat more support for women's political and economic rights than existed 30 years ago (the time of the first IEA Civics Study), but the gaps between males' and females' attitudes remain large. Gender is clearly an identity group for adolescents, and one that intensifies in importance at adolescence (Galambos, Almeida & Petersen, 1990). Countries where women hold many seats in the national legislature tend to have adolescents who are more supportive of women's rights.

SUMMARY

The differentiated picture of country and gender differences presented by these four attitude scales suggests that it was appropriate for us to develop and analyze the four scores separately rather than sum them together into larger scores such as 'tolerance' or 'positive feelings toward government and nation'. Having conducted the more fine-grained analysis, however, we can examine country patterns on the two scales from Domain III (social cohesion and diversity) together. It is important to keep in mind that overall the responses are quite positive on these scales, and that gender differences appear in a substantial number of countries on both of them, a finding that generally confirms previous research with adults and young people.

If we look across the figures in this chapter, it is possible to examine the countries where the students' responses placed their countries *significantly above the international mean on both immigrants' and women's political rights*, and those where the students' responses placed their countries *below the international mean on both scales*. Fourteen-year-olds in Cyprus, Norway, Sweden and the United States are highly supportive of rights for both groups. Countries where support of rights for both groups is low include Bulgaria, Estonia, Hungary, Latvia, Lithuania and the Slovak Republic. The Baltic States and three countries in the Central European region have relatively low levels of support for rights and opportunities for immigrants and women when compared with other participating countries, findings that confirm some recent research. Economic factors, such as a relatively poor economy in which there is competition between groups (men and women, immigrants and non-immigrants) for jobs, should be taken into account when seeking explanations.

What is the potential role of the school in the four attitudinal areas covered in this chapter? Positive feelings about the nation and about political institutions are much more likely to be the subject of instruction than are support for women's political rights or immigrant rights in most countries, according to our Phase 1 results. The Scandinavian countries do place considerable curricular emphasis on women's rights, however. Some countries are also instituting educational programs dealing with student diversity, which may include attempting to foster positive attitudes toward immigrants. In some other countries these are thought of as rather controversial issues for teachers to discuss. Further analysis and research can assist in identifying areas where intensified instructional attention would be appropriate.

Students' Civic
Engagement
and Political
Activities

CHAPTER 6

HIGHLIGHTS RELATING TO CIVIC ACTIVITIES

- Fourteen-year-olds are only moderately interested in politics in most countries. Generally, females are less interested than males, although this is not true in some countries.

- Among 14-year-olds in almost all countries, news broadcasts on television are the most prominent sources of political information. Newspapers rank second, followed by news broadcasts on the radio.

- Voting in national elections is the most preferred future political activity of 14-year-old students. Collecting money for charity work ranks second.

- Only a minority of students—mainly males—believe that they are likely to engage in protest activities such as spray-painting slogans on walls, blocking traffic and occupying buildings. These are activities that would be illegal in most countries.

- A majority (approximately four-fifths) of 14-year olds in all countries *do not* intend to participate in conventional political activities like joining a party, writing letters to newspapers about social and political concerns, and being a candidate for a local or city office.

This chapter deals with a central characteristic of a democracy—political participation in the process by which political demands and objectives are formulated. A prerequisite of responsible participation is political interest and the search for information. This chapter therefore is divided into two sections. The first covers students' political interest and exposure to political news, and the second looks at students' expected participation in political activities.

POLITICAL INTEREST AND EXPOSURE TO POLITICAL NEWS

Relation of this Area to the Study's Design

During Phase 1 of the IEA Civic Education Study, most participating countries mentioned creating political interest in students as a goal of civic education. In addition, countries frequently mentioned reading newspapers, watching news on television, and interpreting material in media messages as important in relation to all three content domains (Torney-Purta, Schwille & Amadeo, 1999). Some countries described programs of media education (or the need for them). Most 14-year-old students are avid consumers of the mass media, and educators recognize the importance of the media in the transmission of civic information and orientations. However, the extent to which students are explicitly encouraged to read or analyze newspapers or view news programs as part of civic education seems to vary across countries.

The 1971 IEA Civic Education Study used a measure of 'interest in public affairs television'. Here, students were asked how likely they would be to watch six different programs dealing with news and current events (embedded in a longer list of program topics). This scale was a positive predictor of civic knowledge and of participation in political discussion in all the participating countries but was not analyzed individually for between-country differences.

Political interest as an attitude toward the political system is part of what Dalton (1996) has called cognitive political mobilization. For example, it is one of the strongest predictors of voting. Political interest among adults and—on a lower level—among adolescents increased in western industrialized societies between the 1960s and the 1990s, and decreased in some countries during the 1990s. The growth of political interest over almost 40 years is, according to Gabriel and van Deth (1995) and Inglehart (1997), related to an increase in post-materialist values. However, the average political interest of young people in most countries is only moderate. It is generally higher in the older and the better-educated students (Dalton, 1996; Nie, Junn & Stehlik-Barry, 1996). In former communist countries like the German Democratic Republic, political interest of students increased dramatically during the times of radical political change and the introduction of democracy, but then decreased during the 1990s as a result of some disillusionment with the democratic system and the free market economy (Oswald, 1999).

Numerous studies in many countries have shown that males are more interested in politics than females. However, there are indications that the gender gap is narrowing in some countries like England, the Netherlands, the United States (Hahn, 1998) and Germany (Kaase, 1989), and among better-educated young people. In addition, there is evidence (Shapiro & Mahajan, 1986) that policy preferences regarding political issues are different for males and females. In a study of young East Germans' political participation, Oswald and Schmid (1998) found that replacing general questions about political interest with questions about specific political topics revealed female students as more interested than males in political issues like ecology, peace and third world problems.

This study therefore examined, first, the adolescents' interest in politics and, second, the extent to which students in different countries report exposure to news media. Interest in politics and exposure to political news (via newspapers, radio and television) may contribute to students' political knowledge. Political interest as well as reading, listening and watching the news may also be related to students' attitudes and concepts of citizenship and democracy. In order therefore to form a predictor of knowledge and attitudes scales (see Chapter 8), students were asked about the frequency with which they read newspapers, listen to the radio and watch television news broadcasts. (For reviews of recent research in the areas of political interest and exposure to political news, see Panels 6.1 and 6.2.)

Putnam answered the question as to why civil society is waning in the United States by proposing 'the culprit is television' (1996, p.46). According to Putnam, the more people watch television in the United States, the less interested they are in politics and the less they participate in political activities. Norris replicated this result (1996). However, she also found that the more people watch television news, the more they engage in political actions. In a review of the literature, Comstock and Paik (1991) reported that exposure to political news (both on television and in newspapers) is associated with higher levels of political knowledge among adults.

In their pioneering work, Chaffee, Ward and Tipton (1970) found that for American adolescents the mass media were by far the most important source of political information compared to parents, friends and teachers. Similar results have since been found in four West-European countries (Hahn, 1998). Using data from surveys and a current events test, Linnenbrink and Anderman (1995) found that American adolescents who watched and read news more frequently than their peers had higher knowledge scores. They also found that depth in understanding news content was more likely to result from reading the news than from viewing news on television. Other research has yielded conflicting results related to the effectiveness of viewing news on television as compared to reading the news, and most studies have included questions about both.

Reading and watching news in the mass media seem to have positive effects on adolescents' political knowledge and political involvement. However, many adolescents are not very interested in obtaining political information. One study in the United States (Bennett, 1998) and two in England (Walker, 1996; Buckingham, 1999) found a marked indifference among young adults and youth to using the media in order to become informed about politics.

Several studies conducted by Chaffee and his associates reported evaluations of programs that encourage students to read newspapers. Chaffee, Morduchowicz and Galperin (1998) evaluated one such program for early adolescents in Argentina and found that newspaper use in class was associated with higher knowledge scores and with more newspaper reading outside class. The effects were maximized when teachers coordinated other classroom activities with media use.

There is some evidence suggesting gender differences in this area. Dowse and Hughes (1971) found a sharp difference between the percentage of English males and females who indicated that they watched news on television: males watched more than females. In a more recent study, Owen and Dennis (1992) found that ten- to 17-year-old males in the United States watched television news and read print sources for political news more frequently than did females. In a German study, males watched more television news and found newspapers more important than did females (Kuhn, 2000). However, the same study found that the reading and watching of news in the media were positively related to political interest, political efficacy and the willingness to engage in political actions for males and females alike. In contrast, an Australian study concluded that the impact of mass media on political attitudes and voting behavior is stronger for adult males than for females (Hayes & Makkai, 1996).

Development of the Items on Political Interest and Exposure to Political News in the 1999 IEA Instrument

Political interest was measured by a single item, 'I am interested in politics', with a four-point scale ranging from 1 = strongly disagree to 4 = strongly agree. Four items (with a four-point scale ranging from 1 = never to 4 = often) assessed the frequency with which students listen to news broadcasts on television and radio and read articles about what is happening in their own country and in other countries in newspapers. An item about using the Internet to obtain news was included as an international option. Because the response patterns of using different media are quite dissimilar, it was not possible to form a summary scale. We therefore report the responses to the questions about the use of newspapers, radio and television as individual items.

Results for Political Interest and Exposure to Political News

Fourteen-year-olds' interest in politics in most countries is moderate. Only in four countries—Colombia, Cyprus, the Russian Federation and the Slovak Republic—do more than 50 percent of the students agree or strongly agree with the item 'I am interested in politics'. In three countries—England, Finland and Sweden—only a quarter (or fewer) of the students give this answer (see Table 6.1).

As in numerous studies across time and nations, males more than females in the majority of countries in our study state that they are interested in politics. However, in ten countries, the gender gap is smaller than reported in previous research. The difference between males and females is not significant in Belgium (French), Bulgaria, Chile, Colombia, Lithuania, Poland, Portugal, Romania, Sweden and the United States (Table 6.1).

In all countries, students watch more television news broadcasts than they listen to radio news broadcasts or read in the newspapers about what is happening in their country (Table 6.2). The most extensive average consumption of television news broadcasts is found in Colombia, the Czech Republic, Hungary, Italy, Norway, Poland, Portugal and the Slovak Republic. The least extensive consumption is found in Australia, Bulgaria, England and the United States.

In most countries, students more frequently read in newspapers about what is happening in their country than they listen to news broadcasts on the radio; in other words, newspapers follow television as the most important source of political information in most countries. However, in six countries the difference between reading about what is happening in the country and listening to news broadcasts on the radio is very small. These countries are Australia, Belgium (French), Germany, Hungary, Poland and Romania (Table 6.2).

In most countries we did not find gender differences in the two most important sources of political information: television and newspapers. In most cases in which we found gender differences, an interesting pattern emerged: males watch more television news than females (in Cyprus, Estonia, Germany and the Slovak Republic), and females read more in newspapers than males (in Belgium/French, the Czech Republic, Latvia and Lithuania). An exception to

Table 6.1 Students' Reports on Their Interest in Politics

Country	Percentage of Students Who 'Agree' or 'Strongly Agree' With the Statement 'I am Interested in Politics'					
	Total		Females		Males	
Australia	▲	31 (1.2)		28 (1.4)		35 (1.7)
Belgium (French)		38 (1.4)		35 (1.8)		41 (2.3)
Bulgaria		40 (1.4)		36 (1.6)		44 (2.2)
Chile		46 (1.4)		46 (1.9)		46 (1.6)
Colombia		63 (1.4)		63 (1.9)		64 (1.7)
Cyprus	▲	66 (0.9)		60 (1.5)		73 (1.4)
Czech Republic	▲	28 (1.0)		20 (1.4)		36 (1.5)
Denmark	▲	30 (1.0)		26 (1.7)		34 (1.2)
England	▲	25 (1.0)		21 (1.5)		28 (1.4)
Estonia	▲	34 (1.1)		30 (1.3)		39 (1.4)
Finland	▲	21 (1.1)		17 (1.5)		26 (1.5)
Germany	▲	42 (1.1)		36 (2.1)		50 (1.6)
Greece	▲	38 (0.9)		32 (1.2)		45 (1.5)
Hong Kong (SAR)	▲	37 (1.2)		29 (1.4)		45 (1.6)
Hungary	▲	39 (1.2)		35 (1.4)		43 (1.8)
Italy	▲	44 (1.0)		38 (1.4)		50 (1.3)
Latvia	▲	41 (1.1)		38 (1.6)		45 (1.5)
Lithuania		40 (1.0)		37 (1.6)		42 (1.4)
Norway	▲	31 (1.1)		25 (1.3)		37 (1.6)
Poland		43 (1.9)		40 (2.7)		46 (3.1)
Portugal		35 (1.2)		32 (1.6)		38 (1.4)
Romania		45 (1.5)		41 (1.7)		49 (1.9)
Russian Federation	▲	54 (1.6)		50 (2.0)		59 (2.1)
Slovak Republic	▲	54 (1.1)		48 (1.7)		62 (1.8)
Slovenia	▲	35 (1.1)		29 (1.3)		40 (1.4)
Sweden		23 (1.5)		20 (1.8)		25 (2.0)
Switzerland	▲	33 (1.1)		25 (1.5)		42 (1.6)
United States		39 (1.4)		37 (1.7)		41 (2.2)
International Sample		39 (0.2)		35 (0.3)		44 (0.3)

( ) Standard errors appear in parentheses. Percentages based on valid responses.

▲ Gender difference statistically significant at .05 level, for direction see text.

Source: IEA Civic Education Study, Standard Population of 14-year-olds tested in 1999.

this pattern was Poland, where females watch slightly more television news than males.

A much clearer gender difference emerged with respect to news broadcasts on the radio. In 15 countries significantly more females than males listen to news on the radio. In no country do males listen more than females.

EXPECTED PARTICIPATION IN POLITICAL ACTIVITIES

Relation of this Area to the Study's Design

Democracy and citizenship comprise the first domain identified in the country reports submitted during Phase 1 of the IEA Civic Education Study. Encouragement of young people to become citizens who vote, participate in other attempts to influence political decision processes or take action in their communities was mentioned in all of the country case studies. It was the central focus of some. Several sub-sections of the content framework of the

Table 6.2 Students' Reports on Their Exposure to Political News

Percentage of Students who Sometimes or Often...

Country	read newspaper articles about own country			watch news broadcasts on television			listen to news broadcasts on the radio		
	Total	Females	Males	Total	Females	Males	Total	Females	Males
Australia	65 (1.2)	67 (1.4)	63 (1.9)	80 (0.8)	81 (1.1)	80 (1.2)	▲ 63 (1.1)	69 (1.4)	55 (1.5)
Belgium (French)	▲ 60 (1.5)	66 (2.0)	55 (1.8)	81 (1.1)	81 (1.6)	81 (1.4)	▲ 56 (1.4)	60 (1.8)	52 (1.6)
Bulgaria	72 (1.4)	75 (1.4)	69 (2.5)	73 (1.7)	74 (1.9)	73 (1.9)	47 (1.4)	48 (1.9)	47 (1.7)
Chile	61 (1.1)	63 (1.7)	59 (1.2)	89 (0.6)	87 (0.9)	90 (0.8)	47 (1.1)	49 (1.6)	46 (1.3)
Colombia	77 (1.3)	78 (1.4)	74 (1.8)	92 (0.7)	92 (0.9)	93 (1.0)	56 (2.3)	55 (3.6)	57 (2.2)
Cyprus	68 (1.1)	67 (1.4)	70 (1.4)	▲ 89 (0.6)	86 (0.9)	93 (0.7)	55 (1.2)	53 (1.5)	57 (1.7)
Czech Republic	▲ 69 (1.1)	73 (1.5)	65 (1.6)	94 (0.5)	94 (0.6)	93 (0.8)	▲ 60 (1.2)	66 (1.4)	55 (1.6)
Denmark	65 (1.1)	67 (1.6)	63 (1.4)	83 (0.7)	81 (1.0)	86 (1.2)	47 (1.2)	49 (1.6)	46 (1.3)
England	70 (1.2)	72 (1.5)	68 (1.8)	78 (0.9)	78 (1.2)	78 (1.3)	▲ 55 (0.8)	59 (1.2)	50 (1.5)
Estonia	75 (1.0)	76 (1.3)	74 (1.1)	▲ 84 (0.8)	81 (1.2)	87 (1.1)	▲ 70 (0.9)	73 (1.2)	67 (1.4)
Finland	73 (1.0)	76 (1.3)	70 (1.5)	89 (0.8)	89 (1.1)	90 (1.0)	▲ 45 (1.1)	53 (1.5)	36 (1.5)
Germany	68 (1.0)	69 (1.4)	67 (1.3)	▲ 83 (0.7)	80 (1.1)	85 (1.1)	▲ 65 (1.0)	70 (1.3)	60 (1.6)
Greece	57 (1.1)	57 (1.4)	58 (1.3)	89 (0.7)	90 (0.7)	88 (1.1)	42 (1.1)	41 (1.3)	43 (1.5)
Hong Kong (SAR)	73 (0.9)	73 (1.0)	73 (1.2)	87 (0.7)	89 (0.8)	86 (0.9)	▲ 59 (0.9)	63 (1.1)	55 (1.2)
Hungary	61 (1.2)	63 (1.4)	58 (1.5)	90 (0.6)	91 (0.8)	90 (0.9)	▲ 59 (0.9)	63 (1.3)	54 (1.5)
Italy	62 (1.2)	65 (1.5)	60 (1.7)	90 (0.7)	91 (0.7)	89 (1.1)	▲ 41 (1.0)	46 (1.5)	36 (1.1)
Latvia	▲ 69 (1.4)	73 (1.8)	64 (1.8)	89 (1.0)	90 (1.0)	88 (1.6)	62 (1.4)	64 (1.5)	60 (2.0)
Lithuania	▲ 71 (1.0)	77 (1.2)	65 (1.3)	84 (0.8)	83 (1.0)	85 (0.9)	52 (1.1)	56 (1.4)	48 (1.6)
Norway	82 (0.9)	83 (1.3)	80 (1.1)	90 (0.6)	91 (0.9)	90 (0.9)	▲ 47 (1.1)	50 (1.5)	43 (1.5)
Poland	73 (0.9)	76 (1.7)	70 (1.7)	▲ 91 (0.6)	93 (0.7)	89 (1.1)	▲ 71 (1.3)	77 (1.6)	64 (1.7)
Portugal	69 (1.0)	68 (1.3)	71 (1.3)	93 (0.5)	93 (0.6)	94 (0.8)	55 (1.0)	56 (1.4)	53 (1.3)
Romania	60 (1.5)	62 (2.0)	58 (1.7)	86 (0.8)	87 (1.1)	86 (1.1)	62 (1.3)	65 (1.4)	59 (1.7)
Russian Federation	75 (1.4)	79 (1.4)	71 (2.1)	89 (0.7)	88 (1.0)	90 (1.1)	57 (1.8)	59 (2.6)	55 (1.7)
Slovak Republic	71 (1.1)	71 (1.4)	70 (1.3)	▲ 92 (0.6)	90 (0.9)	94 (0.7)	58 (1.0)	60 (1.4)	55 (1.3)
Slovenia	65 (1.1)	64 (1.5)	65 (1.3)	84 (1.0)	84 (1.2)	84 (1.3)	56 (1.2)	57 (1.7)	54 (1.7)
Sweden	79 (1.2)	80 (1.9)	78 (1.4)	84 (1.2)	83 (1.2)	86 (1.5)	▲ 47 (1.2)	54 (1.8)	40 (1.3)
Switzerland	65 (1.1)	63 (1.5)	66 (1.3)	84 (0.9)	83 (1.0)	85 (1.3)	59 (1.0)	61 (1.4)	57 (1.4)
United States	62 (1.3)	63 (1.6)	60 (1.8)	79 (1.1)	81 (1.5)	77 (1.2)	▲ 44 (1.6)	48 (1.9)	40 (1.7)
International Sample	68 (0.2)	70 (0.3)	67 (0.3)	86 (0.2)	86 (0.2)	87 (0.2)	55 (0.2)	58 (0.3)	52 (0.3)

( ) Standard errors appear in parentheses. Percentages based on valid responses. ▲ Gender difference statistically significant at .05 level.

Source: *IEA Civic Education Study,* Standard Population of 14-year-olds tested in 1999.

current study deal with participation. Items in the test as well as some of the items measuring concepts of democracy and citizenship in the survey deal with young people's ability to recognize the role of citizens' participation. It is vital, however, to know the extent to which young people actually participate in the activities that are open to them in their communities and the extent to which they expect to participate in adult activities (such as voting) in the future. Panel 6.3 provides a review of previous research relating to participation in political activities.

Development of the Political Activities Items and Scale in the 1999 IEA Instrument

Five items in the final IEA Civic Education survey deal with conventional institutionalized participation. A confirmatory factor analysis identified a three-item scale (join a political party, write letters to a newspaper about social or political concerns, be a candidate for a local or city office). The scale identified by using this method did not include intention to vote. We therefore report intention to vote as a single item in this volume.

Five additional items deal with social movement activities (collect signatures for a petition, participate in a non-violent protest march or rally) and unconventional illegal forms of political behaviors (spray-paint protest slogans on walls, block traffic as a form of protest, occupy public buildings as a form of protest). A last item deals with volunteer commitment for charity causes (collect money for a social cause). As with the voting item, these six items can only be presented singly because they do not fulfill the requirements of Rasch scaling. The answer format of all participation items presented in this chapter was 1 = I will certainly not do this, 2 = I will probably not do this, 3 = I will probably do this, 4 = I will certainly do this.

Results for Expected Participation in Political Activities

Conventional participation

The 'conventional participation' scale comprises three items: join a political party, write letters to a newspaper about social or political concerns, and be a candidate for a local or city office. The majority of students in all countries do not intend to participate in these actions. In the sample across all countries, roughly one-fifth of the students 'agree' or 'strongly agree' with the three items (see Figure B.2i in Appendix B.2).

The highest scores on the conventional participation scale are found in Colombia, Hong Kong (SAR), Latvia, Poland, Romania and the United States (Figure 6.1). Other countries that are significantly above the international mean on this scale are Chile, Cyprus and Portugal. With the exception of the United States, these countries have experienced considerable political changes within the last 30 years. Even in these high-scoring countries, however, only a minority of the students intend to participate in those activities that go beyond voting.

The lowest scores on the conventional participation scale are found in the Czech Republic, Denmark, Germany and Lithuania. Other countries that are significantly below the international mean are Australia, Belgium (French),

PANEL 6.3 Previous Research on Political Activities

The 1971 IEA Study used a single summed score—participation in civic activities. It included listening to political broadcasts, being a candidate in school elections, helping collect money for good causes, asking parents about political parties (and three other items). In the current study, we included a number of scales dealing separately with these different types of participation (for example, exposure to political news and confidence in participation at school). These scales are discussed in other sections of this report. The 1971 study did not ask about expected future activities or about protest activities.

The 'participatory revolution' (Kaase, 1984) of the 1960s in western democracies resulted in a large number of national and cross-national studies about 'protest behavior'. A pioneering and comprehensive study in five western democracies was 'Political Action' (Barnes, Kaase *et al.*, 1979). In this study, Allerbeck, Jennings and Rosenmayr (1979) analyzed intergenerational continuity and change with respect to protest behavior. Seven to eight years later, Jennings and van Deth (1990) replicated the 'Political Action' study in three countries to show that the term 'protest behavior' was no longer appropriate because of the 'normalization of the unconventional' (Fuchs, 1991). Some illegal but non-violent actions like blocking traffic have been termed civic disobedience. In a 1990 article, Kaase differentiated between conventional and unconventional political participation, and, among the latter, between legal and illegal political behaviors. In several chapters of this volume, we refer to unconventional legal behavior as 'social movement activities'.

The communist countries behind the iron curtain saw a long chain of singular protest events, uprisings and subversive actions that were severely oppressed by the authorities. Because the state suppressed the growth of even non-political grassroots movements, a lively tradition of every-day civic activities could not develop in these countries. This situation changed dramatically during the 1980s, with the change beginning in Solidarnosc in Poland and continuing until the iron curtain disappeared as symbolized by the fall of the Berlin Wall. From then on, the different forms of civic and political participation known in the western democracies developed and became accepted in the post-Communist countries (see, for example, Meyer & Ryszka, 1991; McAllister & White, 1994; Flanagan *et al.*, 1999). The development was similar in some countries with former right-wing dictatorships. It is therefore appropriate for the IEA Civic Education Study to administer a survey that includes differentiations between conventional and unconventional (social movement) political activities, and between legal and illegal political activities in all countries included in the study. These differentiations have proved to be valid and have been adopted in recent studies comparing, for example, adolescents' political action potential in West and East Germany, the former Federal Republic of Germany and the former communist German Democratic Republic (Gille & Krüger, 2000).

Some studies using samples of different countries have explained political participation according to characteristics of the individual like age, education, gender, family background, family education and values (Parry, Moyser & Day, 1992; Gundelach, 1995; Topf, 1995; Verba, Schlozman & Brady, 1995; Nie *et al.*, 1996; Flanagan *et al.*, 1998). Other studies have revealed that contextual factors of countries (like organizational affiliation and socioeconomic conditions) seem to predict legal participation but not illegal activities (Huckfeldt & Sprague, 1993; Roller & Wessels, 1996).

Figure 6.1 Expected Participation in Political Activities

Country	Mean Scale Score	8	10	12
Australia	▼ 9.8 (0.05)			
Belgium (French)	▼ 9.7 (0.07)			
Bulgaria	10.0 (0.08)			
Chile	▲ 10.2 (0.05)			
Colombia	▲ 11.1 (0.06)			
Cyprus	▲ 10.4 (0.04)			
Czech Republic	▼ 9.4 (0.04)			
Denmark	▼ 9.5 (0.04)			
England	▼ 9.7 (0.05)			
Estonia	9.9 (0.04)			
Finland	▼ 9.7 (0.05)			
Germany	▼ 9.6 (0.04)			
Greece	9.9 (0.05)			
Hong Kong (SAR)	▲ 10.5 (0.05)			
Hungary	▼ 9.9 (0.04)			
Italy	▼ 9.8 (0.05)			
Latvia	▲ 10.5 (0.07)			
Lithuania	▼ 9.6 (0.05)			
Norway	▼ 9.7 (0.04)			
Poland	▲ 10.5 (0.06)			
Portugal	▲ 10.4 (0.04)			
Romania	▲ 10.5 (0.05)			
Russian Federation	10.0 (0.06)			
Slovak Republic	▼ 9.8 (0.05)			
Slovenia	10.0 (0.04)			
Sweden	▼ 9.8 (0.04)			
Switzerland	▼ 9.7 (0.05)			
United States	▲ 10.5 (0.05)			

( ) Standard errors appear in parentheses.

▲ Country mean significantly higher than international mean of 10.

▼ Country mean significantly lower than international mean of 10.

● = Mean (± 2 SE).

Source: IEA Civic Education Study, Standard Population of 14-year-olds tested in 1999.

England, Finland, Hungary, Italy, Norway, the Slovak Republic, Sweden and Switzerland.

In 19 countries there is no significant gender difference in conventional participation. In nine countries more males than females intend to participate in these conventional political activities, namely Belgium (French), Cyprus, Estonia, Greece, Hong Kong (SAR), Italy, Lithuania, Romania and Switzerland (Figure 6.2). (Note: a figure is presented here because of attention to this issue in previous research.)

The most common conventional political activity among the 14-year-olds is voting (Table 6.3). In all countries, more than half of the students are willing to vote in general elections ('I will probably do this' or 'I will certainly do this'), with a range from 55 percent in Switzerland to 95 percent in Cyprus. More than 90 percent of the students give these answers in Cyprus, Denmark, Hungary and the Slovak Republic. In Belgium (French), Bulgaria, the Czech Republic, Estonia, Germany and Switzerland, less than 70 percent of the 14-

Figure 6.2 Gender Differences in Expected Participation in Political Activities

Country	Mean Score Females	Mean Score Males	8 10 12
Australia	9.8 (0.06)	9.8 (0.07)	
Belgium (French)	9.5 (0.07)	9.9 (0.13)	▲
Bulgaria	9.8 (0.08)	10.2 (0.12)	
Chile	10.1 (0.05)	10.2 (0.08)	
Colombia	11.1 (0.07)	11.1 (0.08)	
Cyprus	10.2 (0.05)	10.6 (0.06)	▲
Czech Republic	9.3 (0.05)	9.6 (0.07)	
Denmark	9.5 (0.05)	9.5 (0.06)	
England	9.7 (0.06)	9.6 (0.08)	
Estonia	9.7 (0.05)	10.2 (0.06)	▲
Finland	9.8 (0.05)	9.6 (0.06)	
Germany	9.6 (0.06)	9.7 (0.05)	
Greece	9.6 (0.06)	10.2 (0.07)	▲
Hong Kong (SAR)	10.3 (0.05)	10.7 (0.07)	▲
Hungary	9.8 (0.05)	10.0 (0.06)	
Italy	9.6 (0.06)	10.0 (0.07)	▲
Latvia	10.3 (0.08)	10.7 (0.09)	
Lithuania	9.4 (0.05)	9.7 (0.08)	▲
Norway	9.7 (0.06)	9.7 (0.06)	
Poland	10.5 (0.05)	10.5 (0.09)	
Portugal	10.4 (0.05)	10.4 (0.05)	
Romania	10.3 (0.07)	10.8 (0.06)	▲
Russian Federation	9.8 (0.07)	10.2 (0.09)	
Slovak Republic	9.8 (0.05)	9.9 (0.06)	
Slovenia	9.9 (0.05)	10.0 (0.07)	
Sweden	9.8 (0.06)	9.7 (0.07)	
Switzerland	9.5 (0.06)	9.9 (0.07)	▲
United States	10.6 (0.06)	10.3 (0.07)	

( ) Standard errors appear in parentheses.

▲ Gender difference statistically significant at .05 level.

├─●─┤ = Mean for Males (± 2 SE).

├─◇─┤ = Mean for Females (± 2 SE).

Source: IEA Civic Education Study, Standard Population of 14-year-olds tested in 1999.

year-olds are potential voters. In all the other countries, between 70 and 90 percent of these young people are potential voters.

In 16 countries significantly more females than males intend to vote. In 12 countries there are no significant gender differences (Table 6.3). However, in Germany and Switzerland more males than females intend to vote, these differences being significant before the Dunn-Bonferroni correction for multiple comparisons.

In some countries in this study, voting is compulsory or is defined as a duty in the constitution, for example, in Australia, Belgium (French), Chile, Greece and Italy. Compulsory voting is generally related to high voter turnout (Lijphart, 1997). With the exception of Belgium (French), the readiness of students to vote is high in these countries but not generally higher than in some other countries where voting is not compulsory. An important point, however, is that the intention to vote or not to vote assessed at age 14 is not necessarily predictive of future voting behavior.

Table 6.3 Students' Reports on Expected Political Activities as an Adult

Percentage of Students who Expect Probably or Definitely to…

Country	vote in national elections			collect money for a social cause			collect signatures for a petition			participate in a non-violent protest march		
	Total	Females	Males	Total	Females	Males	Total	Females	Males	Total	Females	Males
Australia	◄ 85 (1.0)	89 (1.0)	82 (1.4)	◄ 62 (1.3)	72 (1.5)	51 (1.9)	◄ 53 (1.2)	59 (1.8)	47 (1.8)	41 (1.2)	41 (1.6)	40 (1.6)
Belgium (French)	◄ 69 (2.0)	76 (2.2)	62 (2.8)	◄ 47 (1.8)	56 (1.7)	40 (2.5)	◄ 62 (1.4)	71 (1.4)	53 (2.3)	57 (1.4)	58 (1.4)	55 (1.7)
Bulgaria	58 (1.9)	62 (2.4)	55 (2.0)	51 (1.6)	55 (2.1)	48 (1.9)	34 (1.7)	32 (2.1)	37 (2.0)	38 (1.7)	35 (1.8)	42 (2.8)
Chile	74 (1.0)	75 (1.1)	74 (1.3)	◄ 85 (0.9)	89 (1.8)	81 (1.0)	77 (0.8)	78 (1.3)	75 (1.0)	◄ 47 (0.8)	42 (1.6)	51 (1.2)
Colombia	87 (1.3)	89 (1.4)	84 (1.7)	◄ 79 (1.3)	83 (1.4)	73 (1.5)	75 (1.2)	77 (1.1)	72 (1.7)	66 (1.2)	67 (1.6)	65 (1.7)
Cyprus	95 (0.5)	97 (0.5)	94 (0.8)	◄ 82 (0.7)	87 (0.9)	77 (1.2)	64 (1.0)	65 (1.2)	63 (1.5)	86 (1.0)	87 (0.8)	85 (1.1)
Czech Republic	65 (1.7)	63 (1.9)	66 (2.0)	◄ 28 (1.0)	33 (1.4)	24 (1.3)	29 (1.0)	33 (1.7)	24 (1.4)	28 (1.0)	26 (1.6)	31 (1.6)
Denmark	◄ 91 (0.7)	93 (0.7)	89 (1.1)	◄ 51 (1.3)	65 (1.8)	38 (1.5)	43 (1.2)	46 (1.8)	39 (1.4)	46 (1.2)	47 (1.6)	45 (1.5)
England	80 (1.0)	82 (1.2)	78 (1.7)	◄ 57 (1.2)	68 (1.4)	46 (1.6)	45 (1.0)	54 (1.4)	36 (1.4)	28 (1.0)	28 (1.2)	27 (1.4)
Estonia	◄ 68 (1.1)	72 (1.3)	64 (1.7)	◄ 41 (1.2)	46 (1.6)	36 (1.5)	33 (1.2)	35 (1.8)	31 (1.4)	37 (1.2)	34 (1.3)	39 (1.6)
Finland	◄ 87 (0.7)	89 (1.1)	84 (0.9)	◄ 45 (1.3)	57 (2.0)	32 (1.5)	◄ 27 (1.0)	31 (1.5)	22 (1.4)	21 (1.0)	23 (1.6)	19 (1.2)
Germany	67 (1.1)	65 (1.5)	71 (1.3)	◄ 54 (1.2)	62 (1.4)	45 (1.6)	◄ 41 (1.3)	47 (1.7)	35 (1.4)	38 (1.3)	38 (1.6)	37 (1.0)
Greece	◄ 86 (0.9)	91 (1.0)	82 (1.4)	◄ 79 (0.9)	87 (1.2)	71 (1.4)	◄ 46 (1.2)	40 (1.6)	51 (1.6)	78 (1.2)	78 (1.3)	78 (1.0)
Hong Kong (SAR)	80 (1.0)	83 (1.3)	78 (1.2)	78 (0.9)	84 (1.1)	73 (1.1)	◄ 59 (0.8)	59 (1.3)	59 (0.9)	◄ 46 (0.8)	41 (1.1)	52 (1.3)
Hungary	◄ 91 (0.7)	93 (0.7)	89 (1.0)	◄ 46 (1.2)	49 (1.5)	43 (1.5)	◄ 45 (1.1)	51 (1.4)	39 (1.5)	37 (1.1)	35 (1.5)	39 (1.7)
Italy	◄ 80 (1.1)	84 (1.3)	77 (1.6)	◄ 65 (1.2)	73 (1.2)	56 (1.4)	47 (1.0)	50 (1.5)	45 (1.4)	◄ 70 (1.0)	74 (1.0)	66 (1.6)
Latvia	◄ 71 (1.3)	78 (1.4)	64 (1.9)	◄ 57 (1.6)	62 (1.8)	52 (2.1)	44 (1.5)	46 (2.2)	42 (1.7)	39 (1.5)	38 (1.7)	40 (1.9)
Lithuania	◄ 80 (1.1)	83 (1.3)	76 (1.6)	◄ 49 (1.1)	53 (1.3)	43 (1.6)	34 (1.1)	35 (1.4)	34 (1.7)	35 (1.1)	33 (1.4)	37 (1.6)
Norway	◄ 87 (0.7)	89 (1.0)	85 (1.1)	◄ 68 (1.1)	78 (1.4)	58 (1.5)	32 (1.2)	33 (1.5)	31 (1.5)	39 (1.2)	40 (1.7)	38 (1.7)
Poland	◄ 88 (1.2)	92 (0.8)	83 (1.8)	◄ 57 (1.7)	68 (1.7)	45 (2.4)	48 (1.1)	51 (1.3)	44 (2.0)	43 (1.1)	41 (1.8)	45 (1.9)
Portugal	88 (0.8)	87 (1.0)	88 (1.0)	◄ 74 (1.0)	79 (1.2)	70 (1.5)	54 (1.3)	57 (1.8)	51 (1.7)	42 (1.3)	38 (1.8)	45 (1.6)
Romania	82 (1.1)	84 (1.5)	81 (1.6)	73 (1.2)	75 (1.6)	71 (1.6)	46 (1.7)	44 (1.9)	48 (2.1)	◄ 41 (1.7)	32 (1.8)	48 (1.5)
Russian Federation	◄ 82 (1.0)	85 (1.4)	78 (1.5)	56 (1.4)	58 (1.6)	55 (2.0)	34 (1.0)	32 (2.1)	36 (2.2)	◄ 46 (1.0)	41 (1.7)	52 (2.1)
Slovak Republic	◄ 93 (0.6)	95 (0.7)	91 (0.9)	◄ 40 (1.3)	45 (1.7)	35 (1.8)	32 (1.2)	35 (1.8)	30 (1.7)	◄ 39 (1.2)	35 (1.9)	43 (1.6)
Slovenia	◄ 84 (1.0)	87 (1.2)	80 (1.3)	◄ 68 (1.0)	77 (1.2)	60 (1.4)	36 (1.2)	34 (1.5)	38 (1.7)	35 (1.2)	32 (1.4)	38 (1.5)
Sweden	◄ 75 (1.4)	79 (1.9)	71 (1.4)	◄ 42 (1.3)	53 (2.1)	30 (1.9)	31 (1.8)	32 (2.2)	29 (2.1)	36 (1.8)	35 (2.0)	36 (2.5)
Switzerland	◄ 55 (1.3)	52 (1.8)	58 (1.8)	◄ 55 (1.2)	64 (1.6)	46 (1.3)	◄ 42 (1.1)	47 (1.5)	37 (1.4)	40 (1.1)	40 (1.3)	40 (1.5)
United States	◄ 85 (1.0)	89 (0.9)	80 (1.6)	◄ 59 (1.5)	69 (1.8)	49 (2.2)	◄ 50 (1.5)	56 (2.2)	44 (1.8)	39 (1.5)	42 (1.6)	36 (1.8)
International Sample	80 (0.2)	82 (0.3)	77 (0.3)	59 (0.2)	66 (0.3)	52 (0.3)	45 (0.2)	48 (0.3)	43 (0.3)	44 (0.2)	43 (0.3)	45 (0.3)

( ) Standard errors appear in parentheses. Percentages based on valid responses.   ◄ Gender difference statistically significant at .05 level.

Source: IEA Civic Education Study, Standard Population of 14-year-olds tested in 1999.

Uncoventional participation (social movement activities)

The results for two single items relating to social movement activities—collecting signatures for a petition and participating in a non-violent demonstration—are quite different (Table 6.3).

In two countries, Chile and Colombia, three-fourths of all students say they are prepared to *collect signatures*. In six countries, one-third or less of the students are willing to collect signatures, namely in the Czech Republic, Estonia, Finland, Norway, the Slovak Republic and Sweden. The percentages in all the other countries are neither high nor low. Females have higher scores than males in nine countries—Australia, Belgium (French), the Czech Republic, England, Finland, Germany, Hungary, Switzerland and the United States. Only in one country, Greece, do more males than females report their willingness to participate in this way. In 18 countries there are no gender differences.

In four countries (Colombia, Cyprus, Greece and Italy), two-thirds or more of the students expect to *participate in non-violent demonstrations*. In three countries (the Czech Republic, England and Finland), less than one-third intend to act in such a way. The percentages in all the other countries are neither high nor low. In a majority of 22 countries, no gender differences are apparent with respect to non-violent demonstrations. In five countries (Chile, Hong Kong/SAR, Romania, the Russian Federation and the Slovak Republic), more males than females intend to demonstrate; in one country (Italy), more females than males intend to act in this way.

Volunteer commitment for charity or social causes

In all but four countries, more students are willing to collect money for a social cause than to collect signatures, participate in non-violent demonstrations or engage in illegal actions. The four exceptions are Belgium (French), Cyprus, the Czech Republic and Italy. In almost all countries, more students are willing to vote in national elections than to collect money for a social cause. However, in Chile the 14-year-olds mention collecting money more often than they mention voting, and in Switzerland the same percentage of students report their readiness to vote and to collect money.

In a majority of countries, females are more likely than males to express readiness to collect money. However, we did not find significant gender differences in four countries—Bulgaria, Hungary, Romania and the Russian Federation.

Unconventional illegal actions

In most countries only small minorities of students intend to participate in illegal activities such as spray-painting, blocking traffic or occupying buildings (see Table 6.4). Among these three behaviors, 'spray-painting protest slogans on walls' is the most preferred activity. However, in only three countries (Chile, Cyprus and Greece) do as many as 30 percent of the students imagine the possibility of behaving in such a way. In seven countries less than 15 percent of the 14-year-olds speak of spray-painting as a possible activity. In all the other countries, between 15 and 30 percent of the 14-year-olds are potential spray-painters of protest slogans. This type of activity seems to have become a relatively conventional political activity in some countries.

Table 6.4 Students' Reports on Expected Illegal Protest Activities as an Adult

Percentage of Students who Expect Probably or Definitely to…

Country	spray-paint protest slogans on walls			block traffic as a form of protest			occupy buildings as a form of protest		
	Total	Females	Males	Total	Females	Males	Total	Females	Males
Australia	▲ 20 (1.1)	15 (1.1)	26 (1.6)	▲ 18 (1.2)	12 (1.1)	25 (1.7)	▲ 17 (1.1)	11 (1.1)	24 (1.5)
Belgium (French)	▲ 23 (1.3)	17 (1.3)	30 (2.1)	▲ 23 (1.6)	14 (1.6)	31 (2.2)	▲ 22 (1.6)	16 (1.3)	29 (2.4)
Bulgaria	▲ 22 (1.7)	18 (1.7)	26 (2.1)	▲ 22 (1.5)	16 (1.8)	27 (1.9)	▲ 20 (1.7)	15 (1.7)	25 (2.3)
Chile	▲ 31 (0.9)	22 (1.3)	38 (1.2)	▲ 19 (0.8)	14 (0.9)	23 (0.9)	▲ 14 (0.7)	10 (0.7)	18 (1.0)
Colombia	▲ 23 (1.5)	18 (1.5)	30 (1.6)	20 (1.3)	17 (1.7)	23 (1.7)	▲ 15 (1.1)	12 (1.1)	20 (1.6)
Cyprus	▲ 37 (1.1)	33 (1.3)	42 (1.4)	▲ 28 (0.9)	22 (1.3)	34 (1.3)	▲ 28 (1.0)	23 (1.3)	32 (1.6)
Czech Republic	▲ 12 (1.0)	6 (0.9)	18 (1.7)	▲ 7 (0.8)	4 (0.6)	11 (1.3)	▲ 7 (0.8)	3 (0.6)	11 (1.5)
Denmark	▲ 15 (0.9)	9 (0.9)	21 (1.3)	▲ 15 (0.9)	10 (1.0)	20 (1.2)	▲ 12 (0.8)	8 (1.0)	16 (1.2)
England	▲ 14 (0.9)	9 (0.9)	19 (1.3)	▲ 11 (0.8)	8 (0.7)	15 (1.4)	▲ 11 (0.8)	8 (0.9)	15 (1.2)
Estonia	▲ 22 (0.9)	15 (0.9)	30 (1.5)	▲ 12 (0.7)	8 (0.8)	17 (1.4)	▲ 9 (0.7)	6 (0.6)	13 (1.3)
Finland	▲ 10 (0.8)	7 (1.0)	13 (1.4)	▲ 5 (0.7)	3 (0.6)	9 (1.1)	▲ 8 (0.7)	5 (0.7)	12 (1.2)
Germany	▲ 16 (0.9)	12 (1.1)	21 (1.1)	▲ 13 (0.7)	10 (0.9)	16 (1.0)	▲ 12 (0.8)	9 (1.1)	15 (0.9)
Greece	▲ 30 (1.0)	24 (1.3)	36 (1.3)	▲ 42 (1.0)	38 (1.5)	46 (1.3)	▲ 41 (1.1)	37 (1.6)	44 (1.5)
Hong Kong (SAR)	▲ 18 (1.1)	13 (1.0)	23 (1.5)	▲ 17 (1.1)	13 (1.1)	22 (1.5)	▲ 17 (1.2)	12 (1.2)	22 (1.6)
Hungary	▲ 10 (0.7)	5 (0.7)	14 (1.1)	▲ 8 (0.7)	6 (0.8)	11 (1.1)	▲ 7 (0.6)	4 (0.6)	9 (0.9)
Italy	▲ 20 (1.0)	17 (1.2)	24 (1.4)	▲ 18 (1.0)	14 (1.0)	23 (1.5)	▲ 24 (1.0)	22 (1.4)	26 (1.3)
Latvia	▲ 21 (1.3)	13 (1.5)	29 (1.8)	▲ 17 (1.2)	9 (1.0)	25 (2.0)	▲ 15 (1.3)	10 (1.3)	21 (1.8)
Lithuania	▲ 15 (0.8)	10 (0.7)	21 (1.3)	▲ 13 (0.7)	6 (0.7)	20 (1.3)	▲ 10 (0.7)	4 (0.5)	16 (1.4)
Norway	▲ 15 (0.9)	9 (0.9)	20 (1.2)	▲ 12 (0.9)	8 (1.0)	16 (1.2)	▲ 12 (0.7)	6 (0.8)	18 (1.0)
Poland	▲ 18 (0.9)	11 (1.1)	25 (1.4)	▲ 17 (1.1)	9 (1.0)	25 (1.7)	▲ 16 (1.0)	9 (1.1)	22 (1.6)
Portugal	▲ 13 (0.8)	9 (0.8)	17 (1.3)	▲ 11 (0.7)	7 (0.8)	15 (1.2)	▲ 10 (0.7)	7 (0.8)	14 (1.1)
Romania	▲ 15 (1.1)	10 (1.1)	20 (1.6)	▲ 14 (0.8)	8 (1.1)	20 (1.1)	▲ 13 (0.8)	8 (1.2)	17 (1.1)
Russian Federation	▲ 23 (1.1)	19 (1.6)	27 (1.7)	▲ 13 (1.1)	8 (1.1)	18 (1.9)	▲ 9 (0.8)	6 (0.8)	13 (1.5)
Slovak Republic	▲ 13 (0.8)	9 (1.0)	16 (1.2)	▲ 7 (0.7)	5 (0.8)	10 (1.0)	6 (0.7)	4 (0.7)	8 (1.0)
Slovenia	▲ 18 (1.0)	9 (1.0)	27 (1.5)	▲ 12 (0.8)	6 (0.7)	18 (1.3)	▲ 12 (0.9)	5 (0.7)	18 (1.4)
Sweden	▲ 12 (1.2)	8 (1.2)	17 (1.9)	▲ 9 (0.8)	6 (0.9)	12 (1.2)	▲ 10 (1.0)	6 (0.8)	14 (1.6)
Switzerland	▲ 16 (1.1)	12 (1.3)	20 (1.3)	▲ 13 (0.8)	7 (1.0)	17 (1.1)	▲ 12 (0.9)	8 (0.9)	16 (1.4)
United States	▲ 15 (1.2)	9 (1.0)	21 (1.8)	▲ 13 (1.1)	8 (1.1)	18 (1.6)	▲ 14 (1.0)	11 (1.3)	17 (1.5)
International Sample	18 (0.2)	13 (0.2)	24 (0.3)	15 (0.2)	11 (0.2)	20 (0.3)	14 (0.2)	10 (0.2)	19 (0.3)

( ) Standard errors appear in parentheses. Percentages based on valid responses.   ▲ Gender difference statistically significant at .05 level.

Source: IEA Civic Education Study, Standard Population of 14-year-olds tested in 1999.

The results for the two other forms of protest, blocking traffic and occupying buildings, are very similar. One country, Greece, ranks at the top, with slightly over 40 percent of the students reporting the possibility of participating in these forms of illegal action. Three other countries, Belgium (French), Bulgaria and Cyprus, have more than 20 percent (but below 30 percent) of their students ready to participate in these behaviors. Four countries have less than 10 percent of their students willing to undertake such protest—the Czech Republic, Finland, Hungary and the Slovak Republic. The other countries have between 10 and 20 percent of their 14-year-old students ready to block traffic and/or occupy buildings as a protest.

In all countries there is a clear and striking gender difference for the three illegal forms of political actions. Males are more often ready than females to spray-paint protest slogans, block traffic and occupy buildings. In only three cases is the gender difference not statistically significant: in Colombia for blocking traffic, and in Italy and the Slovak Republic for occupying buildings.

SUMMARY

At age 14, adolescents are only moderately interested in politics in most countries. Only in four countries do a majority of the students seem to be interested. In response to the single item 'I am interested in politics', males express more interest than females in 18 countries. No gender difference is evident in ten countries. Television is the most often used source of information for political news. Newspapers rank second.

Voting in national elections is by far the most preferred future political activity of 14-year-old students. Readiness to vote is expressed by a majority of students across all countries. Gender differences, however, vary among countries. The second most frequently reported activity in most countries is charity work (collecting money for a social cause), which is more likely to be preferred by females than males. This activity is followed in importance for students by the legal social movement activities of collecting signatures and participating in non-violent demonstrations. Again, the gender differences vary across countries, with a slight tendency for females to prefer collecting signatures and males to prefer participating in protest marches. The majority of students across all countries do not intend to participate in conventional activities like joining a political party, writing letters to newspapers and being a candidate for a local office. Only a minority of students are ready to engage in illegal activities like spray-painting protest slogans, blocking traffic and occupying buildings. Across all countries, by far more males than females are ready to participate in these activities that would be illegal in most countries. In the area of participation this was the most pronounced gender difference.

The between-country differences in all topics dealt with in this chapter are dramatic evidence of differences in political culture as experienced by young students.

Students' Views of Opportunities for Civic Engagement in Classrooms, Schools and Youth Organizations

HIGHLIGHTS RELATING TO SCHOOLS AND CIVIC EDUCATION

- Fourteen-year-olds generally believe that actions taken by groups of students in school can be effective in school improvement. This sense of 'school efficacy' may be as important as the broader sense of political efficacy relating to the government that has frequently been the subject of civic education research.

- Fourteen-year-olds in general perceive that their schools do not place much emphasis on teaching about the importance of voting in local and national elections.

- About one-quarter of the students say that they are often encouraged to voice their opinions during discussions in their classrooms, but an equal proportion say that this rarely or never occurs. Many of the countries that recently experienced political transitions appear to have a less open climate for discussion.

- Fourteen-year-olds in about one-third of the countries report low rates of participation in civic-related organizations. Charities, volunteer organizations and student councils or parliaments are the most frequent sites for participation in the remaining countries.

Are schools and organizations places where students develop practices of citizenship and confidence in their ability to be effective participants in a broader community? What do students believe they are learning about their country, society and government? Do they feel free to explore their attitudes or beliefs or to discuss issues that they find interesting in their classrooms? And to what extent do they belong to associations in and outside school? These questions all contain elements of the formal and informal aspects of schooling that can be thought of as either outcomes of civic education or influences on it.

RELATION OF THIS AREA TO THE STUDY'S DESIGN

The character of civic education at school and the influence of formal education on outcomes such as civic knowledge and engagement are emphases of the study. The octagon model (see Figure 1.2) identifies this impact at the level of face-to-face interactions with teachers, other students and in informal community settings. All of these interactions were highlighted and interconnected in the Phase 1 case studies. The need to build confidence in students that allows them to participate effectively in groups, ranging from those at school to citizens' groups, was a theme in some but not all countries. Focus groups were conducted with students as part of some Phase 1 case studies. These groups often identified gaps between what the school intended to teach and what the students believed they were learning, highlighting the importance of finding out what the students themselves believe to be the emphases of their schools in this area. There was also widespread acknowledgment among educators of the ideal of a school and classroom atmosphere that would give students a model of democratic process. Many doubted that students were having this experience. Some case studies also highlighted the value of membership in school and out-of-school organizations.

This chapter covers four sections of the survey that deal with these issues—students' responses concerning their confidence in the effectiveness of participation at school, what students perceive they are learning in school, the openness of the classroom climate for discussion, and the organizations in which students participate. Only the first of these, the confidence in participation at school scale, has been identified as an outcome for analysis by country in the same way as the concepts and attitudes covered in the previous chapters. The other three serve as predictors of other scales in Chapter 8. However, country differences in all four sets of items are presented here.

CONFIDENCE IN THE EFFECTIVENESS OF PARTICIPATION AT SCHOOL

The sense of political efficacy is usually defined as the attitude that citizens can make a difference in government decisions. It is often thought of as having two parts. External efficacy is the belief that government officials are responsive to citizen input, while internal efficacy is the belief that the individual can mobilize personal resources to be effective. The sense of efficacy is of long-standing interest in studies of politics and political socialization (for examples of early work in this area, see Campbell, Converse, Miller & Stokes, 1964; Hess & Torney, 1967). The community and the school are among the settings in which such efficacy can be experienced, especially by young people (see Panel 7.1), although the majority of previous research has dealt with efficacy in relation to the government.

Development of the School Confidence Scale in the 1999 IEA Instrument

In developing the area of political efficacy relating to the government, we began with the 1971 IEA items. The final 1999 test included nine efficacy items. We also included a measure in the pilot study that contained 12 items relating to perceptions of school authorities and the student's view of the efficacy of group participation. We reduced this measure to seven items in the final test. The response scale had four points, ranging from 'strongly agree' to 'strongly disagree'.

For political efficacy items about government, the confirmatory factor analysis failed to produce a scale that met IEA standards across countries. In regard to items about efficacy at school, the confirmatory factor analysis revealed two factors. We retained a four-item scale dealing with confidence that groups of students who participate in school-based groups can have an impact on solving school problems.

In her study of political efficacy in relation to the government, Hahn (1998) used a measure of political confidence that focused on a person's belief in his or her ability to influence decisions. The items within this measure were phrased this way: 'I am the kind of person who can influence. . .' followed by 'how others vote' or 'others' decisions'. Hahn found that among the countries she surveyed, students in the United States were most confident, followed by those in Denmark and England, and those in Germany slightly less so. She found small gender effects, with males more confident, perhaps because the emphasis in these items was on using assertiveness to convince someone else of a point of view.

Yeich and Levine (1994) proposed a measure to augment the frequently studied topics of external political efficacy (a belief that the government is responsive to citizens) and internal political efficacy (a belief that the individual citizen can understand political events and have an influence). Their measure involved collective political efficacy, that is, the belief that getting together in groups is effective in solving community problems. They studied adults in the United States who were attempting to mobilize community action.

In a recent study of seven countries, Flanagan, Bowes, Jonsson, Csapo and Sheblanova (1998) used a measure of sense of membership at school that included such items as 'feeling like someone whose opinion counts'. Australian students had the highest sense of membership, followed by students from Bulgaria, Hungary and the United States. Students in the Czech Republic, Sweden and Russia had lower scores. Gender differences tended toward a greater sense of membership among females. Sense of membership at school was an important predictor in some countries of civic commitment (the desire to make a contribution to one's country and society) for both males and females.

Results for Confidence in the Effectiveness of Participation at School

Analysis of scale scores

The items in this scale deal with the value of students working together in groups or as elected representatives to solve school problems. Approximately 30 to 40 percent of students 'strongly agree' and approximately 50 percent 'agree' with these items. To look at this finding another way, only 10 to 15 percent of the students disagree with these items. The large majority of students across countries have had some positive experience with students getting together at school in either formal or informal groups to promote school improvement and solve problems. (For details of scaling and item responses, see Figure B.2j in Appendix B.)

As Figure 7.1 indicates, confidence in the effectiveness of school participation is especially high in Cyprus, Greece and Portugal. Other countries with means significantly above the international mean are Chile, Denmark, Norway, Poland, Romania and Sweden. Confidence in the effectiveness of school participation is relatively low in Germany, Hungary, Latvia and Switzerland. Other countries with means significantly below the international mean are Belgium (French), the Czech Republic, Finland, Hong Kong (SAR), Italy, the

Figure 7.1 Confidence in Participation at School

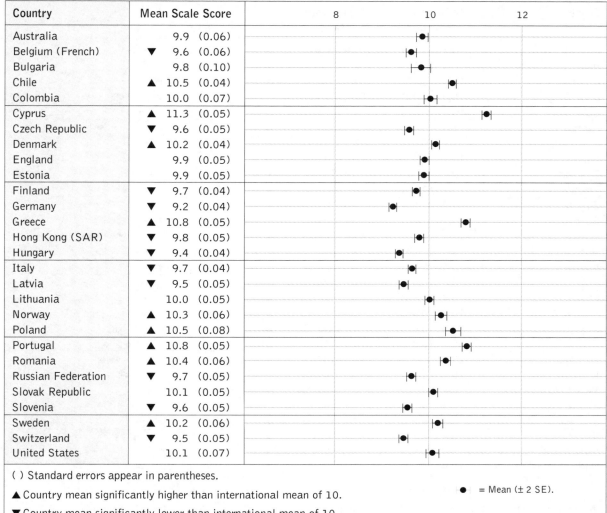

Country	Mean Scale Score		
Australia		9.9	(0.06)
Belgium (French)	▼	9.6	(0.06)
Bulgaria		9.8	(0.10)
Chile	▲	10.5	(0.04)
Colombia		10.0	(0.07)
Cyprus	▲	11.3	(0.05)
Czech Republic	▼	9.6	(0.05)
Denmark	▲	10.2	(0.04)
England		9.9	(0.05)
Estonia		9.9	(0.05)
Finland	▼	9.7	(0.04)
Germany	▼	9.2	(0.04)
Greece	▲	10.8	(0.05)
Hong Kong (SAR)	▼	9.8	(0.05)
Hungary	▼	9.4	(0.04)
Italy	▼	9.7	(0.04)
Latvia	▼	9.5	(0.05)
Lithuania		10.0	(0.05)
Norway	▲	10.3	(0.06)
Poland	▲	10.5	(0.08)
Portugal	▲	10.8	(0.05)
Romania	▲	10.4	(0.06)
Russian Federation	▼	9.7	(0.05)
Slovak Republic		10.1	(0.05)
Slovenia	▼	9.6	(0.05)
Sweden	▲	10.2	(0.06)
Switzerland	▼	9.5	(0.05)
United States		10.1	(0.07)

( ) Standard errors appear in parentheses.

▲ Country mean significantly higher than international mean of 10.

▼ Country mean significantly lower than international mean of 10.

● = Mean (± 2 SE).

Source: IEA Civic Education Study, Standard Population of 14-year-olds tested in 1999.

Russian Federation and Slovenia. A number of these countries' Phase 1 case studies reported attempts, which often met with unexpected difficulties, to enhance students' participation at school.

Analysis of scale scores by gender

Significant gender differences are evident in 16 countries. Figure 7.2 shows that these are all in the direction of females having more confidence than males in the effectiveness of school participation. This finding is the opposite of the gender difference that Hahn (1998) found. She, however, asked students about their individual feelings of confidence or assertiveness and not about whether they thought group participation was likely to be effective.

Figure 7.2 Gender Differences in Confidence in Participation at School

Country	Mean Score Females	Mean Score Males	8	10	12
Australia	10.1 (0.07)	9.6 (0.09)	▲		
Belgium (French)	10.0 (0.07)	9.3 (0.08)	▲		
Bulgaria	10.2 (0.17)	9.5 (0.08)	▲		
Chile	10.6 (0.05)	10.4 (0.05)			
Colombia	10.1 (0.07)	9.9 (0.08)			
Cyprus	11.5 (0.07)	11.0 (0.07)	▲		
Czech Republic	9.7 (0.06)	9.5 (0.06)			
Denmark	10.3 (0.06)	10.0 (0.06)			
England	10.2 (0.07)	9.7 (0.06)	▲		
Estonia	10.1 (0.05)	9.7 (0.06)	▲		
Finland	9.9 (0.06)	9.5 (0.06)	▲		
Germany	9.4 (0.05)	9.1 (0.05)			
Greece	11.1 (0.06)	10.5 (0.08)	▲		
Hong Kong (SAR)	9.9 (0.06)	9.7 (0.07)			
Hungary	9.4 (0.05)	9.3 (0.05)			
Italy	9.8 (0.05)	9.5 (0.06)			
Latvia	9.7 (0.04)	9.3 (0.07)	▲		
Lithuania	10.3 (0.06)	9.8 (0.06)	▲		
Norway	10.5 (0.07)	10.0 (0.07)	▲		
Poland	10.9 (0.06)	10.2 (0.12)	▲		
Portugal	11.0 (0.06)	10.7 (0.07)			
Romania	10.5 (0.06)	10.3 (0.08)			
Russian Federation	9.8 (0.06)	9.5 (0.08)			
Slovak Republic	10.1 (0.06)	10.1 (0.06)			
Slovenia	9.8 (0.06)	9.3 (0.06)	▲		
Sweden	10.4 (0.09)	10.0 (0.08)	▲		
Switzerland	9.7 (0.06)	9.3 (0.05)	▲		
United States	10.4 (0.08)	9.8 (0.09)	▲		

( ) Standard errors appear in parentheses.

▲ Gender difference statistically significant at .05 level.

├●┤ = Mean for Males (± 2 SE).

├◇┤ = Mean for Females (± 2 SE).

Source: IEA Civic Education Study, Standard Population of 14-year-olds tested in 1999.

Source: IEA Civic Education Study, Standard Population of 14-year-olds tested in 1999.

Summary of Confidence in the Effectiveness of Participation at School

Young people daily experience the school as a social and political system. Solving problems that arise there in interaction with others can foster a sense of membership in this community. Confidence that participation at school can make a difference is valuable in itself. Those who prepared the Phase 1 case studies expressed the hope that schools could become more open to such participation, but they also noted the difficulties involved.

For many years, studies in civic education and political socialization have used a measure of political efficacy that asks about the relation of citizens to the national government. The IEA measure of confidence in participation at school seems equally valuable in understanding young people's motivations and actions because it deals with environments that are part of their everyday lives, problems that matter to them, and actions that they can actually undertake rather than anticipate.

The countries that are high on school confidence also score high on scales relating to concepts of citizenship as involving both conventional and social movement activity and on the scale indicating willingness to participate in political activities as adults. We will discuss this matter more fully in Chapter 10.

A question for future analysis is how confidence in effective participation relates to other measures of engagement within countries.

STUDENTS' VIEWS OF THEIR LEARNING

IEA studies in many subject areas since the First International Mathematics Study of more than 40 years ago have used measures of 'opportunity to learn' to ensure the fairness of coverage of a test and to interpret patterns of performance. In these studies, teachers have usually been the ones to rate the extent to which students have studied the material required to answer each test item.

Development of the Views of Learning Items in the 1999 IEA Instrument

'Opportunity to learn' instruments are very time-consuming to administer. In both the 1971 IEA Civic Education Study and the current one there were other reasons for not including an item-by-item rating by teachers of students' opportunity to learn. Civic education is influenced by schooling, but that influence is nested within a much larger set of systems—families, peer groups, community organizations, media presentations and the political culture. Much of the effect of civic education is the product of cumulative learning, not merely of that gained in the current grade but also in previous grades and in a variety of classes including history and mother tongue (and through school and community experience). It would be misleading to discuss opportunity to learn solely on the basis of ratings by a current teacher of one civic-related subject.

Knowing something about the emphases that schools place on learning about civic-related matters is valuable, however. Students were a possible source for this information, but we could not ask them to rate every test item. Based on National Research Coordinators' suggestions, we identified a scale that asked students about what they had learned in school. The scale consisted of seven items, among them 'In school I have learned to cooperate in groups with other students'. Other items dealt with learning to solve community problems, acting to protect the environment, being a patriotic citizen and the importance of voting in national and local elections. We analyzed them as single items.

Results for Students' Views of Their Learning

As Table 7.1 indicates, in many countries the proportion of students who believe they have learned in school about the importance of voting is less than that for the other learning objectives. Specifically, in only 14 countries do the majority of students say they have learned in school about the importance of voting (international mean percentage of 55). In contrast, in 22 countries, the majority of students believe they have learned in school about being a

Table 7.1 Students' Reports on What They Believe They Have Learned in School

Country	Percentage of Students who 'Agree' or 'Strongly Agree' with...						
	In school I have learned to cooperate in groups with other students	In school I have learned to understand people who have different ideas	In school I have learned how to act to protect the environment	In school I have learned to be concerned about what happens in other countries	In school I have learned to contribute to solving problems in the community	In school I have learned to be a patriotic and loyal citizen of my country	In school I have learned about the importance of voting in national and local elections
Australia	90 (0.9)	88 (1.0)	76 (1.1)	70 (1.2)	67 (1.1)	60 (1.0)	55 (1.5)
Belgium (French)	90 (1.1)	80 (1.8)	74 (1.7)	71 (1.7)	62 (1.7)	47 (1.2)	49 (2.5)
Bulgaria	82 (1.3)	77 (1.7)	73 (1.8)	60 (1.5)	65 (1.4)	63 (1.5)	42 (2.2)
Chile	94 (0.5)	94 (0.4)	89 (0.7)	77 (0.9)	81 (0.7)	87 (0.6)	76 (1.1)
Colombia	96 (0.4)	93 (0.6)	94 (0.6)	78 (1.0)	91 (1.0)	90 (0.9)	89 (0.9)
Cyprus	93 (0.6)	88 (0.7)	88 (0.8)	81 (0.9)	80 (0.8)	91 (0.7)	72 (1.1)
Czech Republic	90 (0.9)	74 (1.2)	78 (1.1)	57 (1.5)	69 (1.6)	58 (1.1)	42 (1.6)
Denmark	92 (0.5)	72 (0.9)	78 (1.1)	68 (1.1)	63 (1.0)	44 (1.1)	39 (1.3)
England	94 (0.7)	90 (1.0)	77 (0.9)	74 (1.1)	70 (1.1)	54 (1.3)	41 (1.2)
Estonia	91 (0.7)	84 (0.9)	76 (1.0)	71 (1.1)	54 (1.3)	48 (1.3)	43 (1.5)
Finland	93 (0.6)	83 (0.9)	67 (1.5)	67 (1.2)	32 (1.3)	55 (1.5)	34 (1.4)
Germany	86 (0.7)	77 (1.0)	69 (1.2)	74 (0.9)	69 (1.1)	48 (1.3)	39 (1.3)
Greece	92 (0.6)	87 (0.9)	82 (0.8)	68 (1.0)	83 (0.8)	79 (1.1)	72 (1.1)
Hong Kong (SAR)	91 (0.6)	85 (0.8)	85 (0.8)	72 (0.8)	65 (0.9)	57 (1.1)	71 (1.0)
Hungary	90 (0.6)	71 (1.0)	84 (1.0)	57 (1.2)	45 (1.1)	69 (1.3)	52 (1.2)
Italy	91 (0.7)	87 (0.9)	65 (1.2)	79 (1.1)	77 (1.1)	61 (1.3)	54 (1.2)
Latvia	87 (1.0)	81 (1.1)	76 (1.4)	72 (1.3)	61 (1.5)	52 (1.6)	48 (1.6)
Lithuania	87 (0.8)	79 (1.0)	84 (0.9)	74 (1.0)	62 (1.2)	57 (1.2)	43 (1.3)
Norway	92 (0.6)	79 (1.1)	74 (1.1)	76 (1.0)	61 (1.3)	55 (1.0)	48 (1.3)
Poland	89 (1.1)	79 (1.5)	77 (1.3)	74 (1.7)	74 (2.1)	81 (1.1)	70 (1.4)
Portugal	96 (0.5)	95 (0.5)	92 (0.6)	76 (0.9)	82 (0.9)	84 (0.8)	48 (1.1)
Romania	91 (0.8)	89 (0.8)	93 (0.5)	69 (1.2)	83 (1.2)	88 (1.0)	78 (1.2)
Russian Federation	88 (0.8)	87 (0.8)	80 (1.5)	78 (1.2)	45 (1.2)	66 (1.3)	64 (1.8)
Slovak Republic	95 (0.5)	87 (0.8)	88 (0.8)	76 (1.0)	86 (0.9)	79 (1.1)	68 (1.2)
Slovenia	92 (0.6)	80 (1.0)	78 (1.0)	57 (1.0)	80 (1.1)	64 (1.2)	35 (1.2)
Sweden	91 (1.1)	84 (1.4)	73 (1.5)	76 (1.6)	61 (1.2)	42 (2.0)	57 (1.8)
Switzerland	92 (0.8)	83 (0.8)	64 (1.4)	77 (1.1)	74 (0.9)	48 (1.7)	44 (1.8)
United States	91 (0.9)	89 (1.1)	76 (1.2)	75 (1.1)	73 (1.0)	68 (1.3)	73 (1.4)
International Sample	91 (0.1)	84 (0.2)	79 (0.2)	72 (0.2)	68 (0.2)	64 (0.2)	55 (0.3)

( ) Standard errors appear in parentheses. Percentages based on valid responses.

Source: IEA Civic Education Study, Standard Population of 14-year-olds tested in 1999.

patriotic and loyal citizen (international mean percentage of 64). In 25 countries the majority of students agree that they have learned to solve community problems (international mean percentage of 68). And in all 28 countries, the majority of students agree that they have learned about protecting the environment, what happens in other countries, cooperating in groups, and understanding people (international mean percentages ranging from 72 to 91).

Summary of Students' Views of Their Learning

Schools are places where students believe that they learn to understand and live in harmony with others. This is a vitally important goal, of course. National and local elections are not everyday events, while getting along with others is faced daily. However, in most countries, the importance of voting receives the lowest rating or next to lowest rating of the seven learning objectives. If schools do not explicitly promote this basic level of electoral participation, then students may lack a basic commitment upon which to build later motivation to participate in the political system. Furthermore, as we have noted elsewhere in this volume, students appear to have few opportunities to learn about the kinds of conflict that lead to different political positions and to the debate and discussion that takes place during election campaigns.

In some respects, these findings match the models of good citizenship endorsed by teachers in the early 1990s in Australia, England, Hong Kong (SAR) and the United States (for previous research in this area, see Panel 4.3 in Chapter 4). Getting along with others, involvement in solving community problems, and participation in environmental protection were more acceptable learning objectives for those teachers than instruction about the formal political system. Another reason that some schools may not teach about voting is concern about raising issues of political partisanship. In Chapter 8 we will examine how this measure of students' views on opportunity to learn in school relates to expected civic engagement (likelihood of voting) within the participating countries. In Chapter 10 we will examine the gap between teachers' and students' reports about the opportunity to learn about voting.

OPEN CLASSROOM CLIMATE FOR DISCUSSION

The effectiveness of student participation in the school as a whole and the opportunities for learning about civic processes provided by the curriculum are certainly important. The extent to which students experience their classrooms as places to investigate issues and explore their opinions and those of their peers has been found to be an even more vital part of civic education (see Panel 7.2; also Torney-Purta, Hahn & Amadeo, 2001). One of the most important findings of the 1971 IEA Civic Education Study was that the students' belief that they were encouraged to speak openly in class was a powerful predictor of their knowledge of and support for democratic values, and their participation in political discussion inside and outside school.

The 1971 IEA Civic Education Study used a four-item measure of 'independence of opinion encouraged in the classroom' to assess the classroom climate for discussion. It was an important predictor of all of the study's outcomes, including civic knowledge.

Hahn's (1998) study in five countries' using an augmented set of the IEA classroom climate items' found that students reporting the most issues-related discussion in a supportive classroom were also those students most likely to report high levels of political interest and trust. The ways these discussions took place differed. In Denmark, where the most open classroom climate was reported, elementary children held class meetings to resolve class problems and to advise the school council. Older students conducted inquiries into public policy issues. In the United States, where the climate was moderately open, students were most likely to hold discussions in the context of current events or public policy debates.

Conover and Searing (2000) found through interviews with students in the United States that those from suburban and rural communities were considerably more likely than those from urban or immigrant areas to report that political issues were discussed in their classrooms.

Ichilov (1991) found that Israeli students who participated in classroom discussion were more politically efficacious than those who did not.

There are many ethnographic studies of schools, but one of the few that has focused on citizenship was conducted in Finland and England (Gordon, Holland & Lahelma, 2000). The relationships between the official school, the informal school and the physical school were explored, particularly in terms of the impact on these of depersonalizing student roles, encouraging gendered citizen roles and marginalizing students.

Democratic school practices with respect to the teacher's authority were investigated in the recent seven-country study of adolescents described in Panel 7.1. Students in Australia were most likely to agree that they were encouraged to express their opinions even if they disagreed with those of their teachers. Students in Hungary, Sweden and the United States were in a middle position regarding agreement, while those in Bulgaria, the Czech Republic and Russia were least likely to agree (Jonsson & Flanagan, 2000).

Development of the Open Classroom Climate Scale in the 1999 IEA Instrument

The scale that we developed included 12 items (many of them from the 1971 study) covering classroom climate for open discussion and stress placed by the school on factual learning. The response scale was 1 = never, 2 = rarely, 3 = sometimes, 4 = often.

A confirmatory factor analysis revealed a classroom climate factor with six items about openness for discussion, and also a smaller factor that dealt with the use of lectures and the stress placed on factual learning. This smaller factor did not, however, scale to IEA standards. We therefore retained the classroom climate scale for analysis, leaving the other items for later examination.

Results for Open Classroom Climate for Discussion

Across all countries, between 27 and 39 percent of the students say that they are 'often' encouraged in their schools to make up their own minds, encouraged to express their opinions, free to express opinions that differ from those of other students and of the teacher, and are likely to hear several sides of an issue. A smaller number of students, 16 percent, say that the teacher 'often' encourages discussion of issues about which people have different opinions (see Figure B.2k in Appendix B for these figures and for the item-by-score map). These findings indicate the extent to which emphasis on agreement rather than on discussion of differences of opinion is the practice in many classrooms.

Figure 7.3 indicates that students report especially open climates for classroom discussion in Colombia, Greece, Norway and the United States. Other countries with means significantly above the international mean are Chile, Cyprus, Germany, Italy, Poland, Sweden and Switzerland. In contrast, fewer students on average perceive an open climate for discussion in Belgium (French),

Figure 7.3 Perceptions of Open Classroom Climate for Discussion

Country	Mean Scale Score	8	10	12
Australia	10.1 (0.1)			
Belgium (French)	▼ 9.3 (0.1)			
Bulgaria	▼ 9.3 (0.1)			
Chile	▲ 10.3 (0.1)			
Colombia	▲ 10.8 (0.1)			
Cyprus	▲ 10.4 (0.1)			
Czech Republic	▼ 9.5 (0.1)			
Denmark	10.0 (0.1)			
England	10.0 (0.1)			
Estonia	▼ 9.7 (0.1)			
Finland	10.0 (0.1)			
Germany	▲ 10.4 (0.1)			
Greece	▲ 10.5 (0.1)			
Hong Kong (SAR)	▼ 9.6 (0.0)			
Hungary	▼ 9.4 (0.1)			
Italy	▲ 10.4 (0.1)			
Latvia	▼ 9.6 (0.1)			
Lithuania	▼ 9.8 (0.1)			
Norway	▲ 10.6 (0.1)			
Poland	▲ 10.4 (0.1)			
Portugal	▼ 9.7 (0.1)			
Romania	▼ 9.5 (0.1)			
Russian Federation	10.1 (0.1)			
Slovak Republic	10.2 (0.1)			
Slovenia	▼ 9.3 (0.0)			
Sweden	▲ 10.2 (0.1)			
Switzerland	▲ 10.4 (0.1)			
United States	▲ 10.5 (0.1)			

( ) Standard errors appear in parentheses.

▲ Country mean significantly higher than international mean of 10.

▼ Country mean significantly lower than international mean of 10.

● = Mean (± 2 SE).

Source: IEA Civic Education Study, Standard Population of 14-year-olds tested in 1999.

Bulgaria and Slovenia. Other countries whose means are significantly below the international mean are the Czech Republic, Estonia, Hong Kong (SAR), Hungary, Latvia, Lithuania, Portugal and Romania. The countries where students express little openness in their classroom are primarily those that have experienced considerable changes in civic education over the last decade. The pressure to include new content about democracy and the challenge of preparing teachers who are new to the subject seem to have resulted in little attention to fostering an open climate for classroom discussion in some countries.

There are also significant gender differences across countries (Figure 7.4). In 23 participating countries, females more than males perceive that their classrooms are open to discussion. The exceptions are Belgium (French), Bulgaria, Chile, Hong Kong (SAR) and Romania.

Open classroom climate is used in Chapter 8 as a within-country predictor of student outcomes.

Figure 7.4 Gender Differences in Perceptions of Open Classroom Climate for Discussion

Country	Mean Score Females		Mean Score Males		8	10	12
Australia	10.4	(0.1)	9.7	(0.1)			
Belgium (French)	9.6	(0.1)	9.0	(0.1)			
Bulgaria	9.4	(0.1)	9.2	(0.1)			
Chile	10.5	(0.1)	10.1	(0.1)			
Colombia	11.0	(0.1)	10.5	(0.1)			
Cyprus	10.6	(0.1)	10.3	(0.1)			
Czech Republic	9.8	(0.1)	9.1	(0.1)			
Denmark	10.3	(0.1)	9.7	(0.1)			
England	10.4	(0.1)	9.7	(0.1)			
Estonia	10.0	(0.1)	9.5	(0.1)			
Finland	10.3	(0.1)	9.7	(0.1)			
Germany	10.6	(0.1)	10.1	(0.1)			
Greece	10.8	(0.1)	10.2	(0.1)			
Hong Kong (SAR)	9.7	(0.1)	9.6	(0.1)			
Hungary	9.6	(0.1)	9.2	(0.1)			
Italy	10.8	(0.1)	9.9	(0.1)			
Latvia	9.9	(0.1)	9.3	(0.1)			
Lithuania	10.1	(0.1)	9.5	(0.1)			
Norway	10.9	(0.1)	10.4	(0.1)			
Poland	10.7	(0.1)	10.0	(0.1)			
Portugal	9.9	(0.1)	9.4	(0.1)			
Romania	9.6	(0.1)	9.3	(0.1)			
Russian Federation	10.5	(0.1)	9.7	(0.1)			
Slovak Republic	10.4	(0.1)	9.9	(0.1)			
Slovenia	9.6	(0.1)	9.1	(0.1)			
Sweden	10.5	(0.1)	9.9	(0.1)			
Switzerland	10.7	(0.1)	10.2	(0.1)			
United States	10.8	(0.1)	10.3	(0.1)			

( ) Standard errors appear in parentheses.

▲ Gender difference statistically significant at .05 level.

|—●—| = Mean for Males (± 2 SE).

|—◇—| = Mean for Females (± 2 SE).

Source: IEA Civic Education Study, Standard Population of 14-year-olds tested in 1999.

PARTICIPATION IN CIVIC-RELATED ORGANIZATIONS

The literature on the potential importance of organizational membership in building civil society, 'social capital' and trust or confidence in the government has expanded enormously in the last decade. Special attention should be given, however, to studies that have looked at school-based groups that offer students opportunities for governance or civic experience (see Panel 7.3). Those conducting the Phase 1 case studies saw organizations such as these as particularly important.

Development of the Organizational Participation Items in the 1999 IEA Instrument

Our goal was to develop a list of voluntary organizations inside and outside school to which students might belong. To ensure that the list would be applicable across the range of countries in the study, we had to make some language translations (for example, 'school parliament' for 'school council') and also look for organizations with parallel purposes and types of activities. The National Research Coordinators' input was essential in developing a list of ten organizations for the pilot test, which expanded to 15 organizations in the

---

PANEL 7.3 Previous Research on Civic-related Participation in Organizations

Research on social capital and organizational membership has been conducted in nearly all the countries of Western Europe as well as in the United States (see, for example, Putnam, Leonardi & Nanetti, 1993; Van Deth, Maraffi, Newton & Whiteley, 1999; Pharr & Putnam, 2000; Putnam, 2000). Nearly all the empirical studies have used a similar measure in which respondents are asked to indicate the organizations to which they belong. In some studies, all organizations have been considered in deriving a score (thus, sports teams and musical clubs have been given the same weight as political parties and student government). In other studies, distinctions have been made either between civic-related and non-civic related organizations or between volunteering time or making a special effort as part of one's membership in an organization and being simply a member.

A number of recent studies in the United States have used longitudinal data to trace the links between participation in activities with a civic component during secondary school and later involvement in the community (Verba, Schlozman & Brady, 1995; Youniss, McLellan & Yates, 1997; Hart, Atkins & Ford, 1998). Such a linkage appears to be especially strong for females, according to Damico, Damico and Conway (1998).

Hofer (1999), Marta, Rossi and Boccacin (1999), Oswald (1999), Roker, Player and Coleman (1999) and Yates (1999) presented a picture of organizations through which young people provide service to their communities in Italy, Britain, Germany and the United States. The themes mentioned across countries included the independence of these organizations from political partisanship (and often from connections to political involvement). A sense of civic responsibility and a sense of solidarity are potential results of voluntary involvement. Nearly all the researchers in this area have agreed that giving students a chance to reflect about and discuss their experiences increases the value of the experience itself. Such an opportunity often occurs in the context of connections between school or class work and activities that help others in the community.

---

final. School heads (principals, directors) were given the list of organizations as well, and were asked whether each was available to students. In order to get a picture of peer group activities outside of organizations, students were asked how often they spent time informally with friends after school and also in the evening.

Results for Participation in Civic-related Organizations

Table 7.2 gives the percentages of 14-year-olds answering that they belong to selected civic-related organizations. Twenty-five percent or more of these young people report membership in school parliaments or councils in the following countries: Australia, Cyprus, Denmark, Greece, Hong Kong (SAR), Hungary, Norway, Portugal, Romania, the Russian Federation, Sweden and the United States (with the largest proportions in Cyprus and Greece, more than 55 percent). Only in Cyprus do 20 percent or more of the respondents report

Table 7.2 Students' Reports on Their Participation in Civic-Related Organizations

Country	Percentage of Students who Report Having Participated in...					
	a student council/student government/ class or school parliament	a youth organization affiliated with a political party or union	an environmental organization	a human rights organization	a group conducting voluntary activities to help the community	a charity collecting money for a social cause
Australia	34 (1.4)	4 (0.4)	19 (1.0)	4 (0.6)	33 (1.3)	47 (1.4)
Belgium (French)	22 (1.5)	6 (0.7)	15 (1.3)	8 (1.0)	17 (1.0)	26 (1.5)
Bulgaria	14 (1.0)	4 (0.6)	9 (0.9)	9 (0.8)	8 (0.8)	12 (1.0)
Chile	19 (1.0)	4 (0.4)	21 (1.1)	5 (0.5)	33 (1.4)	24 (1.0)
Colombia	24 (1.4)	4 (0.5)	40 (1.6)	13 (1.3)	34 (1.1)	26 (1.4)
Cyprus	57 (1.1)	25 (1.0)	20 (0.9)	22 (1.2)	22 (0.9)	48 (1.3)
Czech Republic	13 (0.9)	1 (0.2)	13 (1.3)	2 (0.3)	22 (1.0)	18 (1.4)
Denmark	44 (1.3)	4 (0.4)	6 (0.6)	5 (0.5)	32 (1.0)	63 (1.2)
England	19 (0.9)	6 (0.5)	13 (0.8)	5 (0.6)	25 (1.0)	55 (1.4)
Estonia	21 (1.2)	3 (0.4)	8 (0.7)	4 (0.4)	8 (0.6)	10 (0.9)
Finland	22 (1.2)	2 (0.3)	6 (0.7)	2 (0.4)	6 (0.6)	24 (1.0)
Germany	13 (0.8)	5 (0.5)	10 (0.9)	2 (0.3)	16 (0.9)	23 (1.2)
Greece	59 (1.0)	9 (0.6)	32 (1.2)	16 (0.7)	29 (1.0)	53 (1.1)
Hong Kong (SAR)	45 (1.1)	5 (0.5)	12 (0.7)	6 (0.4)	34 (1.1)	37 (1.2)
Hungary	32 (1.5)	4 (0.4)	28 (1.4)	3 (0.4)	23 (1.0)	18 (1.1)
Italy	16 (0.7)	3 (0.3)	7 (0.6)	3 (0.3)	8 (0.6)	6 (0.5)
Latvia	18 (1.0)	2 (0.6)	7 (1.0)	5 (0.9)	12 (1.0)	9 (0.9)
Lithuania	23 (1.0)	1 (0.3)	16 (1.4)	4 (0.4)	7 (0.5)	14 (1.0)
Norway	47 (1.2)	6 (0.5)	16 (0.9)	6 (0.5)	18 (0.9)	84 (0.8)
Poland	19 (0.9)	1 (0.3)	14 (1.6)	3 (0.5)	5 (0.6)	9 (0.8)
Portugal	25 (1.1)	2 (0.3)	25 (1.1)	10 (1.0)	9 (0.7)	20 (1.0)
Romania	37 (2.2)	2 (0.3)	13 (0.9)	8 (0.8)	10 (1.0)	13 (0.9)
Russian Federation	43 (1.9)	2 (0.4)	12 (1.6)	4 (0.8)	11 (1.5)	7 (1.1)
Slovak Republic	3 (0.4)	1 (0.2)	5 (0.7)	1 (0.2)	6 (0.7)	5 (0.9)
Slovenia	18 (0.9)	1 (0.2)	15 (0.8)	4 (0.5)	11 (0.8)	33 (1.5)
Sweden	49 (1.8)	7 (0.6)	15 (1.2)	5 (0.7)	8 (1.0)	25 (1.7)
Switzerland	8 (0.7)	4 (0.5)	10 (0.8)	3 (0.3)	12 (0.7)	27 (1.2)
United States	33 (1.5)	10 (0.9)	24 (1.2)	6 (0.6)	50 (1.4)	40 (1.5)
International Sample	28 (0.2)	5 (0.1)	15 (0.2)	6 (0.1)	18 (0.2)	28 (0.2)

( ) Standard errors appear in parentheses. Percentages based on valid responses.

Source: IEA Civic Education Study, Standard Population of 14-year-olds tested in 1999.

belonging to a youth organization affiliated with a political party or union or to a human rights organization. Twenty-five percent or more of the students report belonging to an environmental organization in Colombia, Greece, Hungary and Portugal. Twenty-five percent or more of the students report belonging to a group conducting voluntary activities in the community in Australia, Chile, Colombia, Denmark, England, Greece, Hong Kong (SAR) and the United States (with the largest proportion in the United States, 50 percent). The most frequent organizational membership relates to charities that collect money for a social cause. This form of membership involves 25 percent or more of students in about half of the countries. However, there are also countries where all types of organizational participation are low: Bulgaria, the Czech Republic, Estonia, Finland, Germany, Italy, Latvia, Lithuania, Poland and the Slovak Republic.

We will explore the relation of school council/parliament membership to civic knowledge and engagement in Chapter 8.

SUMMARY

The majority of students have a moderately positive sense of the effectiveness of students working together to enhance the school and solve problems that may arise there. In their classrooms, many of these young people have an opportunity to participate in the discussion of issues and to feel that their opinions are respected. These discussions are not very frequent, however, especially in some countries that have recently experienced changes in civic education, resulting in teachers new to the subject content of the relevant courses. There seems to be an untapped potential for civic education to provide students with opportunities for meaningful engagement in their schools and classrooms.

In previous chapters of this report, we have noted that young people sometimes seem uncomfortable with disagreements about opinions and have generally poor impressions of organizations such as political parties that propose conflicting ideologies and policy positions. On the one hand, schools must avoid political partisanship, but on the other, before they become voters, students need to acquire a sense of how and why people disagree about issues. Achievement of this objective presents a challenge in some countries.

This chapter has also noted that there is a rich array of experiences in schools and organizations that can be used as predictors of civic knowledge and engagement. We explore this matter further in Chapter 8.

A Model for Explaining Students' Civic Knowledge and Engagement

HIGHLIGHTS RELATING TO THE CORRELATES OF CIVIC KNOWLEDGE AND ENGAGEMENT

- In every country, the civic knowledge of 14-year-olds is a positive predictor of their expressed willingness to vote as adults. It is the most powerful predictor in many countries even when accounting for other factors.

- School practices play an important role in the civic education process. The perception of an open climate for discussion in the classroom is a positive predictor of both civic knowledge and of the likelihood of future voting in about three-quarters of the countries. Participating in a school council or parliament is related to civic knowledge in about one-third of the countries.

- Watching news programs on television is a positive predictor of civic knowledge in about half of the countries and of the likelihood of voting in nearly all countries.

- Fourteen-year-olds from homes with more educational resources have higher civic knowledge in almost all countries. This aspect of the home influences the likelihood of voting in about one-fifth of the countries.

- When other factors are held constant, female students have slightly lower civic knowledge than do males in about one-third of the countries (contrasting with analysis reported in Chapter 3). Females express a greater willingness than males to vote in about one-fifth of the countries.

Although country differences covered in previous chapters enhance our understanding of many civic education processes, numerous questions important to policy-makers, educators and researchers would remain unanswered if differences between students' civic outcomes were not explored. Our purpose therefore in this chapter is to present a model designed to shed light on two of the most important dimensions of citizenship—civic knowledge and civic engagement. The model focuses on between-student differences across and within countries, and examines the relationship of two outcomes to several indicators of home background, school and the individual. The model that we have developed for this volume is a relatively simple one. Its primary purpose is to show the main factors relating to civic knowledge and engagement across countries and to suggest directions for future analysis.

Analysis that attempts to differentiate between school-level effects and student-level effects will be explored in a later volume. More elaborate models that include such variables as extent of family discussion and a wide range of association memberships will also be examined in the future, along with models that look at more complex interactions between civic knowledge, engagement and attitudes. Because of differences between modes of course organization across countries, an analysis of the impact of enrollment in courses with civic-related content will have to be conducted on a within-country basis. Finally, because the same response categories for ethnic group and for parent education could not be used in all 28 countries, the analysis of these effects will also have to be conducted within a country or a small group of countries.

THE MODEL

Panel 8.1 presents the details of the model. In brief, we used two dependent variables: the total score on the knowledge test and the students' stated expectation that they will vote when adults. These have been themes throughout this volume. In addition to linking these variables to explanatory factors, we were interested in analyzing the relationship between the two variables so as to address the question of whether higher levels of civic knowledge are associated with the disposition of students to participate in elections in the future. We chose the relatively narrow variable of the students' response to a question about how likely they would be to vote in the future because of the importance of electoral participation. Future analyses using broader measures will examine the extent to which engagement predicts knowledge (as well as the extent to which knowledge predicts other types of engagement).

We included two background factors in the model: gender and home literacy resources. We reported the results of relatively simple analyses of these variables in Chapter 3 but explore them in more depth here.

Although the study and its policy questions have a focus on schools, it is very likely that particular and different aspects of schooling influence different civic education outcomes. We therefore included four variables from this part of the instrument: expected further education; the students' reports of the extent to which there is an open climate for discussion in their classrooms; the students' reports of opportunities to learn about voting in school; and the students' reported participation in school councils or parliaments (see Panel 8.1). The two variables from outside the school that we included were frequency of 'spending time outside the home with peers in the evening' and frequency of 'watching television news'. Peer group and media experience can be explored with these items. Future analysis will explore in greater detail other organizational memberships, community participation and political information sources.

To compare the size and significance of these effects across countries, we estimated two separate models for each dependent variable. We did this mainly to compare effect sizes across countries in a straightforward way and because for multiple regression models it is possible to compute the correct standard errors using a jackknife procedure.[1] The resulting test statistics were corrected for multiple comparisons. The tables in this chapter include only significant beta coefficients. Panel 8.2 indicates some of the caveats to be considered in interpreting this analysis.

As a first step, we estimated a path regression model based on the calibration sample of 14,000 (500 student respondents chosen randomly from the weighted samples of each of the 28 countries). We then estimated separate regression models using the full weighted sample for each country.

PANEL 8.1 Description of Variables Included in the Model

Dependent variables are (i) the total test score for civic knowledge, and (ii) the expectation of students that they will vote in the future.[2]

The following independent variables were included in the model:

1. Background factors

- *Gender:* Although there are few gender differences in civic knowledge noted in the analysis of Chapter 3, we included this variable for the following reasons. First, in a multivariate model, gender might have effects that do not manifest themselves in a bivariate analysis. Secondly, we found gender differences for participation variables and classroom climate (see Chapters 6 and 7). The variable is coded 0 for males and 1 for females (reversing the coding in the survey booklet).

- *Home literacy resources:* Home literacy resources as measured by students' reports on the number of books at home has a substantial effect on civic knowledge across countries and is the home background indicator in the model (see Chapter 3). The reasons for our focus on this variable are also found in Chapter 3.

2. School factors

- *Expected years of further education:* Students were asked to estimate their years of future education, including vocational and/or higher education. Apart from reflecting the individual's aspiration, this indicator may also reflect the type of school or track the student is in. It also may reflect parental and peer influences. A similar variable was an important predictor of knowledge both in the 1971 IEA Civic Education Study and in Niemi and Junn's (1998) analysis of the National Assessment of Civics in the United States.

- *Open classroom climate for discussion:* This is the international Rasch score presented in Chapter 7. It indicates individual students' perceptions of the atmosphere for expressing opinions and discussion in class, and involves students' relations with peers in the school setting as well as with teachers. This variable was a strong predictor of knowledge, attitudes and participation in the 1971 IEA Civic Education Study. See also Chapter 7.

- *Reported participation in school council or parliament:* This indicator is coded 1 for students who report having participated and 0 for all other students. Our reason for including this variable was based on the assumption from previous research that activities at the school level can enhance civic knowledge and also willingness to engage in future electoral participation. (We considered several other association membership items, but decided that this type of participation seemed to have the most unambiguous meaning across countries.) See also Chapter 7 regarding this variable.

- *Students' reports about having learned about the importance of voting:* Students were asked whether they have learned about this matter in school ('strongly disagree' to 'strongly agree'). We included this variable as a predictor for expectation to vote only. Participation in mock elections in school was an important predictor in Niemi and Junn's (1998) analysis. See also Chapter 7.

3. Students' activities out of school

- *Evenings spent outside home:* Students were asked how often they spent time during the evening with peers outside their homes. 'Almost every day' is coded 4, 'several days a week' is coded 3, 'a few times each month' is coded 2, and 'never' or 'almost never' is coded 1. (This reverses the coding in the survey booklet.) This variable is similar to one in a World Health Organization survey, where it was found to be a predictor of risky or anti-social behavior (Currie, Hurrelmann, Setterobutte, Smith & Todd, 2000). Future analysis will concentrate on more positive peer behaviors and out-of-school associations.

- *Frequency of watching television news:* Students reported how often they watched news broadcasts on television ('never', 'rarely', 'sometimes', 'often'). We chose this variable because television was reported in most countries to be the most important and trusted source of news among 14-year-old students (see Chapters 5 and 6). Future analysis will explore the relative role of newspaper, radio and television information.

PANEL 8.2 Interpreting the Model

The following caveats should be kept in mind when examining the results from this multivariate data analysis:

- Predictors with insignificant effects are included in the model; the explained variance for the dependent variable would be slightly lower if they had been dropped.

- Measurement errors were not taken into account when estimating the model; the structural equation model for the calibration sample is a simple path model.

- Effect sizes of single item predictors may be underestimated in the model.

- This is a single-level analysis, and context effects on the school or class level cannot be disentangled from individual effects. It is not possible to infer from the results whether possible effects of an open classroom climate for discussion are related only through the individual perception of students or whether the common perception of class atmosphere has an effect on the civic knowledge or willingness to vote as an adult.

- The model is strictly recursive, with dependent and independent variables; it is not assumed that a dependent variable might influence an independent or intervening variable. We will explore the reasoning behind this assumption in the 'Technical Report' (Lehmann *et al.*, forthcoming), and explore the models based on other assumptions and on multiple levels of analysis in subsequent volumes.

Figure 8.1 shows the results for the overall model based on the calibration sample data: the (standardized) path coefficients are the same as the beta coefficients for the two separate regression models. For both of the dependent variables, civic knowledge and civic engagement (the likelihood of voting), this model explains about 20 percent of the variance. We checked all independent variables in this overall model for multicollinearity. However, the highest correlation found between two independent variables was only $r = .29$ for home literacy resources and expected education (in the calibration sample).

Figure 8.1 Path Model for Civic Knowledge and Likelihood to Vote

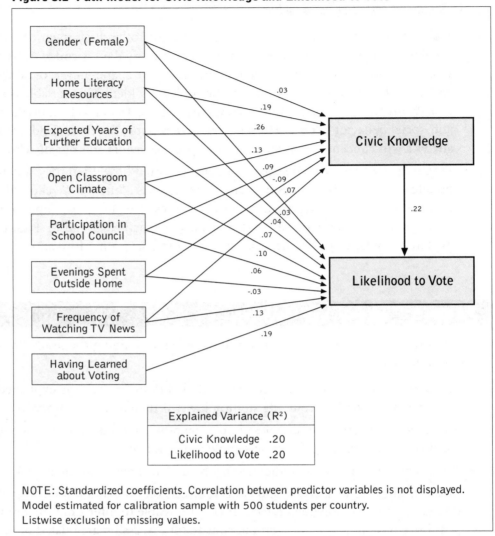

NOTE: Standardized coefficients. Correlation between predictor variables is not displayed.
Model estimated for calibration sample with 500 students per country.
Listwise exclusion of missing values.

Source: IEA Civic Education Study, Standard Population of 14-year-olds tested in 1999.

Predictors of Civic Knowledge in the Sample Containing 28 Countries

In this model for the calibration sample, the most important variable in explaining civic knowledge is expected further education. This variable reflects the future educational aspirations of the individual student, in many cases influenced by parents, schools and peers. In many countries it may also reflect the type of school or program in which the student is enrolled (for example, academic or pre-vocational). In some countries it has a socioeconomic component because programs that prepare students for higher education are more likely to be attended by the children of better-educated or wealthier parents.

The second largest predictor is home literacy resources, as shown in Chapter 3. The more books that students report having in their homes, the higher their level of civic knowledge.

Students' perception of an open classroom climate for discussion is another variable that is positively related to the knowledge score. This variable reflects the individual's perception of the atmosphere in class. As such, perceptions may vary within a class. However, in this area, an individual's view of whether it is a good idea to express an opinion is one factor that is important in determining whether he or she will become involved in class discussion.

Predictors with significant but smaller positive effects on civic knowledge in this model are the reported participation in a school council or parliament and the frequency of watching television news. In the overall model, gender has a relatively small effect on civic knowledge.

Spending evenings outside home is the only independent variable negatively related to civic knowledge. Those students who report that they spend most evenings with peers outside home have lower test scores than others. This negative effect can be interpreted in several ways. Students may have generally lower achievement in school if they spend a lot of time away from home and neglect their studying. The findings relating to this question may also reflect a tendency for some students to orient to the values held by their peers rather than to those held by parents or teachers. Students who do not achieve well at school may focus on peer-groups as a source of identity. The health surveys that have used this question have found that it relates to young people's engagement in risky and sometimes anti-social behavior (see, for example, Currie, Hurrelmann, Setterobutte, Smith & Todd, 2000).

Predictors of Civic Knowledge within Individual Countries

Table 8.1 shows the regression results for civic knowledge separately by countries (using the full sample). The explained variance in civic knowledge ranges from 10 percent in Colombia and 13 percent in Romania, to 33 percent in Hungary and Slovenia and 36 percent in the Czech Republic; the median is 22 percent. The only significant predictor in every country is student's expected level of future educational attainment. Home literacy resources predicts differences in students' civic knowledge in all countries except Hong Kong (SAR). This result corresponds to the findings of the bivariate analysis in Chapter 3.

Those students who perceive an open classroom climate have higher knowledge scores in about three-quarters of the countries. The positive effects of this variable are especially notable in Belgium (French), Denmark, Estonia, the Russian Federation and Sweden. The reported participation in a student council or parliament is a significant predictor in about one-third of the countries in this study, most notably in Australia, Cyprus, Greece and Norway.

Gender (female) has moderate negative effect in 11 countries, which means that controlling for other factors reveals that males have slightly higher knowledge scores than females. This finding leads us to moderate our statements in Chapter 3 about the absence of gender differences. If we assume other factors to be equal, then in some countries gender does make a difference, as shown in the regressions. Among these factors are perceived classroom climate and expected education, both of which are higher for females. This is an important area for further analysis.

Table 8.1 Regression Models for Civic Knowledge Within Individual Countries

Predictor variables	Australia	Belgium (French)	Bulgaria	Chile	Colombia	Cyprus	Czech Republic	Denmark	England	Estonia	Finland	Germany	Greece	Hong Kong (SAR)	Hungary	Italy	Latvia	Lithuania	Norway	Poland	Portugal	Romania	Russian Federation	Slovak Republic	Slovenia	Sweden	Switzerland	United States
Gender (Female)	-	-	-	-.06	-	-.07	-.12	-.09	-	-	-	-.08	-	-	-	-	-	-	-.07	-	-.11	-	-.08	-.06	-	-.08	-.12	-
Home Literacy Resources	.16	.23	.22	.24	.18	.08	.12	.13	.26	.13	.11	.25	.11	-	.16	.18	.14	.14	.17	.14	.19	.10	.21	.15	.10	.20	.22	.23
Expected Years of Education	.20	.22	.26	.27	.20	.33	.50	.28	.18	.26	.36	.28	.40	.17	.43	.27	.28	.32	.26	.41	.28	.25	.13	.36	.43	.26	.27	.27
Open Classroom Climate	.08	.17	-	.11	-	-	.08	.21	.13	.16	-	.13	.11	.08	.06	.13	.14	.13	.13	-	.12	-	.20	.15	.12	.17	.13	.12
Student Council/Parliament	.13	-	-	-	-	.18	-	.10	.07	-	-	.06	.13	-	.06	-	-	-	.13	-	-	-	-	-	.10	.09	-	-
Spending Evenings Outside	-.12	-.11	-	-	-.05	-	-.10	-.15	-.19	-.22	-.12	-.15	-.09	-.21	-.11	-.10	-.10	-.08	-.11	-.07	-.13	-.10	-.09	-	-.07	-.08	-.07	-.10
Watching TV News	.13	.11	-	.08	-	-	-	.07	.10	.07	.10	.08	-	.22	-	.09	.06	.08	.09	.09	-	-	-	.08	.06	-	-	-
R²	.18	.25	.19	.21	.10	.22	.36	.25	.28	.22	.22	.29	.28	.17	.33	.21	.20	.21	.23	.27	.21	.13	.16	.25	.33	.21	.20	.23
Weighted N	2883	1703	2541	5343	4540	2990	3510	2778	2545	3248	2642	3419	3287	4406	3083	3690	2347	3210	2922	3236	3028	2870	2053	3380	2929	2666	2768	2439

NOTE: Standardized (beta) regression coefficients. Not significant coefficients were omitted (-).
The standard errors were estimated using a jackknife procedure for complex sampling; significance tests corrected for multiple comparisons.
Listwise exclusion of missing values.

Source: IEA Civic Education Study, Standard Population of 14-year-olds tested in 1999.

Frequency of watching television news has a significant positive effect in about half of the countries. For students in Hong Kong (SAR), this variable is the strongest positive predictor of civic knowledge. Some previous studies of academic achievement or civil society participation have asked a different question, about total hours of television watching. Those studies assumed that viewing television takes time away from studying or being engaged in the community. Here we are using a different question, about watching television programs that provide information about civic and political matters. In interpreting this positive association, we cannot discount the possibility that students who are more knowledgeable about civic matters are more interested in watching television news (rather than the effect going in the other direction).

Spending evenings outside the home is negatively related to civic knowledge in all but four countries, its effect being strongest in England, Estonia and Hong Kong (SAR). Time spent 'hanging out' with peers seems to be detrimental to achievement, although we cannot be sure as to why (see discussion in previous section).

Some of these findings are quite similar to the multivariate analyses of the data from the IEA Civic Education Study of 1971. Expected further education, perception of the encouragement of expression in the classroom as well as interest in public affairs television were consistently positive predictors for the knowledge score in that study (see Torney, Oppenheim & Farnen, 1975, p.137).

Predictors of the Likelihood of Voting in the Sample Containing 28 Countries

Civic knowledge is the most important variable in explaining the expectation of voting in the future in the calibration sample. Students with higher knowledge scores are more likely to expect to vote when they become adults. The second most important predictor in this model is the student's report of whether he or she has learned in school about the importance of voting. Frequency of watching television news also has a considerable positive relation to the expectation to vote. Perception of an open classroom climate, expected education, and reported participation in a school council/parliament have small positive effects. The effects of home literacy resources, gender and students' reports of spending evenings outside their homes are almost negligible (see Figure 8.1).

Predictors of the Likelihood of Voting within Individual Countries

Table 8.2 presents the model results for the students' expectations that they will vote. The explained variance ranges from 9 percent in Cyprus and 13 percent in Bulgaria and Romania to 28 percent in Belgium (French) and the United States; the median is 20 percent. The score on the civic knowledge test is a significant and positive predictor in every country. It is especially strong in Australia, Belgium (French), the Czech Republic, Estonia and Sweden.

The only other predictor that is significant in every country is the students' reports of having learned about the importance of voting in school. This

Table 8.2 Regression Models for Likelihood to Vote Within Individual Countries

Predictor variables	Australia	Belgium (French)	Bulgaria	Chile	Colombia	Cyprus	Czech Republic	Denmark	England	Estonia	Finland	Germany	Greece	Hong Kong (SAR)	Hungary	Italy	Latvia	Lithuania	Norway	Poland	Portugal	Romania	Russian Federation	Slovak Republic	Slovenia	Sweden	Switzerland	United States
Gender (Female)	-	.08	-	-	-	-	-	-	-	.06	-	-.04	.07	-	-	-	.09	-	-	.07	-	-	-	-	-	.08	-	-
Home Literacy	-	-	-	-	-	-	-	.08	.08	-	-	.11	-	-	-	-	-	-	-	.13	-	-	-	-	-	.12	.13	.12
Expected Years of Education	-	.10	-	-	-	-	.13	.11	.08	.07	.18	-	-	-	-	.10	.14	-	.09	-	.08	-	-	.10	.12	-	.11	.09
Open Classroom Climate	.15	-	-	.11	.16	.10	-	.11	.09	.08	-	.08	.17	.14	.09	.08	.14	.09	.08	-	.08	-	.16	.07	.17	.10	-	.15
Learned to Vote	.12	.17	.12	.29	.18	.09	.23	.15	.16	.22	.29	.20	.09	.18	.17	.16	.20	.08	.15	.14	.14	.17	.13	.15	.17	.20	.20	.20
Student Council/Parliament	-	-	-	-	-	-	-	-	-	-	-	-	-	-	-	-	-	-	-	-	-	-	-	-	-	-	-	.07
Spending Evenings Outside	-.06	-	-	-	-	-	-	-	-	-	-	-	-	-	-	-	-	-	-	-	-	-	-	-	-	-	-	-
Watching TV News	.18	.16	.17	.09	.14	.16	.10	.15	.17	.13	-	.09	.15	.17	.14	.14	.18	.20	.16	.16	.11	.12	.17	.15	.15	.12	-	.13
Civic Knowledge	.27	.27	.18	.15	.14	.13	.32	.23	.21	.27	.12	.26	.20	.20	.20	.26	.19	.20	.25	.23	.22	.21	.16	.18	.17	.27	.17	.21
R²	.26	.28	.13	.18	.15	.09	.27	.21	.21	.22	.20	.21	.16	.20	.18	.21	.21	.16	.21	.20	.14	.13	.17	.15	.15	.27	.16	.28
Weighted N	2519	1477	2020	4608	4276	2773	3017	2256	2126	2653	2180	2926	2971	3751	3009	2956	1864	2453	2440	2954	2659	2540	1810	3171	2542	2120	2167	2168

NOTE: Standardized (beta) regression coefficients. Non-significant coefficients were omitted (-).
The standard errors were estimated using a jackknife procedure for complex sampling; significance tests corrected for multiple comparisons.
Listwise exclusion of missing values.

Source: IEA Civic Education Study, Standard Population of 14-year-olds tested in 1999.

variable is especially important in Chile and Finland, where it is the most substantial predictor. It may be, however, that students who wish to appear engaged in activities that are socially desirable to teachers or other adults respond that they are taught to vote and also that they plan to vote. Future analysis that takes the multi-level structure into account will be especially important in giving insight into the importance of these school factors.

The perception of an open classroom climate has a significant positive effect on the willingness to vote as an adult in 20 countries. Reported participation in a student council or parliament appears as a predictor only in the United States. School parliament did appear as a modest predictor in the previously discussed model based on the calibration sample. This difference in findings may result in part from the fact that school parliaments have not been organized on a widespread basis in some countries. Future analysis should explore the availability of such organizations together with students' reports of their own membership.

Home literacy resources have a moderate positive effect on the reported likelihood of voting in six countries: Denmark, England, Germany, Sweden, Switzerland and the United States. Gender (female) has a significant positive effect in six countries; in these countries female students are more likely to state their expectation of voting in the future than males. In Germany, males are more likely to say that they will vote when they are adults. In half of the countries, expected further education is positively related to expectations to vote; this effect is strongest in Finland. The frequency of watching television news is a significant positive predictor in all but two countries. Spending evenings outside the home is a negative predictor only in Australia.

Four variables are significant predictors of the likelihood of voting in 20 countries or more. These are civic knowledge; the report of the emphasis that schools place on importance of voting as a learning objective; the report of an open climate for classroom discussion; and frequency of watching television news. Three out of four of these are school-related variables.

SUMMARY

A major finding from analysis of the model is the strong relationship between civic knowledge and expectations of participating in elections in the future. The more young people know about the functioning and the values of democracy, the more they expect to exercise this fundamental right of an adult citizen. This reinforces the importance of high-quality and motivating civic education programs to foster knowledge of content and skills in interpreting political communication. The fact that civic knowledge and learning about voting in school are consistent predictors in all the countries suggests that schools play a multifaceted role in this area. Another finding relating to schools is that an open classroom climate is important in fostering both knowledge and intentions to vote, as it was in the 1971 IEA Civic Education Study. Finally, there is the role of the media. The consumption of television news has a positive effect on both civic knowledge and intention to vote in the large majority of the countries participating in this study.

These findings concerning school effects are clear in this analysis in which other factors such as home literacy resources and expected further education are held constant. We can also look at the analysis in another way. When school factors are held constant, students from homes with low educational support and those who do not expect to continue their education have lower knowledge scores in nearly all countries and lower expressed interest in voting in some countries.

These analyses could be refined in many ways. Multi-level analysis would provide clarification of some of the results relating to factors such as classroom climate, participation in a school council or parliament, and opportunity to learn about voting in school. Models showing the ways that civic engagement may foster knowledge should be examined. Different predictors could be included (newspaper reading, a score including activities additional to participation in the school parliament, confidence in the effectiveness of participation, and amount of discussion in the family, to name only a few). Future international publications will include some of these analyses. National volumes can provide in-depth analyses that include variables that were not available across the entire sample of countries (such as ethnic group or type and number of civic-related classes taken).

NOTES

1   The computation of standard errors was done with the program WESVAR 2.11.

2   Although the international Rasch score for the knowledge dimensions is a continuous variable, the item measuring students' expectations to vote is an ordinal four-point-scale. This variable and some others in the analysis were treated as if they were continuous.

CHAPTER 9

The Teaching of
Civic Education

**Bruno Losito and
Heinrich Mintrop**

HIGHLIGHTS RELATING TO TEACHING CIVIC EDUCATION

- There is strong consensus among teachers in all countries that civic education matters a great deal for both students and the country and has its rightful place in the curriculum. However, except for a few countries, there is no overwhelming sentiment that civic education should be its own subject.

- According to teachers in many countries, civic education instruction emphasizes knowledge transmission in reality; by contrast, teachers tend to have a vision that emphasizes critical thinking or values education. Reality and vision are thus incongruent.

- The topics of civic education content that teachers deem important and feel confident teaching are those that receive the most coverage in their classes. This pattern holds across all countries. National history, human and citizens' rights, and environmental concerns are the top-ranking topics; international and social welfare topics are those at the bottom.

- Teacher-centered methods predominate in civic education classrooms according to teacher testimony across many countries. Use of textbooks and recitation are especially prevalent. Written essays and oral participation are the most frequently mentioned forms of assessment. Overall, the degree of standardization of assessment within countries is not very high. Teachers draw from official sources as much as from self-generated sources for civic education material. They heed official authorities, but also see room for negotiations with students.

- Teachers of civic education come to the field from a wide variety of subject-matter backgrounds. Across countries, they nevertheless feel quite confident about their ability to teach in the field. However, in many countries, teachers' most urgent needs for improving civic education revolve around core concerns of content, namely better materials and more subject-matter training.

The IEA Civic Education Study concentrates on students, their civic knowledge, skills and attitudes. Although the study's data from teachers cannot be used to explain student learning, they can illuminate conditions under which civic education instruction takes place in participating countries and thus help readers interpret findings from the previous chapters. Moreover, data collected from teachers are useful in that they can be read as glimpses into the world of civic education teaching.

THE SAMPLE

In a loosely bounded curricular field such as civic education, it is a particular challenge to draw a sample of teachers that is comparable across countries. We knew from Phase 1 case study data that in some countries civic education is affiliated with history; in other countries it is taught by teachers certified to teach mother tongue; or it may actually be integrated into mother tongue instruction. For some countries, civic education is lodged in the domain of religious instruction, while for others it has been developed as a specific amalgamated school subject called social studies that draws teachers from multiple social science disciplinary backgrounds. In some instances, civic education is constructed as an encompassing cross-curricular concern of the whole school. In this case, teachers from all disciplinary backgrounds are seen as obligated to teach in the field.

To ensure a comparable sample across countries, a subject allocation grid was composed that listed the topics from which items for the cognitive part of the student questionnaire were drawn. National Research Coordinators were asked to identify which teachers, teaching which subjects, were primarily responsible for covering these topics in their countries. Each sampled school was asked to administer the teacher questionnaire to three such teachers. Schools were to choose their teachers in this sequence:

1. Three teachers of civic education-related subjects teaching the tested class of students.

2. If three teachers could not be selected this way, then other teachers of civic education-related subjects of a parallel, previous or following grade within the school.

The second condition applied to almost all countries. Selected teachers who declined to participate were not substituted. Thus, the questionnaire was administered to both teachers 'linked' and 'not linked' to the tested class. The analysis for this report, however, is restricted to teachers who reported that they were linked to the tested class.

Because the selection procedure for teacher questionnaires was based on participating students, the sampled teachers do not necessarily represent all teachers from civic-related subjects in a country, but the teachers of the representative samples of *students* sampled for this study. It is important to note that the unit of analysis for all results presented in this chapter is the student and not the teacher. Teacher results were weighted with the number of students they teach. If a student was taught by more than one teacher, the student's weight was distributed equally between the teachers who were teaching the student.[1] All means and percentages describe teachers' reports according to representative student samples and not a representative sample of teachers.

SUBJECT-MATTER BACKGROUND AND CONFIDENCE TO TEACH CIVIC EDUCATION

In the Phase 1 case study reports, experts from many countries described a tenuous disciplinary and subject-matter background of civic education teachers and voiced strong concern about the insufficient training of civic education teachers that leaves them lacking a solid knowledge base in civic education subject matter. The questionnaire therefore inquired about teachers' subject-matter background, their work experience in education generally and in the field of civic education specifically, their training, and their confidence in teaching the field.

What Subjects Constitute the Teaching of Civic Education?

Respondents were asked what civic-related subjects they were teaching at the time of data collection. Using as our basis the sampled teachers' responses, we composed a profile for each country that indicates from which subjects civic education instruction primarily draws. We identified four different profiles: (i) a strong focus on history, (ii) a strong combination of history and civic education, (iii) and (iv) a pattern with no clear emphasis among subjects or disciplines, but which we differentiated into two types, one with and one without religion/ethics in the mix. In most countries, civic education drew from a variety of subjects. Hungary is a prime example of a country in which the civic education teacher sample was very history-based. Australia and Greece are examples of a close combination of history and civics, while religion and ethics, according to teachers' responses, played a considerable role as constituting subjects in Belgium (French), Cyprus, Lithuania, Norway, Slovenia and Sweden.

Table 9.1 shows that for teachers in all countries, the mean number of years in education exceeds the mean number of years of teaching civic education. In all likelihood, a subject different from civic education brought many teachers into their career. While the discrepancies are small for most Western European countries, they are large for all of the participating Eastern European countries, except Bulgaria, Romania and the Slovak Republic. In many Eastern European countries as well as in Chile and Cyprus, there is a five- to ten-year gap, on average, between mean years of work experience in education and mean years of work experience in civic education instruction. Presumably, in the Eastern European countries, large numbers of experienced teachers switched into the civic education field during the last decade and a half when these countries experienced a major regime change. The Lithuania responses show an extreme case of a recently composed teaching force in civic education.

How Confident Do Teachers Feel about Teaching Civic Education Content?

For each country, we computed a score based on teachers' sense of confidence in 20 different civic education topics. We calculated the score by averaging national means for each topic and then computing an average across all topic means. The scale ranged from 1 to 4. The confidence scores in Table 9.1 show that in most countries teachers feel fairly confident teaching civic education. Confidence among sampled teachers from Belgium (French) and Hong Kong (SAR) is relatively low while it is relatively high among teachers from Australia, Cyprus, Germany, Greece, Romania and the Slovak Republic. At the country level, confidence in teaching civic education does not seem to be related either to length of work experience in civic education or participation in professional development (Table 9.1). Countries with low mean work experience in civic education and low participation in professional development (for example, Cyprus and Greece) have a fairly high confidence score, as do countries with higher mean years of work experience and higher participation rates in professional development (for example, Australia and the Slovak Republic).

Table 9.1 Teacher Characteristics

Country	Mean Work Experience (years)		Participation in In-service (in percent)	Mean Confidence Score*	N**
	Total	Civic Education			
Australia	15 (0.7)	14 (0.8)	62 (3.8)	3.0	261
Belgium (French)	19 (1.0)	17 (1.1)	12 (2.6)	2.3	202
Bulgaria	17 (0.6)	15 (0.5)	34 (4.7)	2.6	381
Chile	20 (0.7)	12 (0.8)	8 (1.4)	2.9	455
Cyprus	15 (0.5)	9 (0.7)	15 (2.1)	3.1	292
Czech Republic	19 (0.8)	11 (0.6)	41 (3.1)	2.8	379
Denmark	19 (0.7)	17 (0.6)	100 (0.0)	2.9	328
England	17 (0.6)	14 (0.6)	48 (2.8)	2.9	352
Estonia	21 (0.9)	11 (0.9)	24 (2.3)	2.5	305
Finland	15 (0.8)	14 (0.8)	72 (4.3)	2.9	158
Germany	20 (0.8)	17 (0.8)	22 (2.9)	3.0	246
Greece	13 (0.6)	11 (0.5)	2 (0.9)	3.0	282
Hong Kong (SAR)	12 (0.4)	8 (0.3)	28 (2.2)	2.4	442
Hungary	19 (0.9)	13 (0.8)	28 (3.9)	2.8	149
Italy	16 (0.6)	14 (0.6)	41 (3.1)	2.9	279
Latvia	19 (0.8)	12 (0.8)	56 (3.0)	2.7	342
Lithuania	17 (0.7)	5 (0.6)	49 (3.4)	2.7	303
Norway	18 (0.7)	16 (0.7)	6 (1.7)	2.8	329
Poland	18 (0.7)	13 (0.6)	99 (0.6)	2.8	377
Portugal	9 (0.4)	9 (0.5)	19 (2.0)	2.5	421
Romania	21 (0.7)	17 (0.8)	45 (3.2)	3.0	364
Russian Federation	19 (0.9)	8 (0.7)	42 (3.9)	2.9	233
Slovak Republic	20 (0.7)	16 (0.6)	43 (3.0)	3.0	371
Slovenia	17 (0.5)	8 (0.5)	26 (2.1)	2.9	392
Sweden	14 (1.9)	13 (1.8)	22 (3.7)	2.7	154
Switzerland	19 (0.8)	16 (0.8)	19 (3.3)	2.6	263

( ) Standard errors appear in parentheses.
Means and percentages weighted according to student weights.
* International mean = 2.8. Standard errors < 0.01 for all countries.
** Number of (unweighted) respondents.

Source: IEA Civic Education Study, Standard Population of 14-year-olds tested in 1999.

The teacher questionnaire contained other measures of teachers' training and disciplinary background, but for the most part the data we collected through open response questions were difficult to interpret outside the national context. The enormous variability among countries in the institutional arrangements for civic education made it impossible to standardize these data for the international report. We therefore refer readers to future country reports for further analyses.

CIVIC EDUCATION INSTRUCTION

We were able to gain a rough sketch of civic education instruction across participating countries by asking teachers and schools what content they cover, what methods they use, how they assess students in civic education and from what sources they draw when they prepare for their civic education lessons. To better understand the way civic education content is delivered to students, we asked teachers how frequently they use a variety of teaching methods. In case study reports from Phase 1, country experts ventured that civic education lessons lack variety in instructional formats and are mostly teacher-centered. Phase 1 reports also alerted us to the problematic role of assessments in civic education. In some country reports, a lack of formal assessments was seen as an indication of the diminished status of the subject and the diminished importance attached to civic education knowledge.

It was noted in Phase 1 country reports that civic education content is often less codified and less formalized compared to other subjects. This, the reports suggested, leaves it to teachers to select materials that they deem appropriate. In the teacher questionnaire, we asked teachers about their use of teacher-made materials and unofficial sources versus packaged materials and official sources. Teacher discretion in the selection of materials may have the positive consequence of giving teachers increased autonomy, but it may also portend an insufficient material base for instruction, as some country reports noted. This question was further explored when we asked teachers to check those areas in which they saw the greatest need for improvement.

What Is the Content of Civic Education Instruction and How Do Teachers Gauge Students' Opportunity to Learn this Content?

The questionnaire asked teachers to respond to 20 civic education topics by assessing each topic's importance, their confidence in teaching it, and their students' opportunity to learn it. The topics covered areas such as history, political systems, citizens' and human rights, economic affairs, international affairs, and media.

Table 9.2 indicates that 16 of the 20 listed topics have mean importance ratings of 3.0 or higher, indicating that teachers think these topics are important ones to teach. Using the same mean criterion, teachers describe themselves as confident in teaching only five topics, and believe that students have considerable opportunity to learn only one topic (national history).

Topics vary with regard to teachers' coverage of them and students' opportunity to learn them (see Table 9.2 and Table E.1 in Appendix E). The topics teachers believe to be the most important are those they are most likely to cover with students. Teachers rank history and citizens' and human rights as well as environmental issues at the top of their importance list and estimated coverage list. They deem topics in the areas of international and economic affairs less important and are also less likely to cover them. In most countries, they deem international migration and labor unions very low in importance relative to other topics, and give them relatively little coverage. Teachers' low ratings for international organizations in many European countries contrast with the heightened concern that Phase 1 experts from these countries attached to the supra-national 'European dimension' in civic education content.

Which Methods of Instruction Do Teachers of Civic Education Use in Their Lessons?

Ten different methods were listed on the teacher questionnaire (eight of which appear in Table 9.3). The teachers were asked to rate these methods according to the frequency with which they use them in the classroom. In a large majority of the 26 countries, there is evidence of a preponderance of teacher-

Table 9.2 Teachers' Assessment of Civic Education Content: Importance, Confidence to Teach and Opportunity to Learn

	Topic	Importance[1]	Confidence to Teach[2]	Opportunity to Learn[3]
National History	National History	3.4	3.2	3.0
Constitution and Political Systems	National Constitution	3.3	2.8	2.4
	Conceptions of Democracy	3.1	2.8	2.3
	Electoral Systems	3.0	2.8	2.3
	Political Systems	3.0	2.8	2.3
	Judicial System	3.0	2.5	2.1
Citizen and Human Rights	Citizens Rights	3.6	3.1	2.7
	Human Rights	3.6	3.0	2.7
	Equal Opportunities	3.2	3.0	2.5
	Cultural Differences	3.2	2.8	2.5
International Organizations and Relations	International Organizations	2.9	2.6	2.3
	International Problems	3.1	2.7	2.3
	Migration	2.7	2.6	2.3
Economics and Welfare	Economic Issues	2.9	2.6	2.3
	Social Welfare	3.0	2.7	2.3
	Trade Unions	2.6	2.6	2.0
Media	Dangers of Propaganda	3.3	2.9	2.4
	Media	3.3	3.0	2.6
Others	Environmental Issues	3.4	2.9	2.9
	Civic Virtues	3.2	2.9	2.6

1 Mean of students' teacher ratings on four-point-scale (1='not important' to 4='very important') weighted according to student weights.

2 Mean of students' teacher ratings on four-point-scale (1='not at all' to 4='very confident') weighted according to student weights.

3 Mean of students' teacher ratings on four-point-scale (1='not at all' to 4='very much [opportunity]') weighted according to student weights.

Standard errors < 0.01 for all countries.

Source: IEA Civic Education Study, Standard Population of 14-year-olds tested in 1999.

centered formats. A combination of textbooks with recitation (and sometimes worksheets) is used with the highest frequency. In Australia, Chile, Denmark, Hong Kong (SAR), Norway, Poland, Slovenia and Sweden students are also taught using group work. Across countries, teachers testify to a fairly frequent occurrence of discussions of controversial issues in their civic education classrooms, and a far less frequent occurrence for role-plays and projects.

How Do Teachers of Civic Education Assess Their Students?

Teachers were asked to check which forms of assessment they primarily use in civic education. The questionnaire gave respondents six options of which they were to select two. This forced-choice format resulted in a fairly high number of missing values in some countries. Data from these countries therefore were omitted from the analysis.

Across countries, the most common form of assessment is a combination of written composition and oral participation (see Table E.2 in Appendix E). Although overall not as popular as essays and oral participation, multiple

Table 9.3 Teachers' Reports on Frequency of Instructional Methods*

Country	Textbooks	Recitation	Lectures	Worksheets	Group Work	Projects	Role Play	Controvers. Issues
Australia	2.6 (0.07)	2.9 (0.06)	2.3 (0.05)	2.7 (0.06)	2.8 (0.05)	2.7 (0.06)	2.4 (0.06)	2.8 (0.05)
Belgium (French)	1.6 (0.08)	2.9 (0.07)	1.7 (0.08)	2.7 (0.09)	2.3 (0.08)	2.2 (0.07)	1.6 (0.07)	2.5 (0.06)
Bulgaria	3.4 (0.05)	3.3 (0.03)	2.7 (0.06)	3.0 (0.06)	2.3 (0.06)	2.3 (0.07)	2.0 (0.06)	2.9 (0.05)
Chile	3.0 (0.08)	3.1 (0.05)	2.6 (0.06)	3.1 (0.05)	3.2 (0.06)	2.8 (0.06)	2.8 (0.07)	3.0 (0.06)
Cyprus	3.7 (0.04)	3.2 (0.05)	2.7 (0.06)	2.7 (0.05)	2.3 (0.05)	2.2 (0.04)	1.7 (0.04)	2.7 (0.06)
Czech Republic	2.7 (0.05)	3.1 (0.04)	2.3 (0.06)	2.1 (0.05)	2.2 (0.04)	2.1 (0.04)	2.2 (0.05)	2.7 (0.07)
Denmark	2.6 (0.04)	2.5 (0.04)	2.1 (0.05)	2.1 (0.05)	2.9 (0.04)	2.7 (0.04)	1.9 (0.05)	2.8 (0.05)
England	2.4 (0.05)	2.9 (0.04)	1.9 (0.04)	2.8 (0.05)	2.5 (0.05)	2.4 (0.04)	2.3 (0.04)	2.7 (0.04)
Estonia	3.1 (0.04)	3.1 (0.04)	2.3 (0.06)	2.6 (0.06)	2.3 (0.05)	2.1 (0.03)	2.2 (0.05)	2.7 (0.04)
Finland	2.8 (0.06)	3.1 (0.05)	2.4 (0.06)	1.9 (0.07)	2.4 (0.06)	2.1 (0.04)	1.6 (0.06)	2.9 (0.07)
Germany	3.0 (0.06)	2.8 (0.04)	1.5 (0.05)	3.0 (0.05)	2.3 (0.05)	2.0 (0.05)	1.9 (0.06)	2.9 (0.06)
Greece	3.5 (0.04)	3.5 (0.04)	2.7 (0.07)	2.9 (0.06)	2.0 (0.05)	2.2 (0.05)	1.3 (0.03)	3.1 (0.06)
Hong Kong (SAR)	2.8 (0.06)	3.7 (0.02)	2.6 (0.06)	3.4 (0.04)	3.0 (0.04)	2.7 (0.04)	2.5 (0.04)	3.0 (0.03)
Hungary	3.1 (0.06)	2.9 (0.06)	2.3 (0.06)	2.0 (0.06)	2.3 (0.05)	2.1 (0.05)	1.9 (0.05)	2.9 (0.05)
Italy	3.1 (0.05)	3.2 (0.04)	2.9 (0.05)	2.4 (0.05)	2.4 (0.05)	2.0 (0.05)	1.6 (0.05)	3.0 (0.04)
Latvia	3.1 (0.05)	3.0 (0.04)	2.3 (0.04)	2.7 (0.05)	2.4 (0.04)	2.2 (0.03)	2.1 (0.04)	2.6 (0.04)
Lithuania	2.8 (0.05)	2.9 (0.05)	2.1 (0.05)	3.0 (0.06)	2.5 (0.05)	2.0 (0.04)	2.3 (0.05)	3.0 (0.04)
Norway	3.2 (0.03)	2.7 (0.05)	2.5 (0.04)	3.0 (0.04)	2.7 (0.04)	2.6 (0.05)	2.0 (0.04)	2.5 (0.04)
Poland	3.1 (0.08)	3.3 (0.06)	2.8 (0.08)	2.5 (0.06)	3.1 (0.05)	2.9 (0.06)	2.7 (0.08)	3.2 (0.07)
Portugal	3.3 (0.04)	3.1 (0.04)	2.5 (0.04)	2.9 (0.03)	2.3 (0.02)	2.2 (0.02)	1.9 (0.03)	2.5 (0.03)
Romania	3.5 (0.05)	3.5 (0.04)	3.2 (0.05)	2.5 (0.05)	2.2 (0.06)	1.9 (0.04)	2.1 (0.05)	3.0 (0.05)
Russian Federation	3.1 (0.07)	3.3 (0.04)	2.9 (0.05)	2.6 (0.07)	2.1 (0.05)	2.2 (0.05)	2.1 (0.05)	2.8 (0.05)
Slovak Republic	3.3 (0.04)	3.1 (0.04)	1.8 (0.05)	2.1 (0.05)	2.3 (0.04)	2.2 (0.03)	2.4 (0.05)	2.4 (0.04)
Slovenia	2.7 (0.05)	2.6 (0.04)	1.9 (0.05)	2.8 (0.05)	2.7 (0.04)	2.2 (0.03)	2.3 (0.04)	3.0 (0.03)
Sweden	3.0 (0.07)	2.6 (0.10)	2.2 (0.07)	2.5 (0.08)	2.7 (0.07)	2.7 (0.07)	2.0 (0.06)	2.5 (0.09)
Switzerland	2.6 (0.07)	2.6 (0.05)	1.6 (0.05)	2.9 (0.05)	2.5 (0.06)	2.2 (0.04)	1.9 (0.06)	2.5 (0.05)
International Sample	**3.0 (0.01)**	**3.0 (0.01)**	**2.4 (0.01)**	**2.6 (0.01)**	**2.5 (0.01)**	**2.3 (0.01)**	**2.1 (0.01)**	**2.8 (0.01)**

() Standard errors appear in parentheses.

* Mean of students' teachers' ratings on four-point-scale (1 'never' to 4 'very often') weighted according to student sample weights.

Source: IEA Civic Education Study, Standard Population of 14-year-olds tested in 1999.

choice tests are a more popular feature in a number of Eastern European countries but are a negligible feature in most Western European countries. Within participating countries, variety prevails over uniformity in the forms of assessment used in civic education. Teachers seem to have wide discretion in selecting an appropriate way of assessing students. Hence, no category was chosen by the large majority of teachers in a given country, a pattern that could have been expected if mandatory forms of assessment existed for this field, as they may exist in core subjects. The strength of oral participation bolsters the view of civic education as a pragmatic and highly communicative field of instruction.

What Sources Do Teachers Use to Prepare for Civic Education-Related Activities?

The questionnaire asked respondents to rate the level of importance they would attribute to eight different sources. Some of these are more externally generated (for example, official curricula, textbooks) while others are more internally generated (for example, teachers' own ideas, self-produced materials).

When teachers plan for civic education, they draw from a variety of sources. The extent to which they draw from internally and externally generated materials is in balance in most countries (see Table E.3, Appendix E). Media and original sources are sometimes even more important than official curricula and textbooks. Materials provided by publishers or foundations seem to be relatively less important to sampled teachers from all countries in this sample. Experts from some post-Communist countries interviewed during Phase 1 mentioned civic education materials provided by foundations, especially from Western Europe and North America. But there is not a corresponding difference between regions in teachers' reports of the use of commercial or foundation-provided materials. In summary, teachers of civic education seem to have a high degree of flexibility as to the sources for their lesson planning, and they draw from both external and internal sources.

What Needs to Be Most Urgently Improved about Civic Education?

The teacher questionnaire listed ten areas in which respondents might wish for improvement. Teachers were asked to select the top three choices (see Table 9.4).

The top-ranked need encompassed 'better materials and textbooks' followed by 'additional training in content' and 'more time for instruction'. Thus, in many countries, teachers' most urgent needs refer to core activities of the subject, and more strongly to concerns relating to content than to instructional methods. Extension of time for instruction is a priority in some countries. Assistance with special projects and activities is of lesser concern. Some

Table 9.4 Teachers' Reports on Needed Improvements*

Country	Better Materials	More Materials	More Instructional Time	Training in Teaching	Training in Content	More Collegial Cooperation	Special Projects	More Autonomy
Australia	55 (4.0)	19 (3.2)	38 (3.9)	27 (3.4)	36 (3.9)	25 (2.6)	29 (3.7)	10 (2.2)
Belgium (French)	10 (2.7)	27 (5.1)	45 (5.2)	32 (4.9)	43 (5.1)	25 (4.2)	26 (4.5)	13 (2.9)
Chile	37 (3.8)	24 (3.3)	43 (3.7)	44 (3.4)	55 (3.5)	28 (3.0)	14 (2.0)	16 (2.9)
Cyprus	58 (3.1)	9 (1.8)	31 (3.4)	27 (2.6)	31 (3.1)	24 (2.8)	22 (3.0)	27 (3.2)
Czech Republic	51 (4.2)	33 (4.4)	6 (2.1)	29 (2.8)	40 (3.4)	23 (3.3)	17 (3.1)	15 (2.6)
England	40 (2.6)	25 (2.5)	23 (2.3)	32 (2.6)	47 (3.0)	33 (3.0)	26 (2.3)	15 (2.2)
Estonia	61 (3.4)	25 (2.9)	12 (2.6)	36 (3.7)	36 (3.3)	34 (3.4)	19 (2.5)	17 (2.7)
Finland	34 (4.4)	11 (2.7)	55 (5.0)	27 (4.1)	19 (3.4)	26 (3.8)	37 (4.6)	2 (1.1)
Germany	42 (4.8)	6 (1.8)	43 (4.0)	41 (4.7)	25 (3.9)	22 (3.5)	37 (4.4)	24 (3.9)
Greece	55 (3.5)	8 (1.7)	27 (3.0)	36 (3.2)	54 (3.2)	11 (2.1)	31 (3.6)	12 (2.2)
Hong Kong (SAR)	53 (2.3)	23 (2.4)	39 (2.6)	41 (2.4)	50 (2.9)	22 (2.2)	8 (1.4)	17 (1.9)
Hungary	72 (3.7)	9 (2.3)	53 (4.6)	29 (3.9)	52 (4.0)	18 (3.3)	17 (3.2)	7 (2.2)
Italy	19 (2.5)	6 (1.6)	50 (3.4)	41 (3.4)	14 (2.1)	55 (3.6)	26 (3.4)	16 (2.5)
Norway	26 (2.9)	10 (1.9)	13 (2.2)	55 (2.9)	52 (3.2)	41 (3.0)	18 (2.8)	17 (2.2)
Romania	71 (3.0)	25 (2.6)	23 (2.6)	17 (2.2)	20 (2.5)	34 (3.3)	17 (2.5)	26 (2.6)
Russian Federation	57 (3.7)	46 (4.4)	55 (4.0)	38 (3.7)	36 (2.6)	13 (2.0)	3 (1.2)	12 (2.3)
Slovenia	47 (3.1)	23 (2.4)	9 (1.5)	41 (2.9)	54 (3.2)	31 (2.6)	28 (2.5)	13 (2.1)
Sweden	23 (4.9)	12 (4.2)	46 (6.0)	27 (5.1)	54 (6.2)	38 (5.5)	44 (5.5)	8 (3.4)

( ) Standard errors appear in parentheses. Percentages based on valid responses.

* Percentage of students whose teachers chose a specific improvement as one of their three choices.

Data are not available for Bulgaria, Denmark, Latvia, Lithuania, Poland, Portugal, Slovak Republic, Switzerland.

Source: IEA Civic Education Study, Standard Population of 14-year-olds tested in 1999.

countries, however, differ from this pattern. For example, teachers in Italy are especially concerned about improved collegial cooperation. In Sweden, the number of teachers expressing need for support in special projects is relatively high. Teachers in most countries express relatively little concern with autonomy in decision-making, an area that has received much attention from policy-makers. According to civic education teachers, improvements should be made that have an impact on daily classroom experience by enhancing their subject-matter expertise, the quality of materials available to students, and time available for instruction.

THE INSTITUTIONAL FRAMEWORK OF CIVIC EDUCATION

A repeated theme in the case study reports from Phase 1 was the precarious status held by civic education as a subject in schools. This issue is related to the uncertainty in conceptualizing civic education knowledge due to the amalgamated disciplinary base of the subject and teachers' varied subject-matter backgrounds that we discussed earlier. How, then, do teachers frame civic education in the institutional context of the school? We explored the status and broader conceptualization of civic education in the school by looking at teachers' beliefs about the place of civic education in the curriculum, about the solidity and orientation of civic education knowledge, and about the effect of civic education instruction on students. With regard to its place in the curriculum, civic education may be structured as its own subject, as a field integrated into the social sciences or into the curriculum as a whole, or as a primarily extra-curricular endeavor. Each model may have considerable repercussions for the kinds of knowledge and methods that become emphasized in civic education instruction. Thus, teachers' preferences as to the place of civic education in the curriculum may indicate the degree to which they construct civic education as a traditional subject or as an interdisciplinary set of civic skills or dispositions.

To pursue this line of inquiry further, we explored how teachers conceptualized civic education knowledge and its pedagogical purposes. One dimension of knowledge conceptualization is the degree to which civic education knowledge is seen as contested or consensual. Comparative studies of school subjects (for example, Stodolsky, 1988) have shown that social-science-based subject matter is highly contested relative to other subjects. It is conceivable that this situation may be especially true in countries that have undergone political transitions in the recent past.

Teachers engage in civic education instruction with certain pedagogical purposes in mind. Phase 1 reports mentioned a number of them: transmission of knowledge, exercise of critical thinking, encouragement to undertake political action, and strengthening of values. Many country experts concluded that the prevailing goal of civic education in their country was knowledge transmission.

What Should Be the Place of Civic Education in the Curriculum?

The questionnaire asked respondents to rate the extent of their agreement to four options: should civic education be taught as a separate subject, be integrated into the social sciences, be integrated into all subjects, or be an extracurricular activity? The responses are shown in Table 9.5. It is apparent that the extra-curricular model is the least popular among teachers, and that a model that integrates civic education into other social sciences is the most popular. Civic education as a separate subject is particularly appealing to teachers in the Czech Republic, Estonia, Romania, the Russian Federation and the Slovak Republic, while it holds very little appeal in Denmark and Norway. Generally, when respondents envision a place for civic education in the curriculum, they in some respects reflect the institutional status quo in their countries, that is, they advocate a version of civic education that leans on another social science-based subject while not completely rejecting other options. Overall, the support for civic education as its own subject is overshadowed by teachers' support for the integration model.

How Do Teachers Conceptualize Civic Education Knowledge?

The study inquired about competing versions of civic education knowledge. Civic education knowledge can be constructed as contested. A corresponding emphasis of civic education instruction might be the fostering of critical thinking or political activism. Civic education knowledge can also be constructed as consensual, in which case knowledge transmission may be a more likely emphasis of instruction.

When civic education teachers were asked whether there was broad consensus in their society as to what is worth learning in civic education, they tended to doubt societal consensus. Skepticism about societal consensus regarding civic education knowledge prevails among teachers from established western democracies as well as post-Communist countries. This skepticism notwithstanding, respondents believe that agreement on what is worth learning is nevertheless possible. A great majority of teachers across many participating countries stress official curricula as points of orientation. This orientation, however, does not stand in the way of teachers' willingness to negotiate with students over what is to be studied in civic education (see Table E.4, Appendix E).

Another way of understanding teachers' conceptualization of civic education knowledge is to look at the broad objectives of instruction revolving around knowledge transmission, critical thinking, political participation, and values. The questionnaire asked respondents to share their perceptions of which of these four broad objectives is currently emphasized in their schools and which they would like to see emphasized. The question was presented in a forced choice format with only one possible choice for the '*is*' and '*should*' columns respectively. Many teachers presumably felt unable to make a single choice of which objective is and which should be accorded the most emphasis. As a result, the number of missing cases is quite high.

Table 9.6 reveals an interesting pattern. It can be seen that teachers overwhelmingly report that most emphasis in civic education instruction is placed on knowledge transmission. By contrast, the percentages of teachers who think that this ought to be the case are very low, making the differences rather stark between responses on what is and what ought to be. In 14 countries not even 10 percent of responding teachers feel that the greatest

Table 9.5 Teachers' Reports on their Preference for the Place of Civic Education in the Curriculum

Country	Percentage of Students whose Teachers 'Agree' or 'Strongly Agree' that Civic Education Should Be Taught...			
	as a specific subject	integrated into social sciences	integrated into all subjects	as an extra-curricular activity
Australia	46 (3.7)	89 (2.2)	58 (3.5)	14 (2.8)
Belgium (French)	57 (4.6)	92 (2.3)	72 (4.8)	28 (4.5)
Bulgaria	56 (3.4)	76 (3.1)	40 (4.5)	26 (3.8)
Chile	64 (3.1)	84 (2.5)	80 (2.9)	13 (2.3)
Cyprus	72 (2.9)	78 (2.4)	49 (3.2)	34 (3.2)
Czech Republic	86 (2.3)	67 (4.0)	49 (3.9)	12 (2.1)
Denmark	4 (1.4)	94 (1.6)	64 (3.3)	6 (1.6)
England	33 (3.0)	90 (1.7)	79 (2.1)	23 (2.9)
Estonia	85 (2.3)	88 (2.1)	58 (3.6)	26 (3.3)
Finland	61 (4.4)	77 (4.0)	54 (4.9)	7 (2.6)
Germany	66 (3.9)	75 (4.2)	59 (4.2)	85 (3.4)
Greece	73 (3.5)	82 (2.8)	63 (3.3)	26 (3.1)
Hong Kong (SAR)	68 (2.8)	84 (1.9)	69 (2.1)	57 (2.4)
Hungary	49 (4.1)	78 (3.2)	28 (3.7)	6 (2.1)
Italy	50 (3.5)	80 (2.5)	59 (3.3)	63 (3.5)
Latvia	45 (2.8)	92 (1.7)	69 (2.6)	41 (3.4)
Lithuania	73 (2.3)	81 (2.6)	50 (3.4)	35 (3.0)
Norway	5 (1.3)	97 (0.9)	82 (2.5)	5 (1.4)
Poland	71 (3.7)	71 (2.5)	43 (2.7)	5 (1.4)
Portugal	56 (2.8)	71 (2.6)	90 (1.5)	16 (2.1)
Romania	85 (2.2)	64 (3.7)	41 (2.9)	10 (1.8)
Russian Federation	88 (2.5)	83 (3.5)	50 (3.4)	59 (4.8)
Slovak Republic	94 (1.4)	40 (3.6)	28 (3.2)	7 (1.5)
Slovenia	57 (2.8)	83 (2.1)	67 (2.4)	11 (1.7)
Sweden	33 (6.2)	94 (3.7)	85 (4.6)	4 (1.6)
Switzerland	24 (2.8)	95 (1.4)	46 (3.9)	78 (3.1)

() Standard errors appear in parentheses. Percentages based on valid responses.

Source: IEA Civic Education Study, Standard Population of 14-year-olds tested in 1999.

emphasis should be placed on knowledge transmission. In most of these countries, the majority feels that knowledge is the current emphasis, however. In Italy, the tension between reality and vision is more acute than in any other of the participating countries: Teachers, teaching 82 percent of the Italian students, think that knowledge transmission guides instruction, but a proportion of teachers, teaching only 2 percent of the students, feel this is the ideal.

Across countries, *critical thinking* is the most often selected vision, but not decidedly so. Values and, to a lesser degree, *political participation* find approval among sizable numbers of teachers as well. In a few countries, such as Belgium (French), Bulgaria, Chile, England and Slovenia, a plurality of teachers report that, instead of knowledge transmission, values are in fact emphasized. The discrepancy in these countries between reality and vision is not as great as for countries in which knowledge transmission is reported as the prevailing mode of instruction.

Table 9.6 Teachers' Reports on Emphasis in Civic Education*

Country	Knowledge		Critical Thinking		Participation		Values	
	Is placed	Should be placed	Is placed	Should be placed	Is placed	Should be placed	Is placed	Should be placed
Belgium (French)	24 (7.3)	24 (6.5)	29 (6.5)	23 (6.1)	12 (5.9)	25 (6.5)	34 (7.0)	28 (6.0)
Bulgaria	33 (4.0)	18 (3.3)	22 (4.9)	22 (3.6)	6 (2.0)	25 (4.0)	40 (4.3)	35 (4.7)
Chile	41 (5.6)	13 (3.3)	7 (2.5)	33 (6.5)	6 (2.8)	25 (4.6)	45 (6.2)	29 (5.3)
Cyprus	78 (5.1)	7 (4.2)	4 (2.2)	11 (5.8)	4 (2.0)	59 (9.7)	15 (4.0)	23 (8.1)
Czech Republic	51 (3.3)	3 (1.0)	18 (3.1)	42 (3.5)	4 (2.4)	18 (4.1)	27 (3.7)	38 (3.9)
Denmark	48 (4.1)	10 (2.0)	27 (3.8)	44 (4.3)	2 (1.1)	17 (3.2)	22 (3.3)	28 (3.3)
England	35 (4.0)	12 (2.8)	14 (3.1)	35 (4.2)	9 (2.6)	17 (2.7)	42 (4.6)	37 (4.4)
Estonia	61 (4.8)	5 (1.9)	18 (3.9)	35 (4.7)	4 (1.6)	24 (4.2)	16 (3.5)	36 (5.3)
Finland	79 (3.5)	15 (3.4)	13 (2.5)	59 (4.6)	3 (1.8)	6 (2.2)	5 (1.8)	20 (3.9)
Germany	59 (6.0)	4 (2.5)	21 (5.5)	30 (5.5)	1 (0.1)	44 (5.5)	19 (5.0)	22 (4.9)
Greece	65 (2.9)	9 (2.0)	17 (2.6)	39 (3.2)	5 (1.4)	24 (3.1)	13 (2.0)	28 (3.2)
Hong Kong (SAR)	49 (4.4)	9 (2.9)	10 (2.1)	42 (5.5)	12 (2.7)	6 (2.2)	29 (3.9)	43 (4.9)
Hungary	71 (4.2)	10 (2.7)	12 (2.8)	39 (4.2)	4 (1.8)	23 (3.5)	13 (3.0)	28 (3.8)
Italy	82 (2.7)	2 (0.9)	12 (2.3)	69 (2.8)	1 (0.7)	10 (1.9)	5 (1.6)	19 (2.4)
Latvia	52 (3.6)	8 (1.8)	14 (2.7)	41 (4.5)	11 (2.2)	18 (3.1)	22 (3.3)	32 (3.3)
Lithuania	40 (5.4)	6 (2.2)	16 (3.9)	31 (3.8)	14 (4.4)	32 (4.0)	30 (4.8)	31 (4.2)
Norway	80 (3.6)	7 (2.7)	3 (1.7)	41 (4.8)	3 (1.3)	25 (3.9)	14 (2.9)	28 (3.9)
Portugal	63 (2.9)	40 (2.6)	13 (2.0)	29 (2.6)	4 (1.2)	19 (2.1)	21 (2.6)	12 (2.0)
Romania	77 (2.5)	3 (1.0)	16 (2.5)	43 (4.0)	2 (0.7)	24 (4.3)	5 (1.5)	31 (3.3)
Russian Federation	58 (3.6)	10 (2.2)	11 (3.0)	19 (3.0)	5 (1.7)	11 (2.3)	26 (3.8)	59 (4.3)
Slovak Republic	60 (5.1)	9 (2.0)	17 (3.5)	34 (4.8)	1 (0.9)	17 (3.3)	22 (4.2)	39 (4.7)
Slovenia	30 (3.7)	8 (1.9)	30 (3.5)	34 (3.0)	5 (1.8)	18 (2.4)	35 (3.7)	40 (3.2)
Sweden	71 (6.6)	18 (5.0)	16 (5.0)	60 (6.3)	0 (0.2)	0 (0.2)	13 (4.3)	22 (5.3)
Switzerland	54 (9.0)	9 (4.1)	23 (6.7)	46 (9.2)	5 (3.2)	10 (4.1)	18 (5.5)	36 (7.6)

( ) Standard errors appear in parentheses. Percentages based on valid responses.

The Australian questionnaire used a different format for this question.

Because of the low number of valid responses, data from Poland were omitted.

* Percentage of students whose teachers chose one out of four answers.

Source: IEA Civic Education Study, Standard Population of 14-year-olds tested in 1999.

How Much Does Civic Education Matter?

Fairly uniformly across countries, students are taught by teachers who strongly affirm that schools are places where civic education ought to be taught and can be taught effectively (see Table 9.7). For large proportions of respondents, civic education matters a great deal in facilitating students' civic development, and teachers therefore fulfill an important role for their country.

When asked to assess specific attitudes and skills that make up civic education instruction, the majority of teachers attest to their own effectiveness (see Table E.5, in Appendix E). They agree that students learn to understand people, to cooperate, to solve problems, to protect the environment, to develop concern about the country, and to know the importance of voting. These attitudes are learned in school, according to teachers' judgment, despite the perceived emphasis on knowledge transmission in many countries. An exception is the development of feelings of patriotism and loyalty. A majority of teachers in Western European countries (and Hong Kong/SAR) see little effect of civic education instruction in this area. Attitudes towards patriotism seem to

Table 9.7 Teachers' Reports on the Relevance of Civic Education

Country	Percentage of Students Whose Teachers 'Agree' or 'Strongly Agree' that...		
	teaching civic education makes a difference for students' political and civic development	teaching civic education matters a great deal for our country	schools are irrelevant for the development of students' attitudes and opinions about matters of citizenship
Australia	98 (1.0)	90 (2.0)	5 (1.9)
Belgium (French)	99 (0.5)	94 (1.8)	5 (1.9)
Bulgaria	98 (0.9)	91 (2.3)	15 (4.0)
Chile	83 (2.8)	98 (0.8)	27 (3.6)
Cyprus	65 (2.8)	96 (1.3)	18 (1.9)
Czech Republic	53 (4.3)	81 (2.8)	6 (1.5)
Denmark	94 (1.5)	91 (1.7)	4 (1.4)
England	90 (1.7)	81 (2.3)	9 (1.7)
Estonia	98 (0.9)	94 (1.4)	17 (2.4)
Finland	98 (1.0)	93 (2.3)	2 (0.8)
Germany	88 (3.1)	97 (1.4)	9 (3.0)
Greece	94 (1.6)	86 (2.2)	11 (2.0)
Hong Kong (SAR)	96 (1.0)	96 (1.2)	12 (1.7)
Hungary	94 (2.1)	70 (3.9)	1 (1.0)
Italy	97 (1.0)	95 (1.5)	7 (1.6)
Latvia	99 (0.5)	95 (0.9)	5 (1.2)
Lithuania	99 (0.5)	95 (1.3)	5 (1.5)
Norway	98 (0.7)	96 (1.2)	2 (0.8)
Poland	96 (2.3)	92 (2.4)	7 (2.1)
Portugal	99 (0.4)	98 (0.6)	3 (0.9)
Romania	98 (0.9)	97 (1.0)	15 (2.2)
Russian Federation	98 (1.1)	96 (1.6)	7 (1.2)
Slovenia	87 (1.8)	81 (2.2)	12 (1.9)
Sweden	97 (2.4)	100 (0.5)	14 (2.8)
Switzerland	82 (3.7)	86 (2.5)	12 (3.6)

( ) Standard errors appear in parentheses. Percentages based on valid responses.
Data are not available for Slovak Republic.

Source: IEA Civic Education Study, Standard Population of 14-year-olds tested in 1999.

differentiate teachers from this region from other participating countries. In general, however, teachers across all participating countries testify to the worth of their work and the important status of civic education instruction in schools and society.

VIEWS OF CITIZENSHIP

Teachers' views on what students should learn to become good citizens may strongly influence civic education instruction. The value that teachers place on specific civic behaviors may translate into learning goals and objectives that teachers pursue in their classrooms. Some of these behaviors speak to conventional forms of political allegiance and participation. Others imply a more activist stance. Teachers, as well as students (see Chapter 4), were asked to give their opinion on the same civic behaviors so that cross-referencing would be possible.

What Should Students Learn to Become Good Citizens?

Teachers rated the importance of 15 items that described qualities of a good citizen (eight of which appear in Table 9.8). The item that receives nearly unanimous approval among teachers across all countries is 'knowing about the country's national history'. This response corresponds with the history background of many teachers, and the importance they attach to historical events as a topic of civic education. Students, in contrast, do not see history as such a high priority (refer to Chapter 4). Students and teachers across countries agree, however, about the importance of obedience to the law. Agreement that this item is highly important is almost universal across countries. Protecting the environment and promoting human rights are other highly important qualities of a good citizen according to teachers across most participating countries.

'Joining a political party' is the item universally perceived as least important among the 15 choices. Except for Cyprus, large majorities of teachers reject the importance of party membership. Students also rate party membership as a low priority for good citizenship for adults (see Chapter 4). Responses to 'willingness to serve in the military to defend the country' differ among countries. Ratings from most Western European countries are low. Probably as a reflection of the political situation, willingness to defend one's country receives its highest rating in Cyprus. Teachers in Greece and some Eastern European countries also give a relatively high rating to this item.

SUMMARY

The IEA Civic Education Study was begun with a set of policy-relevant questions. For the teaching of civic education, these questions revolved around teacher preparation and training, characteristics of classroom instruction, the institutional framework of civic education in the organization of schools, and democratic citizenship. We found that subject matter background, work experience in civic education and participation in professional development vary widely across the participating countries. Nevertheless, in most countries, teachers' level of confidence in teaching major civic education topics is fairly high, even though their greatest articulated needs have to do with the provision of better materials, more subject-matter training, and more instructional time. This study seems to suggest that, in a large number of countries, improvement efforts need to concentrate on instructional essentials.

A look at markers of classroom instruction reveals a fairly high level of uniformity across countries and a fairly low level of standardization within countries. In civic education, it seems that teachers have discretion in emphasizing specific topics, choosing materials and forms of assessments and employing instructional methods. Content that teachers deem important tends to get more coverage. In many countries, teachers express willingness to negotiate curricular topics with students. Teachers use self-produced materials and materials gleaned from the media as well as official sources. Teachers across countries also use a variety of assessments, but essays and oral participation prevail. Civic education classrooms appear to be largely teacher-centered, but, according to teachers, this does not preclude discussions of controversial issues.

Table 9.8 Teachers' Perceptions of the Effects of Selected Learning Goals for Good Citizens*

Country	Percentage of Students whose Teachers 'Agree' or 'Strongly Agree' that to Become a Good Adult Citizen Students Should Learn to Recognize the Importance of...							
	knowing national history	obeying the law	joining a political party	serving the military	participating in peaceful protest	promoting human rights	ignoring a law that violated human rights	protecting the environment
Australia	98 (1.2)	97 (1.2)	16 (2.7)	20 (2.9)	83 (2.9)	94 (1.7)	63 (3.8)	98 (1.1)
Belgium (French)	98 (1.0)	98 (1.3)	8 (2.3)	16 (3.6)	74 (4.3)	97 (1.4)	93 (2.2)	97 (1.5)
Bulgaria	99 (0.4)	100 (0.4)	12 (2.3)	89 (1.9)	81 (3.4)	96 (1.0)	84 (2.4)	99 (0.6)
Chile	100 (0.0)	99 (0.6)	18 (2.3)	49 (3.5)	68 (2.9)	96 (1.1)	60 (3.8)	99 (0.9)
Cyprus	100 (0.0)	99 (0.3)	51 (3.4)	98 (0.8)	96 (1.3)	100 (0.0)	85 (2.5)	98 (0.8)
Czech Republic	99 (0.8)	100 (0.3)	6 (1.9)	81 (2.5)	84 (1.9)	95 (1.5)	85 (2.4)	98 (0.9)
Denmark	95 (1.5)	95 (1.3)	16 (2.2)	23 (2.6)	58 (3.1)	84 (2.5)	73 (3.1)	84 (2.5)
England	94 (1.2)	96 (1.3)	16 (2.3)	23 (2.6)	76 (2.5)	81 (2.3)	56 (3.4)	94 (1.5)
Estonia	100 (0.4)	100 (0.4)	11 (2.0)	92 (1.8)	75 (2.6)	93 (1.2)	87 (2.6)	n.a. (n.a.)
Finland	100 (0.0)	100 (0.3)	6 (1.7)	61 (4.5)	58 (4.6)	94 (2.2)	68 (3.9)	92 (2.6)
Germany	99 (0.5)	97 (1.3)	18 (3.3)	44 (4.2)	81 (3.7)	93 (2.1)	74 (4.3)	94 (2.3)
Greece	100 (0.3)	97 (1.2)	19 (2.9)	95 (1.7)	93 (1.7)	99 (0.5)	56 (3.3)	98 (0.8)
Hong Kong (SAR)	97 (0.9)	100 (0.0)	11 (1.4)	55 (2.4)	75 (2.1)	87 (1.8)	46 (2.7)	97 (0.8)
Hungary	100 (0.0)	100 (0.0)	3 (1.4)	60 (3.9)	64 (4.2)	93 (2.1)	30 (3.6)	94 (2.6)
Italy	98 (0.8)	97 (1.0)	13 (2.1)	59 (3.3)	90 (2.1)	96 (1.3)	80 (2.7)	96 (1.4)
Latvia	100 (0.2)	99 (0.4)	13 (2.5)	80 (2.4)	80 (2.7)	94 (1.8)	81 (2.6)	97 (1.3)
Lithuania	99 (0.7)	95 (1.4)	10 (1.8)	85 (2.5)	77 (2.3)	96 (1.4)	85 (2.1)	74 (2.6)
Norway	98 (0.9)	98 (0.6)	21 (2.8)	46 (3.0)	67 (2.7)	86 (2.0)	98 (0.9)	93 (1.7)
Poland	96 (2.5)	98 (0.8)	10 (2.5)	84 (3.2)	79 (3.2)	95 (1.3)	100 (0.4)	99 (0.5)
Portugal	96 (1.0)	99 (0.5)	8 (1.2)	40 (2.4)	85 (1.8)	99 (0.4)	57 (2.9)	100 (0.0)
Romania	99 (0.4)	100 (0.2)	32 (2.9)	95 (1.1)	88 (2.1)	97 (1.0)	64 (3.5)	99 (0.7)
Russian Federation	100 (0.0)	100 (0.0)	15 (2.8)	94 (1.5)	74 (3.3)	95 (1.9)	78 (3.2)	n.a. (n.a.)
Slovak Republic	99 (0.6)	100 (0.3)	5 (1.2)	84 (2.3)	85 (2.1)	97 (0.9)	85 (2.8)	100 (0.2)
Slovenia	99 (0.6)	97 (0.8)	4 (1.0)	65 (2.9)	72 (2.7)	96 (1.0)	69 (2.5)	98 (0.9)
Sweden	93 (2.8)	99 (0.5)	20 (5.5)	30 (5.4)	86 (5.0)	97 (2.3)	83 (4.4)	87 (4.8)
Switzerland	96 (1.4)	93 (1.8)	11 (2.4)	42 (4.1)	65 (3.7)	82 (3.0)	76 (2.9)	81 (3.0)

() Standard errors appear in parentheses. Percentages based on valid responses.

* Percentage of students whose teachers chose one out of four answers.

Source: IEA Civic Education Study, Standard Population of 14-year-olds tested in 1999.

These discussions notwithstanding, civic education is reportedly a matter of knowledge transmission in most of the countries that participated in the study whereas critical thinking and political engagement are said to receive less attention. Teachers in most countries see this state of affairs negatively. For those who advocate a different kind of civic education, the gap between reality and vision might be a good leverage point for reform and for the development of materials and training.

Content related to national history and human and citizens' rights tops the agenda in almost all countries. While the teaching of history speaks to the traditional connectedness of civic education to history in many countries, teachers, it seems, have moved away from the traditional pattern of civic education involving instruction about government institutions. Human rights and the environment are topics of importance. But the fairly low profile of international concerns may worry those who see civic education as a prime area of instruction that should prepare students for a life in a globalized world.

Lower perceived importance and less coverage of economic issues might give rise to similar concerns. It is conspicuous that civic ideals, attitudes and concerns for individual citizens and the community are favored and tend to receive agreement across countries, while traditional institutions are either less favored (for example, political parties, unions) or rated differently across countries (for example, the military).

For teachers from the participating countries, there is widespread consensus that civic education is a curricular field that belongs in schools and matters a great deal for the well-being of students and country. In the survey, teachers give testimony to the meaningfulness of their work and the relevance of their field for society. To play this important role, civic education does not necessarily have to be a separate subject according to teachers' sentiments in many countries, but civic education knowledge should be part of the regular curriculum. Society's contestations make it difficult, in the eyes of many teachers from many countries, to ascertain what should be learned in civic education, but official curricula and standards can rally consensus. Thus, despite much teacher discretion and autonomy, policy plays a crucial role in orienting teachers and forging a firm base for the field.

Many civic education teachers across the participating countries see themselves as autonomous instructors who do not eschew controversy, who wish to emphasize the pragmatic and critical aspects of the field and who attach themselves to an agenda of individual rights. Yet they also feel beholden to national traditions and constrained to teach in a way that makes knowledge transmission central.

NOTE

1   Teacher data from Colombia and the United States have been omitted from all tables in this chapter due to country-specific problems in ascertaining the linkage between teachers and classes of students. Data from one or more countries with many missing or uncodable responses have been omitted from single tables.

Civic Knowledge and Engagement: A Synthesis

SUMMARY OF HIGHLIGHTS RELATING TO THE 1999 IEA CIVIC EDUCATION STUDY

- Students in most participating countries demonstrate knowledge of fundamental democratic ideals and processes and moderate skill in interpreting political materials. Their understanding, however, is often superficial or detached from life. About one-third of the students are unable to interpret a simple election leaflet, for example.

- Differences between countries in civic knowledge and skills are not as large as in cross-national studies in mathematics. There are no simple explanations for differences in countries' levels of performance in civic knowledge. The high-performing group includes some countries that have experienced massive political transitions during the lifetimes of these 14-year-olds, as well as other countries that are long-standing democracies.

- Within countries there is a substantial positive relationship between students' knowledge of democratic processes and institutions and their reported likelihood of voting when they become adults.

- Educational practices play an important role in preparing students for citizenship. Schools that operate in a participatory democratic way, foster an open climate for discussion within the classroom and invite students to take part in shaping school life are effective in promoting both civic knowledge and engagement. Many students, however, do not perceive this participatory climate in their classrooms or these opportunities in their schools.

- Teachers of civic-related subjects are largely favorable to civic education and consider it important for both their students and their country. Teachers in many countries believe that better materials, more subject-matter training and more instructional time would improve civic education.

- Young people agree that good citizenship includes the obligation to obey the law and to vote. In fact, most students report that they intend to vote when they are adults. However, it is the perception of many young people that their schools teach little about the importance of voting. When students perceive that their schools emphasize this topic, the proportion who say they are likely to vote increases.

- Except for voting, students are unlikely to think that conventional political participation is very important. The large majority of young people say they are unlikely to join a political party, consider writing a letter to a newspaper about a social concern or become a political candidate in the future.

- Across countries, students are open to less traditional forms of civic and political engagement such as collecting money for a charity and participating in non-violent protests or rallies. A small minority of students would be willing to participate in protest activities that would be illegal in most countries, such as blocking traffic or occupying buildings.

- Students are likely to get their major exposure to news through television, and in most countries they tend to trust that medium somewhat more than newspapers. The frequency of watching news programs on television is associated with higher civic knowledge in about half the participating countries. It is also related to students' projected likelihood of voting in nearly all countries.

- The trust in government expressed by youth is similar to adult attitudes in the different countries. The courts and the police are trusted the most, while political parties are trusted the least. Across countries, students have generally positive attitudes toward the political and economic rights of women and toward immigrants' rights.

- In about one-third of the countries males have slightly higher civic knowledge scores than females. Female students are much more likely than male students to support women's political and economic rights and rights for immigrants. Males are more willing to engage in illegal protest behavior activities than females. Females are more likely to collect money for and be involved with social causes.

- In almost all the participating countries, students from homes with more educational resources possess more civic knowledge, and in about one-fifth of the countries they are more likely to say they will vote.

The IEA Civic Education Study was initiated in the mid-1990s by the International Association for the Evaluation of Educational Achievement to examine the ways in which young people are prepared for the rights and responsibilities of citizenship in their societies, many of them undergoing rapid change. The preparation of young people for civic participation is a complex task. While the school has an important role, it does not stand alone in this process. Rather, it is nested within a set of systems and influences. The political culture includes political and economic values that influence young people's views; this culture increasingly is influenced by global processes. The practices of citizenship are absorbed and refined through experience in many kinds of communities and with the mass media. In this study we have examined several aspects of adolescents' experience. In looking at homes, our focus has been on the resources that families provide to foster literacy and educational achievement. In schools our focus has been on what the curriculum prescribes for students to learn, on the climate for discussions within classrooms, and on organizations important in the lives of students and their peers. We included many of the dimensions identified as important in the earlier case study phase of the research (Torney-Purta, Schwille & Amadeo, 1999).

In this chapter we will first examine the IEA Civic Education Study's overall accomplishments, next look at some country differences, and finally present a synthesis across chapters indicating reasons for optimism and for pessimism.

WHAT THE STUDY ACCOMPLISHED

The IEA Civic Education Study was massive, both in terms of number of respondents and in breadth of coverage. Nearly 90,000 14-year-olds in 28 countries were surveyed during 1999 on topics ranging from their knowledge of democratic principles to their trust in government. The analysis of this information has enriched our understanding of what youth know about democracy, citizenship, national identity and diversity, and addressed most of the policy questions with which we began the study. Although we cannot predict future behavior, we have gained a picture of some current beliefs and activities of young people, as well as their future intentions.

One of the study's purposes has been to point in a constructive way to some of the high points and low points of specific countries' experience with civic education for adolescents. We have investigated some of the potential predictors of knowledge and engagement within countries. Participating countries will issue national reports, and there will also be further in-depth international reports. It is our hope that the data (to be released in 2002) will be a resource to researchers cross-nationally to conduct additional analysis.

Civic education was not high on some countries' agendas in 1993 when we began the study. There is evidence that it has come to the forefront in many places, often as the process of consolidating democracy has intensified. We have developed tools that can be used across democratic countries to assess the major dimensions of young people's civic understanding, attitudes and engagement. Case studies formulated during Phase 1 identified in the participating countries a common core of content that focused on democracy, national identity and diversity. From this we developed the content framework and then designed a reliable and valid test and survey of civic education. In collaborating with educators and researchers from 28 countries, we learned the importance of viewing citizenship as composed of several relatively independent dimensions. These dimensions include knowledge of fundamental ideas about democracy, skills in analyzing media communication, concepts of how democracy works, trust in government institutions, supportive attitudes toward rights for groups experiencing discrimination, and expectations of adult participation. Just as we identified and measured these different aspects of citizenship, we have also explored a differentiated set of conditions that might foster them. This work has taken us beyond country rankings based on the knowledge scores of youth. It has also taken us beyond much of the research on adults based on a limited set of attitudinal measures.

HOW STUDENTS RESPONDED IN DIFFERENT COUNTRIES

There were some areas of the instrument in which students' responses across countries were similar. In most areas, however, students in different countries demonstrated different patterns of performance (refer to Chapters 3 through 7). To depict these we have divided countries into three groups on each scale in the test and survey: (i) a group significantly above the international mean; (ii) a group not significantly different from the international mean; and (iii) a group significantly below the international mean. This analysis is summarized in Table 10.1 and will be discussed separately for civic knowledge, civic engagement and civic attitudes. Multifaceted patterns of strengths and weaknesses can then be identified.

Civic Knowledge

Students from a diverse set of countries score at each of the three levels *on civic knowledge*, the total score based on knowledge of civic content and skills in interpreting political communication. Those *countries significantly above the mean* are Cyprus, the Czech Republic, Finland, Greece, Hong Kong (SAR), Italy, Norway, Poland, the Slovak Republic and the United States (column 3 of Table 10.1). This high-performing group includes countries with substantial traditions of democratic government and civic education and also countries that have experienced recent and major political transitions (in several cases within the lifetimes of 14-year-olds). The high-scoring countries seem to have in common educational systems that successfully promote reading literacy (although some countries with high literacy levels scored less well). The post-Communist countries that perform well include those that experienced transitions mobilizing considerable attention within the country. These countries were also able to organize school-based civic education programs relatively quickly after these transitions.

The countries *at the international mean in performance on civic knowledge* are Australia, Bulgaria, Denmark, England, Germany, Hungary, the Russian Federation, Slovenia, Sweden and Switzerland. This group of countries is again diverse, and it includes several where deficiencies in civic education have recently been identified and new initiatives planned.

Table 10.1 Civic Knowledge, Civic Engagement and Civic Attitudes Across Countries

Country	Civic Knowledge			Civic Engagement				Civic Attitudes and Other Concepts						
	Content knowledge (subscale)	Interpretative skills (subscale)	Total civic knowledge	Conventional citizenship	Social movement citizenship	Expected participation in political activities	Confidence in participation in school	Economy-related government responsibilities	Society-related government responsibilities	Positive attitudes toward immigrants	Positive attitudes toward one's nation	Trust in government-related institutions	Support for women's political rights	Open climate for classroom discussion
Australia		▲		▲	▲	▲	▲	▲	▲		▲	▲	▼	▲
Belgium (French)		▼		▲	▲	▲		▲		▲			▲	▲
Bulgaria	▲	▲	▲	▼	▼	▼	▼	▼		▼	▼		▲	▼
Chile	▼	▲	▼	▼	▼	▼	▼		▼	▼	▼	▼		▼
Colombia	▼	▼	▼	▼	▼	▼	▼	▲	▲		▼	▲	▼	▼
Cyprus				▲	▲	▲		▲		▲	▼	▼		▲
Czech Republic				▲	▲	▲					▼			
Denmark	▲	▲	▲	▲	▲	▲	▲	▲	▲	▲	▼	▲	▲	▲
England	▼	▼	▼	▲	▼	▲	▼	▲	▲	▲	▲	▲	▼	▲
Estonia					▼	▲	▼	▲	▲	▲	▼		▼	▲
Finland	▲	▲	▲	▲	▲	▲	▲	▲	▼	▲	▲	▲	▲	▲
Germany	▼	▼	▼	▼	▼	▼	▼	▼	▼	▼	▼		▼	▲
Greece	▲	▲	▲	▲	▲	▲	▲	▲	▲	▲	▼	▲	▲	▲
Hong Kong (SAR)	▼	▼	▼	▲	▲	▲	▲	▲	▲	▲	▲	▲	▲	▲
Hungary	▲	▲	▲	▲	▲	▼	▲	▲	▲	▼	▲	▲	▲	▲
Italy	▼	▼	▲	▼	▼	▼	▼	▼	▼	▼	▲		▲	▲
Latvia	▼	▼	▼	▼	▼	▼	▼	▼	▼	▼	▼	▼	▼	▼
Lithuania	▼	▼		▲	▲	▲	▼	▲	▼	▼	▼	▲	▼	▼
Norway	▲	▲		▲	▲	▲	▲	▲	▲	▲	▲	▲	▲	▲
Poland	▼	▼		▼	▼	▼	▼	▼	▼	▼	▼	▼	▲	▲
Portugal	▼	▼		▼	▼	▼	▼	▼	▼	▼	▼	▼	▲	▼
Romania					▲	▼	▼	▼		▼	▼	▲	▼	▼
Russian Federation					▼	▲	▲	▼		▲	▼	▼	▲	
Slovak Republic	▼	▼	▼	▼	▼	▲	▼	▼	▲	▲	▲	▲	▲	▲
Slovenia	▲			▲	▲	▼	▲			▼	▲		▲	▼
Sweden		▼		▲	▲	▼	▼			▲	▲	▲	▲	▲
Switzerland				▲	▲	▼	▲	▲		▲	▲	▲	▲	▼
United States	▼	▼	▼	▲	▲	▼	▲	▼		▼	▲	▼	▲	▼

▲ Country mean significantly higher than international mean.

▼ Country mean significantly lower than international mean.

Source: IEA Civic Education Study, Standard Population of 14-years-olds tested in 1999.

CHAPTER 10 CIVIC KNOWLEDGE AND ENGAGEMENT: A SYNTHESIS

The countries *below the international mean in performance on civic knowledge* are Belgium (French), Chile, Colombia, Estonia, Latvia, Lithuania, Portugal and Romania. This mixed group of Latin American, Western European, Baltic and other post-Communist countries has experienced considerable changes in government within the last 10 to 30 years. Belgium (French), Chile and Portugal tested relatively young samples, which may partially account for their position.

In looking at all these differences, we need to remember that the amount of variation between countries' performance on the total civic knowledge score is relatively small—more similar to that found in the IEA study of literacy than in IEA studies in mathematics (TIMSS and TIMSS-R). This finding suggests that the family, the community and the media are important sources of learning in addition to school-based civic education.

It is also possible to examine the two civic knowledge sub-scales separately (Table 10.1, columns 1 and 2). A look at the content knowledge sub-scale alone reveals that Hungary and Slovenia would be added to the high-performing countries mentioned in the previous section. If we look at skill in interpreting political communication, then it is evident that Australia, England and Sweden would be added to the list of high-performing countries mentioned in the previous section.

Although there are significant differences across countries in students' knowledge, there are also basic ideas associated with democracy on which there is consensus across countries. These areas of agreement can be identified by examining some of the items endorsed in all countries as part of *the concept of democracy*. There is consensus on the part of the average student across countries about the importance to democracy of free elections, civil society, lack of constraint on expressions of opinion, the rule of law and the presentation of different points of view in the press.

Both the data on knowledge and on concepts suggest that 14-year-olds in these countries grasp most of the fundamental principles involved in the ideal functioning of democracy, but in many countries their understanding is relatively superficial.

Civic Engagement

A second important dimension of citizenship is the students' interest and engagement in various types of participation in the different systems to which they belong.

First, it should be noted that these young people believe that good citizenship for adults includes the obligation to obey the law and to vote (see Chapter 4). Although there are considerable differences between countries, the obligations of loyalty to the country, serving in the military and working hard are also endorsed by the average student. Conventional participatory actions such as engaging in political discussion and joining a political party are relatively infrequently endorsed as important for adult citizens.

In the case of voting, we can look at both students' views and teachers' views of the extent to which the topic is discussed in schools. Teachers within a country are more likely to say that they teach about voting than students are to say that they learn about voting in school (compare Table 7.1 with Table E.5 in Appendix E). This difference between students' and teachers' reports of a curricular focus on voting is especially striking in the Czech Republic, Denmark, Estonia, Finland, Germany, Hungary, Norway and Sweden. In these countries there is a difference of more than 30 percent between the proportion of teachers who say students have an opportunity to learn about voting and the lower proportion of students who perceive that they have had such an opportunity. Student respondents in seven out of eight of these countries (except Hungary) also have scores on concepts of conventional citizenship that are significantly below the international mean. (See Chapter 4.)

In contrast, there are some countries where voting and other conventional citizenship activities are thought to be relatively important by students: Bulgaria, Chile, Colombia, Cyprus, Greece, Italy, Lithuania, Poland, Portugal, Romania, the Slovak Republic and the United States (Table 10.1). Many of these countries have experienced dramatic political events during the last several decades, and all have made some recent efforts at highlighting or improving civic education.

Citizenship responsibilities relating to participation in social movement groups are very likely to be endorsed. Students in a wide range of countries support these activities in connection with environmental or community service groups. In previous studies the assumption was often made that conventional activities form the basic or minimum level of citizenship participation. To this cluster of activities the especially interested citizen might add membership and action connected to social causes. The 14-year-olds in this study seem instead to be primarily attracted by social movement groups and to place little emphasis on conventional participatory activities apart from voting.

Although these conventional participatory activities that citizens may choose to undertake are not frequently endorsed, other attributes traditionally associated with citizenship, such as patriotism or loyalty to the country and willingness to serve in the military, are rated as important in many countries.

It is easier to grasp some of the country differences in civic engagement by looking across scales. There are *four scales from the survey that deal with participation*, three with participation in the political or social system and one with school participation. These are (i) the concept of citizenship as involving conventional participation, (ii) the concept of citizenship as involving social movement participation, (iii) expected political activities as an adult, and (iv) confidence in the effectiveness of participation at school. Table 10.1, columns 4–7, summarizes for each country whether each of these four scores is significantly above, not different from, or below the international mean. Four of these columns (conventional citizenship, social movement citizenship, expected political activities, and confidence at school) relate to active participation.

In the following countries *three or four of these participation scales are significantly above the international mean:* Chile, Colombia, Cyprus, Greece, Poland, Portugal, Romania and the United States. Young people in these countries seem more willing than those in other countries to participate in several ways and at several levels of the social and political system. This group includes both of the Latin American countries, the Southern European countries (with the exception of Italy), two post-Communist countries and the United States. This group, where civic engagement is relatively high, includes countries that perform significantly above the mean on the knowledge test (Cyprus, Greece, Poland and the United States), and also countries that perform significantly below the mean on the knowledge test (Chile, Colombia, Portugal and Romania).

In the following countries, either three or four of the participation scales are significantly below the international mean: Australia, Belgium (French), the Czech Republic, Denmark, England, Finland, Germany, Slovenia, Sweden and Switzerland. Note that this group, where students appear less engaged in a civic sense, includes all of the Northern European countries except Norway and two of the post-Communist countries.

These countries where students are relatively low in civic participation do not have a common level of performance on the knowledge test; the Czech Republic and Finland score high on knowledge, while Belgium (French) scores low. The other countries in the group have knowledge scores near the international mean.

Already we can see that no single measure of citizenship can adequately represent the complexity of the performance and behavior of students in these 28 countries. Certainly, knowledge scores alone do not tell the entire story; neither does current or intended participation. Furthermore, the post-Communist countries that might have been expected a decade ago to have similar scores in this study show quite diverse patterns of performance in civic knowledge and civic engagement. Previous history of democracy, the organization of the Communist system, the way in which transitions took place, recent economic conditions, and initiatives toward civic education reform should be examined in attempting to understand these patterns. These findings suggest the importance of multiple indicators of civic education's success and of multiple routes in improving civic education.

Civic Attitudes

The attitude scales included in the study were varied—positive national feeling, trust in government-related institutions, support for the rights of immigrants and support for political rights for women. There are substantial similarities between the results for these 14-year-olds and the results for adult samples tested in the past decade using similar measures. For example, trust in political parties is lower than trust in institutions such as the national parliament, and substantially less than trust in courts and police (Chapter 5). To take another example of similarity between adults and young people, trust in government-related institutions is below the international mean in countries with short histories of democracy, especially the post-Communist countries. These young people already seem in many respects to be members of their countries' political cultures.

Trust in the media is also relatively low in most of the countries that are in the process of consolidating democracy. There are interesting patterns of differential trust when television, radio and newspapers are considered separately. For example, television and radio are trusted as much or more than newspapers as sources of news by these 14-year-olds in all countries except the United States (Chapter 5).

Those countries where trust in government-related institutions is low nevertheless tend to maintain relatively positive attitudes about the nation (Chapter 5 and Table 10.1). Only Estonia and Latvia are significantly below the international mean both on trust in government-related institutions and on positive attitudes toward the nation. There seems to be a reservoir of support either for the nation or for government-related institutions among young people in the large majority of these countries.

Concepts of the proper responsibilities of the government also show substantial similarity to results of studies with adults. For example, there is a high level of endorsement of government responsibilities for society-related matters such as providing education, and a somewhat lower level of endorsement for the government assuming certain responsibilities related to the economy. Respondents in Australia, Belgium (French), Denmark, Germany, Greece, Hong Kong (SAR), Norway, Switzerland and the United States are the least likely to believe that it is appropriate for the government to intervene in economic matters such as reducing income disparities, guaranteeing jobs and controlling prices (Chapter 4 and Table 10.1). Young people may be reflecting support for the free market that is part of the political culture of adults in their country.

In the area of endorsement of political rights and opportunities for immigrants and for women, there are, as Table 10.1 shows, relatively low scores in several countries facing economic difficulties. The scores on both of these scales are below the international mean in Bulgaria, Estonia, Hungary, Latvia, Lithuania and the Slovak Republic (Chapter 5). It is important, however, that the average 14-year-old even in these countries is more likely to have a positive than a negative attitude toward rights for both immigrants and women. There are gender differences in these scales that are more substantial than for any other measures in the instrument, with females having more positive attitudes.

The particular groups experiencing discrimination differ between nations (immigrants in many countries, but also racial, linguistic and religious groups, among others). There is a less ambiguous basis for examining attitudes toward groups experiencing discrimination within a nation or a small group of nations than internationally, and further analysis of these data is indicated.

GROUNDS FOR OPTIMISM AND PESSIMISM IN CIVIC EDUCATION

There are both positive and negative aspects of the civic knowledge, skills, concepts, attitudes and activities of these adolescents surveyed just before the end of the 1990s.

On the positive side, students in some countries perform well when asked to demonstrate their understanding of the fundamental ideas and principles of democracy. However, if one moves beyond these basics, understanding appears to be superficial. Substantial numbers of young people, especially in some countries, fail to attain even this grasp. Among the most telling gaps are those dealing with understanding policy positions of potential candidates in elections.

Also on the positive side, students from some countries that have recently experienced major transitions following decades of non-democratic rule score in the top group on the knowledge test. High levels of literacy, national political cultures that moved in visible ways to support democratic institutions and efforts to reform curricula and train teachers may be among the reasons.

There is no simple and compelling explanation for the countries whose students appear in the top-scoring group, however. A number of countries in the middle- and low-scoring groups have recently recognized deficiencies in civic education and instituted programs of reform. These new initiatives did not take effect in time to be reflected in students' performance in 1999, but the IEA results can serve as benchmarks for future evaluations of programs in these countries.

Furthermore, on the optimistic side, this study shows that knowledge of content and skills in interpreting political information are valuable in themselves and also positively associated with young people's assessment of how likely they will be to vote as adults. The context in which this knowledge is imparted is important, however. A classroom climate in which the student is free to discuss opinions and different points of view is associated with both higher knowledge scores and with intent to vote in the majority of countries. This finding about the value of encouraging free discussion in the classroom has been replicated from the 1971 IEA Civic Education Study in a much more diverse set of countries.

Teachers report that recitation, textbooks and worksheets designed to transmit knowledge still form the predominant mode of instruction. In contrast, teachers' vision for civic instruction focuses on students discussing and being critical about information. They favor more subject-matter preparation, better materials and more instructional time to close this gap.

Civic engagement also shows a differentiated pattern. Students across countries show an acceptance of the rule of law in the importance they attach to citizens' obligation to obey the law. Young people in some countries appear ready to take advantage of several avenues for participation—conventional activities in the political system, social movement groups in the community and joining with others to solve problems in school. However, the more pessimistic view reveals in some countries a marked disinclination toward such participation and a lack of the necessary infrastructure for engagement.

Returning to the positive viewpoint, we see that the majority of students express a willingness to vote (especially when schools stress its importance and when they are knowledgeable about civic-related topics). In most countries, young people's views of political parties are relatively negative, however. In place of giving allegiance to parties and to what many perceive as hierarchical political organizations ruled by an older generation, they are instead gravitating to social movements as the arenas in which good citizenship can be manifested. For example, many are willing to join voluntary groups to raise money or to assist the needy in their communities.

Environmental organizations are also popular in some countries. Youth may reject certain types of conventional political organizations, especially those that do not give a relatively immediate sense of feedback. Other research also suggests that young people want particularistic face-to-face engagement and not universalistic and more distant relations, in this case to government or political parties. It is impossible, however, to predict the long-term implications for society if there is a decline in conventional participation.

When we look at what makes a difference to students' scores within a country, it is clear that equipping young people with knowledge of basic democratic principles and with skills in interpreting political communication is important in enhancing their expectation that they will vote. School organizations such as councils and parliaments seem to play a small but positive role in preparing students for the responsibilities of adult citizenship. In some countries, young people seem ready to grasp new participation opportunities that are open to them. Conversely, in some countries, the infrastructure for this kind of participation appears to be lacking. Phase 1 of the study suggested that although a vision of skill-focused learning and participation in school governance is widely endorsed, concrete movement in this direction may be viewed with ambivalence. The idea that schools should be models of democracy is often stated but difficult to put into practice.

Young people are frequent consumers of the electronic media. The 14-year-olds who watch more news on television are both more knowledgeable about civic matters and more likely to say that they will vote when they become adults. Although newspaper reading is probably also a positive influence, these young people report that they are more likely to watch or listen to news than to read newspapers. In most countries, they also report more trust in news on television than in what appears in newspapers. On the pessimistic side, only a little more than half the students place much trust in media sources, and many are not interested in political news.

Support for opportunities for immigrants and for women's political rights is widespread, especially among females. In every country, however, a small number of young people would restrict opportunities for immigrants and for women.

A moderate amount of trust in governmental institutions is widely acknowledged as an important supportive factor for democracy. Young people in countries that have recently experienced political transitions express low levels of trust, but in most there is a reservoir of support in the form of positive feelings toward the nation.

Gender differences appear to be less sizeable than those found in previous studies. In some countries, when other factors are controlled, males are somewhat more knowledgeable about civic-related topics and females more likely to expect to vote. A very substantial gender difference in support for women's rights continues to exist. In a substantial number of countries, females are more likely than males to support social movement involvement as important for adult citizens and to be willing to collect money for social causes. Males have more positive national attitudes in a number of countries and are more likely to engage in protest activities that would be illegal in many countries. Differences in both knowledge and engagement associated with home educational background and expected education are also significant.

Another positive finding of the current study is that teachers feel that civic education at this age level is valuable both for students' development and for that of their countries. They give a more positive picture of this process than that provided by the experts interviewed during Phase 1 of the study. Civic-relevant topics are often integrated into courses in history or taught as part of social science or social studies. There is no widespread sentiment for civic education as a separate subject, but neither is a totally cross-curricular approach without anchors to subject matter popular. Teachers are responsive to official curriculum, materials and authorities, but they also find their own materials and negotiate with their students about what is relevant to learn. On the negative side, good materials, subject-matter training for teachers and sufficient instructional time are seen as lacking in many countries.

Civic education across these 28 countries has many facets, among them civic content knowledge, skills in understanding political communication, civic engagement of several types, and attitudes of trust and tolerance. The average student in most countries has a base of knowledge and positive attitudes upon which to build. There is no single approach inside or outside school that is likely to enhance all of these facets of citizenship. A focus on didactic instruction, issues-centered-classroom discussion, students' participation in school councils or other organizations, education about the media, or community-based projects may enhance one outcome without influencing (or even at the expense of) others. The school is a valuable focus for a significant number of these activities, however, indicated by the extent to which school factors predict civic knowledge and engagement. Our hope is that individual countries will examine their own students' positions in relation to the various dimensions identified in this study, conduct further analysis and involve policy-makers, educators and the public in a dialogue about the ways that curriculum, teacher training and community involvement can better prepare young people for citizenship.

Appendices

APPENDIX A EXAMPLES OF ITEMS FROM THE CIVIC KNOWLEDGE TEST

Figure A.1a   Item Example: Which of the following is a fact?

Country	Correct Answers (in %)	Example 1 (Item #38) Type 2: Skills in Interpretation
Australia	58 (1.5)	
Belgium (French)	42 (1.5)	
Bulgaria	44 (2.5)	
Chile	26 (1.1)	
Colombia	26 (1.6)	
Cyprus	63 (1.3)	**38.** Three of these statements are opinions and one is a fact. Which of the following is a **FACT** [the factual statement]?
Czech Republic	46 (1.6)	
Denmark	54 (1.0)	
England	54 (1.1)	
Estonia	46 (1.2)	A. People with very low incomes should not pay any taxes.
Finland	68 (1.0)	B. In many countries rich people pay higher taxes than poor people.*
Germany	53 (1.5)	
Greece	53 (1.3)	
Hong Kong (SAR)	57 (1.6)	
Hungary	48 (1.4)	C. It is fair that some citizens pay higher taxes than others.
Italy	55 (1.4)	D. Donations to charity are the best way to reduce differences between rich and poor.
Latvia	42 (1.5)	
Lithuania	35 (1.6)	
Norway	59 (1.2)	
Poland	50 (3.2)	
Portugal	25 (1.6)	
Romania	39 (2.4)	
Russian Federation	52 (2.4)	
Slovak Republic	44 (1.5)	
Slovenia	44 (1.2)	
Sweden	54 (1.8)	
Switzerland	56 (1.5)	
United States	69 (1.6)	
International Sample	49 (0.3)	

( ) Standard errors appear in parentheses.
* Correct answer.

Source: IEA Civic Education Study, Standard Population of 14-year-olds tested in 1999.

Figure A.1b Item Example: Which is an example of discrimination in pay equity?

Country	Correct Answers (in %)	Example 2 (Item #26) Type 2: Skills in Interpretation
Australia	66 (1.4)	
Belgium (French)	47 (1.6)	
Bulgaria	33 (2.4)	
Chile	31 (1.2)	
Colombia	32 (2.0)	
Cyprus	56 (1.3)	
Czech Republic	48 (1.6)	
Denmark	67 (1.2)	
England	64 (1.1)	
Estonia	41 (1.3)	
Finland	75 (1.0)	
Germany	51 (1.2)	
Greece	49 (1.5)	
Hong Kong (SAR)	65 (1.6)	
Hungary	56 (1.4)	
Italy	48 (1.4)	
Latvia	33 (1.8)	
Lithuania	42 (1.5)	
Norway	57 (1.3)	
Poland	68 (2.3)	
Portugal	41 (1.4)	
Romania	32 (1.9)	
Russian Federation	29 (2.4)	
Slovak Republic	29 (1.6)	
Slovenia	46 (1.2)	
Sweden	68 (1.6)	
Switzerland	57 (1.8)	
United States	76 (1.6)	
International Sample	50 (0.3)	

26. Two people work at the same job but one is paid less than the other. The principle of equality would be violated if the person is paid less because of ...

A. fewer educational qualifications.
B. less work experience.
C. working for fewer hours.
D. gender [sex].*

( ) Standard errors appear in parentheses.
* Correct answer.

Source: IEA Civic Education Study, Standard Population of 14-year-olds tested in 1999.

Figure A.1c Item Example: Result if large publisher buys many newspapers

Country	Correct Answers (in %)	Example 4 (Item #18) Type 1: Knowledge of Content
Australia	59 (1.4)	
Belgium (French)	50 (1.6)	
Bulgaria	55 (1.6)	
Chile	40 (1.1)	
Colombia	49 (2.1)	
Cyprus	71 (1.0)	18. Which of the following is most likely to happen if a large publisher buys many ofthe [smaller] newspapers in a country?
Czech Republic	51 (1.4)	
Denmark	70 (0.9)	
England	49 (1.3)	
Estonia	61 (1.0)	
Finland	48 (1.2)	A. Government censorship of the news is more likely.
Germany	62 (1.1)	
Greece	71 (1.1)	B. There will be less diversity of opinions presented.*
Hong Kong (SAR)	70 (1.3)	
Hungary	54 (1.2)	
Italy	44 (1.2)	C. The price of the country's newspapers will be lowered.
Latvia	57 (1.6)	
Lithuania	65 (1.1)	D. The amount of advertising in the newspapers will be reduced.
Norway	65 (0.8)	
Poland	78 (1.5)	
Portugal	34 (1.0)	
Romania	39 (1.9)	
Russian Federation	66 (1.9)	
Slovak Republic	61 (1.3)	
Slovenia	55 (1.2)	
Sweden	69 (1.0)	
Switzerland	56 (1.2)	
United States	59 (1.6)	
International Sample	57 (0.3)	

( ) Standard errors appear in parentheses.
* Correct answer.

Source: IEA Civic Education Study, Standard Population of 14-year-olds tested in 1999.

Table A.1 Domain Content Categories and Short Titles for Items in Final Test

I A: Democracy and Its Defining Characteristics

Domain Content Category	Item #	Short Titles for Items	Correct Answers (in %)	Item Parameter
Identify defining characteristics of democracy	12	...who ought to govern in democracy (also IEA, 1971)	71	88
	19	...necessary feature of democratic government	65	96
Identify limited and unlimited government, undemocratic regimes	17	...what makes a government non-democratic	53	106
Evaluate strengths and weaknesses of democratic systems	14	...main message of cartoon about democracy	61	100
Identify incentives to participate in the form of factors undermining democracy	9	...most serious threat to democracy	72	90
Identify problems in transitions of government from non-democratic to democratic	29	...most convincing action to promote democracy	54	106

Table A.1 (continued)

I B: Institutions and Practices in Democracy

Domain Content Category	Item #	Short Titles for Items	Correct Answers (in %)	Item Parameter
Identify characteristics and functions of elections and parties	11	...function of having more than one political party	75	88
	22	...function of periodic elections (also IEA, 1971)	42	113
Identify qualifications of candidates for positions and making up one's mind during elections	23	...which party issued political leaflet	65	97
	24	...what issuers of leaflet think about taxes	71	91
	25	...which policy issuers of leaflet likely to favor	58	100
Identify a healthy critical attitude toward officials and their accountability	30	...example of corruption in national legislature	66	96
	33	...main message of cartoon about political leader	77	84
Identify basic character of parliament, judicial system, law, police	2	...an accurate statement about laws	78	84
	13	...main task of national legislature	67	94
Identify provisions of constitution	28	...what countries' constitutions contain	62	99
Understand basic economic issues and their political implications	27	...essential characteristic of market economy	47	110
	38	...a fact (not an opinion) about taxes	49	109

Table A.1 (continued)

I C: Citizenship: Rights and Duties

Domain Content Category	Item #	Short Titles for Items	Correct Answers (in %)	Item Parameter
Identify general rights, qualifications, and obligations of citizens in democracies	3	...a political right	78	85
Identify citizens' rights to participate and express criticism and their limits	10	...illegal activity for a political organization	59	101
	15	...violation of civil liberties in democracy (also IEA, 1971)	53	107
Identify obligations, civic duties of citizens in democracy	1	...role of citizen in democratic country	79	83
Understand the role of mass media in democracy	4	...which of a reporter's rights was violated	70	92
	18	...result if large publisher buys many newspapers	57	103
Identify network of associations and differences of political opinion	7	...why organizations are important in democracy	69	93
	34	...main point of article about factory being shut	35	121
Identify the human rights defined in international documents	6	... purpose of Universal Declaration of Human Rights	77	86
	20	...what is in Convention on Rights of the Child	77	84
Identify rights in the economic sphere	8	...purpose of labor unions	64	98
Demonstrate awareness of tradeoffs	35	...economic objections to factory being shut	67	93

II A: National Identity

Domain Content Category	Item #	Short Titles for Items	Correct Answers (in %)	Item Parameter
Recognize sense of collective identity	32	...an opinion (not a fact) about flags	66	95
Recognize that every nation has events in its history of which it is not proud	36	...main message of cartoon about history textbooks	58	102

Table A.1 (continued)

II B: International Relations

Domain Content Category	Item #	Short Titles for Items	Correct Answers (in %)	Item Parameter
Recognize international economic issues and organizations (other than inter-governmental) active in dealing with matters with economic implications	21	...who owns multinational businesses	47	110
	31	...an opinion (not a fact) about the environment	53	106
Recognize major inter-governmental organizations	16	...major purpose of United Nations (also IEA, 1971)	85	77

III A: Social Cohesion and Diversity

Domain Content Category	Item #	Short Titles for Items	Correct Answers (in %)	Item Parameter
Recognize groups subject to discrimination	5	...an example of discrimination in employment	65	97
	26	...an example of discrimination in pay equity	50	108
	37	...a fact (not an opinion) about women and politics	72	89

APPENDIX B ITEM-BY-SCORE MAPS FOR SCALES REPORTED IN CHAPTERS 5 THROUGH 7

Item-by-Score Map and International Item Percentages

This section contains additional information on the scales presented in Chapters 4 to 7. The item-by-score map links scale scores to item responses; tables with international item frequencies show how students in the participating countries answered the scaled items. We have scaled the attitudinal items using the IRT (Item Response Theory) 'Partial Credit Model'. We then transformed the resulting person parameters (logits) for the latent dimensions to international scales with a mean of 10 and a standard deviation of 2 across all countries (equally weighted). The scale scores are always to be seen as relative to the international mean, and in themselves do not reveal any substantial meaning regarding the item response categories.

Generally, items differ according to the extent of endorsement along the latent dimension. Thus, for example, in a measurement of altruism, respondents will probably more readily agree with 'donating smaller amounts of money' than with 'spending time after work in community service'. Both items may measure the same dimension, but respondents usually will score higher on the latent dimension when they agree with the second item.

To illustrate the meaning of these international scale scores for every scale, we have provided a so-called 'Item-by-Score Map'. From the item parameters of the Rasch model it is possible to determine which response can be expected for each item given a certain scale score. Figure B.1 shows how the item-by-score map should be interpreted.

The vertical lines indicate for each of the scale scores at the top of the figure which response a student is most likely to give. If, for example, a respondent has a score of 10 in this example, he or she is likely to agree with Items 1 and 2 but to disagree with Item 3. Likewise, a respondent with a scale score of 8 will probably disagree with Item 1 and 2 and disagree strongly with Item 3, whereas a respondent with a scale score of 12 will probably strongly agree with Items 1 and 2 and agree with item 3.

In addition to providing the item-by-score maps, we also give the international percentage for each scaled item. These percentages are based on equally weighted samples from all 28 participating countries and include only valid responses, excluding 'don't know' and missing. The international percentages enable the reader to see the average level of endorsement for each of the scaled items. Figure B.1 shows a fictitious example, and consequently does not contain any percentages.

Figure B.1 Example of Item-By-Score Map

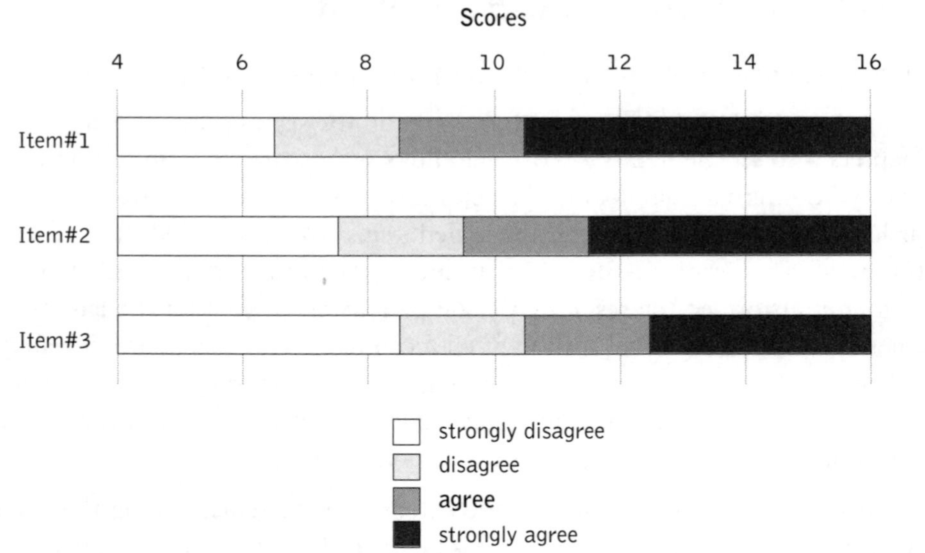

Examples of how to interpret the item-by-score map:

#1: A respondent with score 6 is expected to disagree strongly with all three items.

#2: A respondent with score 8 is expected to disagree with Items 1 and 2 and disagree strongly with Item 3.

#3: A respondent with score 10 is expected to agree with Items 1 and 2 but disagree with Item 3.

#4: A respondent with score 12 is expected to agree strongly with Items 1 and 2 and agree with Item 3.

#5: A respondent with score 14 is expected to agree strongly with all three items.

Source: *International Coordinating Center of the IEA Civic Education Study.*

Figure B.2a Item-By-Score Map for Importance of Conventional Citizenship

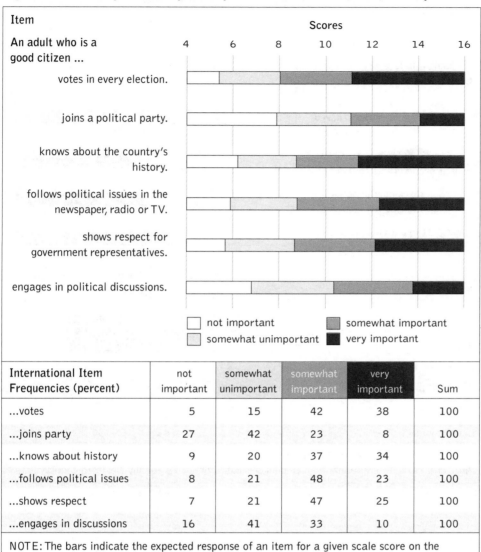

International Item Frequencies (percent)	not important	somewhat unimportant	somewhat important	very important	Sum
...votes	5	15	42	38	100
...joins party	27	42	23	8	100
...knows about history	9	20	37	34	100
...follows political issues	8	21	48	23	100
...shows respect	7	21	47	25	100
...engages in discussions	16	41	33	10	100

NOTE: The bars indicate the expected response of an item for a given scale score on the horizontal axis. International item frequencies based on all 28 equally weighted country data.

Source: IEA Civic Education Study, Standard Population of 14-year-olds tested in 1999.

Figure B.2b Item-By-Score Map for Importance of Social Movement-related Citizenship

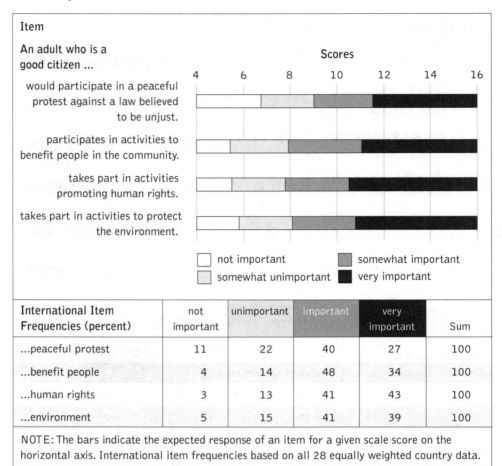

International Item Frequencies (percent)	not important	unimportant	important	very important	Sum
...peaceful protest	11	22	40	27	100
...benefit people	4	14	48	34	100
...human rights	3	13	41	43	100
...environment	5	15	41	39	100

NOTE: The bars indicate the expected response of an item for a given scale score on the horizontal axis. International item frequencies based on all 28 equally weighted country data.

Source: IEA Civic Education Study, Standard Population of 14-year-olds tested in 1999.

**Figure B.2c Item-By-Score Map for Concept of Society-related Government
Responsibilities**

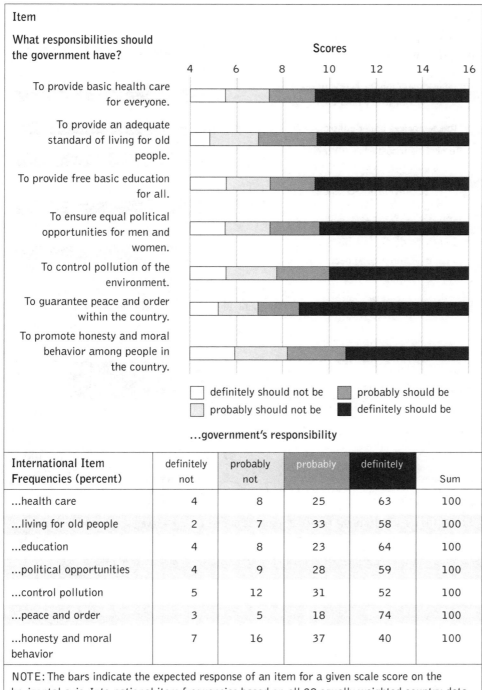

International Item Frequencies (percent)	definitely not	probably not	probably	definitely	Sum
...health care	4	8	25	63	100
...living for old people	2	7	33	58	100
...education	4	8	23	64	100
...political opportunities	4	9	28	59	100
...control pollution	5	12	31	52	100
...peace and order	3	5	18	74	100
...honesty and moral behavior	7	16	37	40	100

NOTE: The bars indicate the expected response of an item for a given scale score on the horizontal axis. International item frequencies based on all 28 equally weighted country data.

Source: IEA Civic Education Study, Standard Population of 14-year-olds tested in 1999.

Figure B.2d Item-By-Score Map for Concept of Economy-related Government Responsibilities

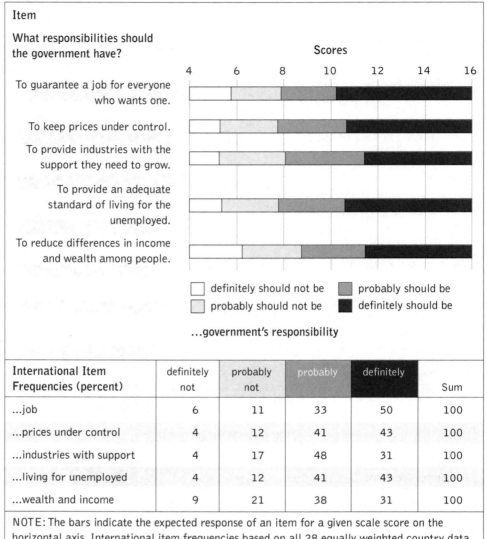

Item What responsibilities should the government have?					Scores

To guarantee a job for everyone who wants one.

To keep prices under control.

To provide industries with the support they need to grow.

To provide an adequate standard of living for the unemployed.

To reduce differences in income and wealth among people.

☐ definitely should not be   ▓ probably should be

☐ probably should not be   ■ definitely should be

...government's responsibility

International Item Frequencies (percent)	definitely not	probably not	probably	definitely	Sum
...job	6	11	33	50	100
...prices under control	4	12	41	43	100
...industries with support	4	17	48	31	100
...living for unemployed	4	12	41	43	100
...wealth and income	9	21	38	31	100

NOTE: The bars indicate the expected response of an item for a given scale score on the horizontal axis. International item frequencies based on all 28 equally weighted country data.

Source: IEA Civic Education Study, Standard Population of 14-year-olds tested in 1999.

Figure B.2e Item-By-Score Map for Trust in Government-related Institutions

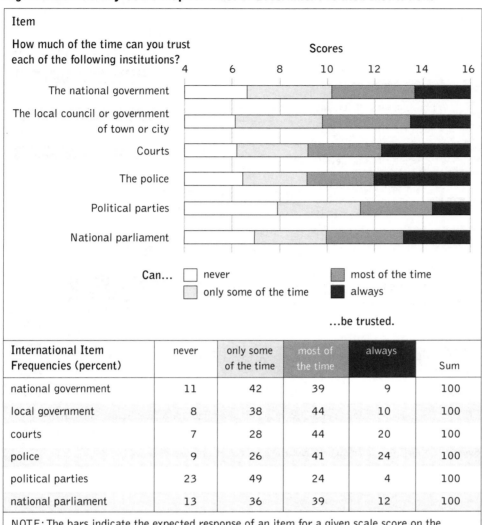

International Item Frequencies (percent)	never	only some of the time	most of the time	always	Sum
national government	11	42	39	9	100
local government	8	38	44	10	100
courts	7	28	44	20	100
police	9	26	41	24	100
political parties	23	49	24	4	100
national parliament	13	36	39	12	100

NOTE: The bars indicate the expected response of an item for a given scale score on the horizontal axis. International item frequencies based on all 28 equally weighted country data.

Source: IEA Civic Education Study, Standard Population of 14-year-olds tested in 1999.

Figure B.2f Item-By-Score Map for Positive Attitudes toward One's Nation

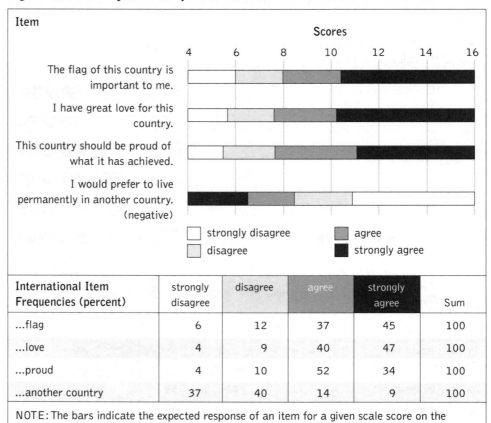

International Item Frequencies (percent)	strongly disagree	disagree	agree	strongly agree	Sum
...flag	6	12	37	45	100
...love	4	9	40	47	100
...proud	4	10	52	34	100
...another country	37	40	14	9	100

NOTE: The bars indicate the expected response of an item for a given scale score on the horizontal axis. International item frequencies based on all 28 equally weighted country data.

Source: *IEA Civic Education Study,* Standard Population of 14-year-olds tested in 1999.

Figure B.2g Item-By-Score Map for Positive Attitudes toward Immigrants

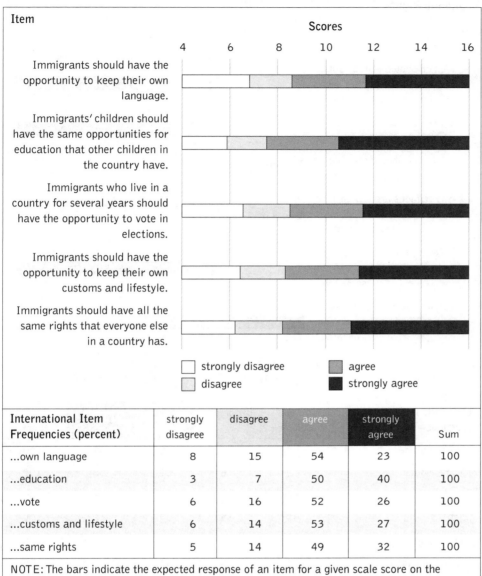

International Item Frequencies (percent)	strongly disagree	disagree	agree	strongly agree	Sum
...own language	8	15	54	23	100
...education	3	7	50	40	100
...vote	6	16	52	26	100
...customs and lifestyle	6	14	53	27	100
...same rights	5	14	49	32	100

NOTE: The bars indicate the expected response of an item for a given scale score on the horizontal axis. International item frequencies based on all 28 equally weighted country data.

Source: IEA Civic Education Study, Standard Population of 14-year-olds tested in 1999.

Figure B.2h Item-By-Score Map for Attitudes toward Women's Political and Economic Rights

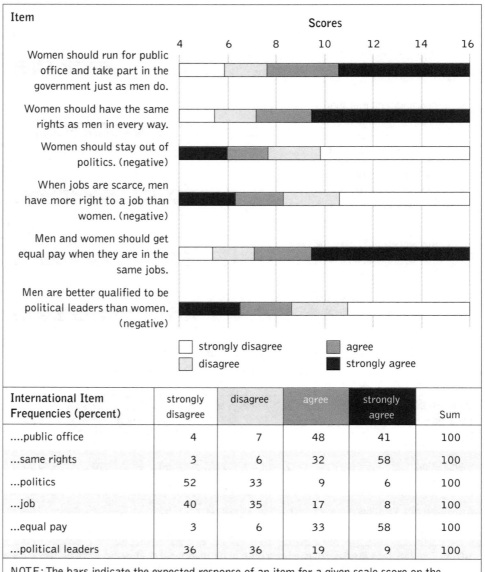

International Item Frequencies (percent)	strongly disagree	disagree	agree	strongly agree	Sum
....public office	4	7	48	41	100
...same rights	3	6	32	58	100
...politics	52	33	9	6	100
...job	40	35	17	8	100
...equal pay	3	6	33	58	100
...political leaders	36	36	19	9	100

NOTE: The bars indicate the expected response of an item for a given scale score on the horizontal axis. International item frequencies based on all 28 equally weighted country data.

Source: IEA Civic Education Study, Standard Population of 14-year-olds tested in 1999.

Figure B.2i Item-By-Score Map for Political Activities

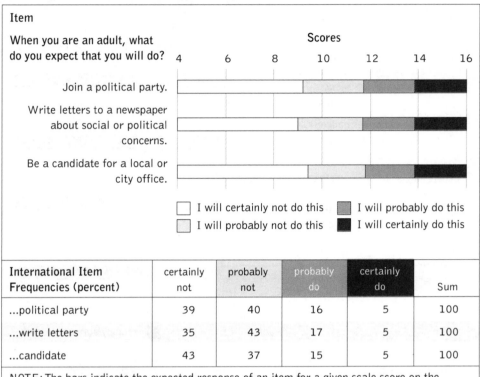

International Item Frequencies (percent)	certainly not	probably not	probably do	certainly do	Sum
...political party	39	40	16	5	100
...write letters	35	43	17	5	100
...candidate	43	37	15	5	100

NOTE: The bars indicate the expected response of an item for a given scale score on the horizontal axis. International item frequencies based on all 28 equally weighted country data.

Source: IEA Civic Education Study, Standard Population of 14-year-olds tested in 1999.

Figure B.2j Item-By-Score Map for Confidence in Participation at School

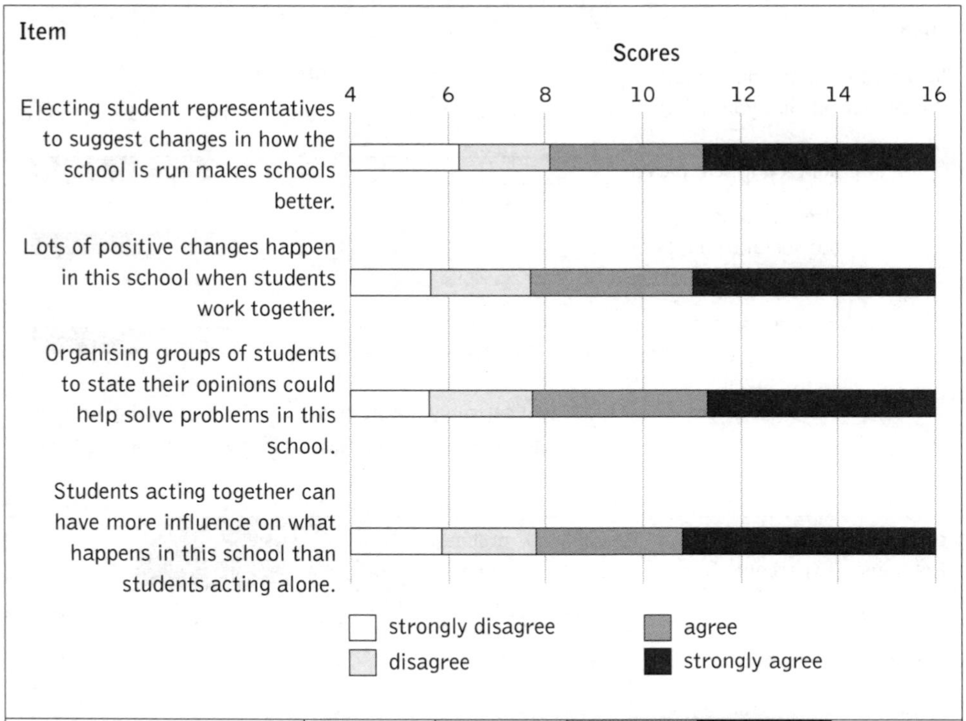

Item

International Item Frequencies (percent)	strongly disagree	disagree	agree	strongly agree	Sum
...electing students	5	11	54	30	100
...working together	3	10	54	34	100
...organising groups	3	10	58	29	100
...acting together	3	10	50	37	100

NOTE: The bars indicate the expected response of an item for a given scale score on the horizontal axis. International item frequencies based on all 28 equally weighted country data.

Source: IEA Civic Education Study, Standard Population of 14-year-olds tested in 1999.

Figure B.2k Item-By-Score Map for Open Classroom Climate for Discussion

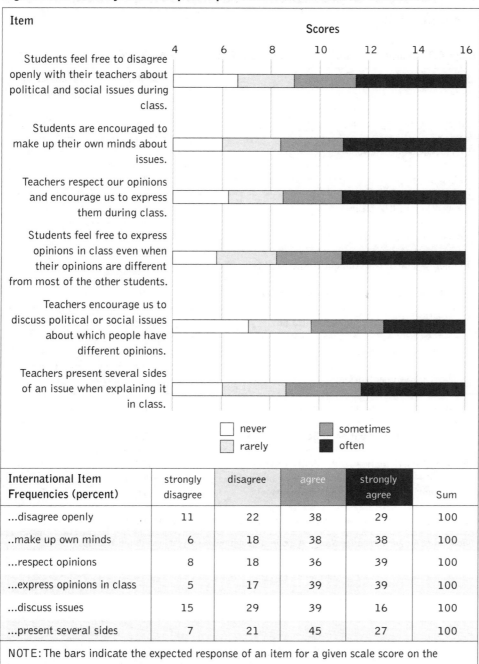

International Item Frequencies (percent)	strongly disagree	disagree	agree	strongly agree	Sum
...disagree openly	11	22	38	29	100
..make up own minds	6	18	38	38	100
...respect opinions	8	18	36	39	100
...express opinions in class	5	17	39	39	100
...discuss issues	15	29	39	16	100
...present several sides	7	21	45	27	100

NOTE: The bars indicate the expected response of an item for a given scale score on the horizontal axis. International item frequencies based on all 28 equally weighted country data.

Source: IEA Civic Education Study, Standard Population of 14-year-olds tested in 1999.

APPENDIX C CLASSICAL PSYCHOMETRIC INDICES (SELECTED)

Table C.1 Cronbach's Alpha Reliability Coefficients for All Scales

Scale Name	Alpha	Number of Items in Scale
Total Civic Achievement	.88	38
Civic Knowledge Subscale	.84	25
Skills in Interpreting Political Communicationas	.76	13
Conventional Citizenship	.67	6
Social Movement Citizenship	.63	4
Economy-related Government Responsibility	.55	5
Society-related Government Responsibility	.70	7
Trust in Government-related Institutions	.78	6
Positive Attitudes toward One's Nation	.68	4
Support for Women's Rights	.79	6
Positive Attitudes toward Immigrants	.82	5
Confidence in Participation in School	.69	4
Expected Participation in Political Activities	.73	3
Open Climate for Classroom Discussions	.76	6
Coefficients computed for calibration sample of 500 students per country.		

Source: IEA Civic Education Study, Standard Population of 14-year-olds tested in 1999.

Table C.2 Cronbach's Alpha Reliability Coefficients Within Countries: Civic Knowledge Subscales and Overall Test

Country	Content Knowledge	Skills in Interpreting Political Communication	Total Civic Knowledge
Australia	.85	.80	.90
Belgium (French)	.82	.76	.88
Bulgaria	.85	.73	.89
Chile	.80	.77	.87
Colombia	.79	.74	.86
Cyprus	.81	.73	.87
Czech Republic	.83	.71	.88
Denmark	.86	.78	.90
England	.83	.77	.88
Estonia	.79	.71	.86
Finland	.83	.72	.88
Germany	.84	.74	.89
Greece	.84	.78	.89
Hong Kong (SAR)	.88	.81	.91
Hungary	.81	.74	.87
Italy	.83	.73	.88
Latvia	.82	.71	.87
Lithuania	.82	.70	.87
Norway	.86	.74	.90
Poland	.86	.77	.90
Portugal	.81	.68	.86
Romania	.83	.65	.87
Russian Federation	.86	.79	.90
Slovak Republic	.79	.70	.86
Slovenia	.82	.71	.87
Sweden	.84	.74	.89
Switzerland	.82	.71	.87
United States	.86	.81	.90
Median	**.83**	**.74**	**.88**
Number of items	*25*	*13*	*38*

Source: IEA Civic Education Study, Standard Population of 14-year-olds tested in 1999.

APPENDIX D STANDARD DEVIATIONS OF TOTAL CIVIC KNOWLEDGE

Table D.1 Standard Deviations of Total Civic Knowledge

Country	Overall		Females		Males	
	Mean	Standard deviation	Mean	Standard deviation	Mean	Standard deviation
Australia	102 (0.8)	20	103 (0.9)	18	101 (1.1)	22
Belgium (French)	95 (0.9)	18	97 (1.1)	17	93 (1.3)	19
Bulgaria	98 (1.3)	20	99 (1.5)	20	97 (1.2)	20
Chile	88 (0.8)	17	88 (0.8)	16	89 (0.8)	17
Colombia	86 (1.2)	15	87 (1.3)	15	86 (1.1)	16
Cyprus	108 (0.5)	19	108 (0.7)	19	108 (0.6)	20
Czech Republic	103 (0.8)	19	102 (0.8)	18	104 (1.0)	19
Denmark	100 (0.5)	21	99 (0.7)	20	102 (0.7)	22
England	99 (0.7)	19	99 (0.8)	18	100 (1.0)	20
Estonia	94 (0.5)	16	95 (0.6)	16	93 (0.7)	17
Finland	109 (0.6)	21	110 (0.9)	19	108 (0.8)	22
Germany	100 (0.5)	19	99 (0.6)	18	101 (0.7)	19
Greece	108 (0.7)	21	109 (0.8)	21	107 (0.9)	22
Hong Kong (SAR)	107 (1.0)	23	108 (1.1)	21	106 (1.4)	24
Hungary	102 (0.7)	18	102 (0.7)	17	101 (0.8)	18
Italy	105 (0.7)	19	106 (0.9)	19	104 (1.1)	20
Latvia	92 (0.8)	17	93 (0.9)	17	90 (0.9)	16
Lithuania	94 (0.7)	17	95 (0.8)	16	92 (0.8)	17
Norway	103 (0.4)	20	103 (0.6)	19	103 (0.7)	22
Poland	111 (1.7)	22	112 (2.2)	22	109 (1.5)	23
Portugal	96 (0.7)	17	96 (0.8)	16	97 (0.9)	17
Romania	92 (0.7)	17	92 (1.0)	17	91 (0.9)	16
Russian Federation	100 (1.3)	21	99 (1.2)	20	100 (1.7)	22
Slovak Republic	105 (0.7)	17	105 (0.8)	17	105 (0.9)	17
Slovenia	101 (0.4)	18	102 (0.6)	17	99 (0.6)	18
Sweden	99 (0.7)	20	100 (0.8)	18	99 (1.1)	21
Switzerland	98 (0.8)	17	97 (0.8)	16	100 (0.9)	18
United States	106 (1.0)	22	107 (1.2)	21	106 (1.3)	24

( ) Standard errors appear in parentheses.

Source: IEA Civic Education Study, Standard Population of 14-year-olds tested in 1999.

Table E.1 Teachers' Perceptions of Students' Opportunities to Learn

| Country | Percentage of Students whose Teachers Perceive 'Considerable' or 'Very Much' Opportunity to Learn About… | | | | | | | | | |
| | Constitution and political system | | | | | | Citizen and human rights | | | |
	National history	National constitution	Democracy	Electoral systems	Political systems	Judicial system	Citizen rights	Human rights	Equal opportunities	Cultural differences
Australia	70 (3.8)	18 (3.2)	28 (3.7)	32 (3.7)	21 (3.3)	22 (3.2)	43 (3.5)	38 (3.6)	42 (3.9)	50 (3.8)
Belgium (French)	31 (5.0)	3 (1.7)	18 (3.9)	8 (2.9)	13 (3.5)	7 (2.8)	30 (5.2)	40 (5.3)	26 (5.0)	26 (5.0)
Bulgaria	88 (1.8)	33 (3.2)	26 (3.2)	23 (2.8)	34 (4.1)	12 (2.4)	40 (3.6)	45 (4.9)	n.a. (n.a.)	n.a. (n.a.)
Chile	84 (3.4)	35 (3.6)	32 (3.4)	32 (3.8)	25 (3.2)	22 (3.1)	58 (4.1)	56 (4.0)	63 (3.4)	63 (3.4)
Cyprus	80 (2.7)	24 (2.6)	26 (3.4)	28 (2.6)	26 (2.7)	12 (1.7)	58 (3.4)	74 (2.8)	57 (3.5)	57 (3.5)
Czech Republic	84 (2.5)	68 (3.6)	51 (4.2)	60 (4.5)	45 (4.5)	35 (4.1)	89 (2.5)	91 (2.1)	57 (3.7)	61 (3.5)
Denmark	91 (1.8)	79 (2.5)	77 (3.0)	63 (2.7)	80 (2.6)	70 (2.6)	84 (2.3)	89 (1.8)	85 (2.1)	84 (2.3)
England	82 (2.1)	22 (2.6)	25 (2.7)	22 (2.6)	36 (2.8)	19 (2.7)	43 (3.0)	50 (3.1)	64 (2.5)	64 (2.5)
Estonia	83 (3.3)	29 (3.8)	21 (3.4)	24 (3.5)	21 (3.2)	18 (2.9)	46 (3.9)	47 (4.1)	32 (3.9)	32 (3.9)
Finland	91 (2.7)	11 (2.9)	36 (4.3)	16 (3.2)	35 (4.0)	12 (2.4)	17 (3.2)	36 (4.1)	21 (3.5)	21 (3.5)
Germany	56 (4.9)	26 (3.9)	18 (3.5)	43 (3.9)	30 (4.0)	23 (3.1)	48 (4.4)	50 (4.3)	44 (5.0)	44 (5.0)
Greece	91 (2.0)	31 (3.6)	27 (3.2)	21 (2.9)	27 (3.3)	10 (2.0)	60 (3.4)	61 (3.4)	55 (3.3)	32 (3.2)
Hong Kong (SAR)	51 (2.3)	10 (1.7)	13 (1.7)	36 (2.4)	11 (1.8)	29 (2.5)	59 (2.3)	40 (2.4)	35 (2.4)	35 (2.4)
Hungary	77 (3.9)	40 (4.1)	30 (4.1)	36 (3.8)	41 (4.3)	24 (3.8)	44 (4.0)	37 (3.8)	33 (3.8)	30 (4.1)
Italy	71 (3.1)	51 (3.4)	42 (3.5)	22 (2.7)	28 (3.0)	18 (2.5)	66 (2.8)	69 (3.1)	46 (3.5)	46 (3.5)
Latvia	81 (3.0)	20 (2.6)	37 (3.3)	18 (2.3)	25 (2.9)	5 (1.5)	44 (3.7)	40 (3.6)	31 (2.9)	31 (2.9)
Lithuania	78 (3.0)	20 (2.4)	15 (2.5)	13 (2.8)	16 (3.1)	12 (2.2)	48 (3.3)	48 (3.4)	26 (3.1)	26 (2.9)
Norway	92 (1.9)	72 (3.1)	47 (3.1)	65 (3.3)	64 (3.2)	59 (3.3)	60 (3.7)	88 (2.2)	87 (2.2)	78 (3.1)
Poland	96 (1.4)	88 (2.1)	61 (3.5)	74 (3.3)	59 (4.6)	54 (4.4)	88 (2.4)	87 (2.4)	65 (4.0)	65 (4.0)
Portugal	72 (2.4)	23 (1.7)	34 (2.7)	17 (2.0)	38 (2.6)	6 (1.3)	47 (2.6)	52 (2.5)	38 (2.9)	43 (2.6)
Romania	91 (1.9)	54 (3.6)	34 (3.2)	30 (3.7)	24 (2.6)	16 (2.3)	61 (3.3)	55 (3.3)	32 (3.3)	32 (3.3)
Russian Federation	93 (1.9)	87 (3.2)	74 (3.6)	62 (3.5)	63 (3.9)	58 (4.1)	94 (1.6)	92 (2.0)	60 (3.6)	60 (3.6)
Slovak Republic	62 (3.1)	96 (1.2)	87 (2.5)	80 (2.9)	58 (3.4)	59 (3.1)	98 (1.2)	95 (1.5)	74 (2.9)	74 (2.9)
Slovenia	86 (1.9)	36 (2.9)	57 (2.8)	20 (2.4)	40 (2.8)	7 (1.6)	72 (2.8)	77 (2.1)	70 (2.6)	70 (2.6)
Sweden	87 (4.0)	86 (4.0)	87 (3.7)	87 (4.0)	81 (4.9)	98 (0.6)	96 (1.5)	92 (2.1)	83 (5.0)	83 (5.0)
Switzerland	63 (4.8)	36 (3.9)	33 (4.2)	47 (4.8)	42 (3.8)	16 (2.4)	51 (4.8)	63 (4.3)	53 (4.0)	53 (4.8)

() Standard errors appear in parentheses. Percentages based on valid responses.

Data from Colombia and the United States are omitted from all tables in this appendix due to country-specific problems in ascertaining the linkage between teachers and classes of students.

Source: IEA Civic Education Study, Standard Population of 14-year-olds tested in 1999.

Table E.1 (continued) Teachers' Perceptions of Students' Opportunities to Learn

Country	International organizations and relations			Economics and welfare			Media		Others	
	International organizations	International problems	Migrations	Economic issues	Social welfare	Trade unions	Dangers of propaganda	Media	Environmental issues	Civic virtues
Australia	16 (2.4)	28 (3.4)	33 (3.6)	20 (3.1)	24 (3.1)	12 (2.7)	30 (3.7)	54 (3.7)	68 (3.8)	34 (4.0)
Belgium (French)	6 (1.7)	15 (3.7)	17 (3.4)	17 (4.3)	4 (1.9)	1 (0.8)	27 (5.0)	41 (5.7)	47 (4.8)	32 (5.2)
Bulgaria	38 (5.4)	n.a. (n.a.)	n.a. (n.a.)	n.a. (n.a.)	n.a. (n.a.)	n.a. (n.a.)	n.a. (n.a.)	n.a. (n.a.)	n.a. (n.a.)	n.a. (n.a.)
Chile	38 (3.5)	25 (3.4)	24 (3.0)	34 (3.7)	40 (4.1)	13 (2.8)	34 (3.1)	65 (3.5)	87 (2.3)	73 (3.2)
Cyprus	47 (3.0)	24 (2.8)	23 (2.6)	15 (2.0)	34 (3.3)	14 (1.9)	30 (2.9)	53 (3.3)	73 (2.4)	71 (3.0)
Czech Republic	44 (4.3)	63 (3.6)	33 (3.6)	29 (3.3)	42 (4.0)	16 (2.9)	55 (4.3)	66 (3.4)	88 (2.2)	76 (3.1)
Denmark	71 (3.1)	73 (2.8)	82 (2.6)	57 (3.1)	79 (2.6)	64 (3.1)	83 (2.4)	92 (1.9)	90 (1.8)	76 (2.9)
England	31 (2.8)	39 (2.9)	38 (2.2)	42 (2.5)	43 (2.9)	24 (2.7)	57 (2.5)	61 (2.9)	70 (2.4)	19 (2.5)
Estonia	22 (3.1)	25 (3.1)	20 (2.8)	31 (3.3)	36 (3.8)	13 (2.6)	20 (3.3)	48 (3.9)	69 (3.5)	38 (4.0)
Finland	29 (3.9)	63 (3.9)	38 (4.2)	19 (3.0)	10 (2.6)	7 (2.4)	45 (4.5)	30 (4.0)	17 (3.2)	12 (2.9)
Germany	11 (3.3)	22 (3.5)	19 (3.0)	35 (3.2)	27 (2.7)	14 (3.2)	33 (4.1)	54 (4.2)	69 (4.6)	22 (3.9)
Greece	16 (2.6)	18 (2.8)	36 (3.6)	13 (2.6)	30 (3.4)	12 (2.3)	23 (3.1)	63 (3.4)	78 (2.9)	41 (3.8)
Hong Kong (SAR)	8 (1.6)	12 (1.9)	26 (2.1)	34 (2.7)	33 (2.2)	9 (1.6)	25 (2.1)	42 (2.2)	62 (2.4)	61 (2.5)
Hungary	29 (3.5)	31 (3.9)	21 (3.7)	31 (3.9)	29 (3.7)	31 (4.0)	25 (3.8)	37 (3.9)	43 (4.2)	35 (3.9)
Italy	39 (3.4)	27 (3.1)	59 (3.1)	36 (2.9)	34 (2.9)	17 (2.1)	40 (3.2)	63 (2.8)	74 (2.7)	44 (3.5)
Latvia	21 (3.2)	26 (2.9)	26 (3.0)	62 (3.1)	45 (3.2)	9 (1.6)	15 (2.8)	42 (3.4)	69 (3.2)	47 (3.2)
Lithuania	11 (1.8)	12 (1.9)	12 (2.2)	27 (3.5)	34 (3.2)	3 (1.1)	10 (2.2)	35 (3.3)	50 (3.2)	60 (3.1)
Norway	49 (3.2)	66 (3.1)	33 (3.2)	28 (3.0)	16 (2.5)	36 (3.6)	65 (3.5)	80 (3.0)	83 (2.8)	87 (2.3)
Poland	64 (3.6)	54 (3.3)	34 (5.1)	39 (5.2)	52 (3.4)	43 (5.8)	49 (3.9)	72 (2.7)	91 (2.2)	79 (3.0)
Portugal	33 (3.0)	32 (2.6)	42 (2.9)	34 (2.4)	8 (1.5)	9 (1.6)	29 (2.5)	40 (2.5)	69 (2.3)	41 (2.9)
Romania	30 (2.5)	30 (2.9)	43 (3.0)	43 (3.1)	44 (3.4)	18 (2.5)	20 (2.7)	60 (3.4)	69 (2.4)	53 (2.8)
Russian Federation	54 (3.8)	48 (4.1)	27 (3.9)	58 (4.8)	59 (3.0)	28 (3.2)	38 (3.0)	58 (4.1)	75 (3.0)	84 (2.8)
Slovak Republic	59 (3.7)	66 (3.5)	39 (3.3)	62 (3.7)	70 (3.1)	37 (3.8)	81 (2.8)	84 (2.4)	96 (1.4)	87 (2.4)
Slovenia	50 (3.2)	47 (2.8)	48 (2.9)	26 (2.2)	29 (2.6)	16 (2.1)	46 (3.1)	69 (2.8)	86 (2.0)	52 (3.0)
Sweden	69 (6.7)	79 (4.9)	58 (5.7)	79 (4.3)	76 (5.9)	55 (5.9)	90 (3.8)	88 (4.0)	87 (4.5)	96 (1.7)
Switzerland	25 (4.8)	33 (3.8)	38 (4.1)	29 (3.5)	23 (3.3)	14 (2.9)	47 (4.6)	65 (4.5)	63 (4.4)	19 (4.4)

Percentage of Students whose Teachers Perceive 'Considerable' or 'Very Much' Opportunity to Learn About…

() Standard errors appear in parentheses. Percentages based on valid responses.

Source: IEA Civic Education Study, Standard Population of 14-year-olds tested in 1999.

Table E.2 Teachers' Reports of Type of Assessment Used (two choices, percent chosen)

Country	Percentage of Students whose Teachers Report to Rely Primarily on...					
	Written compositions	Multiple-choice tests	Oral assessments	Oral participation	Other	No specific assessment
Australia	75 (3.5)	14 (2.3)	35 (3.3)	33 (3.9)	32 (3.8)	1 (0.4)
Belgium (French)	45 (4.7)	12 (3.5)	16 (3.7)	54 (5.0)	11 (3.3)	13 (3.5)
Chile	48 (3.1)	32 (3.4)	24 (3.3)	53 (3.6)	28 (3.2)	3 (1.1)
Cyprus	42 (3.0)	36 (3.5)	17 (2.7)	83 (2.3)	11 (1.9)	1 (0.7)
Czech Republic	37 (3.1)	27 (3.1)	39 (2.8)	77 (2.5)	10 (2.1)	0 (0.1)
England	38 (2.4)	4 (1.2)	39 (2.6)	66 (3.0)	11 (1.7)	12 (2.0)
Estonia	52 (3.7)	23 (3.1)	53 (3.6)	40 (3.8)	11 (2.3)	4 (1.4)
Finland	91 (2.0)	7 (1.7)	8 (2.2)	90 (2.4)	4 (1.7)	n.a. (n.a.)
Germany	81 (3.3)	2 (1.1)	27 (3.9)	71 (4.3)	10 (2.8)	2 (1.1)
Greece	72 (3.2)	9 (2.1)	26 (3.4)	83 (2.6)	5 (1.0)	0 (0.0)
Hong Kong (SAR)	25 (2.0)	15 (2.0)	12 (1.8)	73 (1.9)	24 (2.3)	10 (1.6)
Hungary	62 (4.1)	17 (3.3)	58 (4.2)	45 (4.6)	4 (1.8)	1 (1.0)
Italy	15 (2.3)	19 (2.6)	73 (2.5)	68 (2.8)	2 (0.9)	3 (1.1)
Norway	84 (2.2)	9 (1.6)	4 (1.3)	86 (2.4)	14 (2.4)	n.a. (n.a.)
Romania	35 (3.2)	50 (3.6)	42 (3.2)	58 (3.1)	3 (0.9)	1 (0.6)
Russian Federation	55 (3.1)	46 (3.8)	77 (3.7)	14 (2.6)	6 (1.6)	n.a. (n.a.)
Slovenia	37 (2.5)	12 (2.1)	23 (2.7)	59 (2.9)	7 (1.4)	18 (2.2)
Sweden	79 (5.3)	n.a. (n.a.)	28 (6.2)	58 (5.8)	19 (5.0)	n.a. (n.a.)

() Standard errors appear in parentheses.

Data are not available for Bulgaria, Denmark, Latvia, Lithuania, Poland, Portugal, Slovak Republic and Switzerland.

Source: IEA Civic Education Study, Standard Population of 14-year-olds tested in 1999.

Table E.3 Teachers' Reports on the Importance of Sources for Planning Civic Education-related Activities

Country	Percentage of Students whose Teachers Consider as 'Important' or 'Very Important'						
	Curricular guidelines	Approved textbooks	Original sources	External materials	Media	Personal assessment	Self-produced materials
Australia	79 (2.7)	77 (3.1)	86 (3.0)	50 (3.9)	97 (1.1)	82 (3.1)	78 (3.3)
Belgium (French)	25 (4.8)	60 (5.3)	98 (1.3)	53 (5.9)	97 (1.3)	78 (5.0)	23 (4.8)
Bulgaria	92 (1.8)	93 (1.4)	96 (1.3)	38 (2.8)	77 (3.5)	84 (3.1)	77 (3.2)
Chile	87 (2.4)	94 (1.6)	98 (0.5)	73 (3.3)	97 (1.6)	77 (4.0)	89 (3.5)
Cyprus	88 (2.4)	93 (1.8)	96 (1.5)	50 (3.6)	91 (1.7)	90 (1.7)	88 (2.0)
Czech Republic	80 (3.9)	77 (2.9)	92 (2.1)	23 (3.0)	80 (2.9)	84 (2.5)	58 (3.6)
Denmark	81 (2.4)	61 (3.3)	92 (1.8)	22 (2.5)	99 (0.6)	88 (1.7)	75 (3.0)
England	52 (3.0)	57 (2.6)	69 (2.8)	50 (2.9)	89 (1.8)	75 (2.4)	82 (2.4)
Estonia	87 (2.8)	89 (2.1)	97 (1.2)	47 (3.4)	94 (1.9)	88 (2.4)	81 (3.2)
Finland	67 (4.5)	83 (3.7)	82 (3.3)	44 (4.8)	100 (0.0)	99 (0.5)	93 (2.2)
Germany	84 (3.3)	92 (2.1)	94 (2.3)	56 (4.4)	99 (0.5)	81 (3.2)	87 (3.1)
Greece	92 (1.8)	100 (0.3)	97 (1.1)	78 (2.9)	95 (1.5)	90 (2.0)	94 (2.0)
Hong Kong (SAR)	56 (2.7)	52 (2.8)	59 (2.7)	51 (2.6)	81 (2.0)	85 (1.6)	72 (2.6)
Hungary	78 (3.6)	79 (3.4)	93 (2.3)	21 (3.6)	95 (1.8)	89 (2.5)	81 (3.2)
Italy	56 (3.0)	64 (3.5)	97 (1.1)	43 (3.6)	92 (1.9)	76 (3.0)	62 (3.6)
Latvia	84 (2.3)	84 (2.4)	95 (1.3)	44 (3.1)	94 (1.6)	89 (2.2)	78 (2.8)
Lithuania	84 (2.4)	87 (2.5)	98 (0.7)	31 (3.0)	90 (2.3)	86 (2.1)	83 (2.5)
Norway	88 (2.2)	88 (1.9)	83 (2.1)	43 (2.6)	97 (0.9)	82 (2.1)	56 (2.6)
Poland	87 (3.2)	78 (3.1)	100 (0.3)	65 (3.6)	94 (2.5)	82 (3.2)	83 (2.7)
Portugal	77 (2.4)	73 (2.4)	94 (1.3)	83 (1.7)	97 (0.9)	90 (2.0)	80 (1.8)
Romania	78 (2.3)	97 (0.9)	97 (0.7)	55 (3.5)	92 (1.6)	89 (1.8)	84 (2.3)
Russian Federation	91 (2.1)	87 (2.6)	100 (0.4)	20 (3.2)	94 (2.3)	82 (3.3)	74 (3.9)
Slovak Republic	93 (1.5)	88 (2.0)	95 (1.6)	22 (2.8)	80 (2.5)	87 (2.0)	62 (3.4)
Slovenia	84 (2.2)	89 (1.9)	94 (1.2)	71 (2.5)	92 (1.6)	87 (2.0)	83 (2.0)
Sweden	94 (2.3)	57 (5.0)	71 (5.8)	25 (4.4)	96 (2.4)	97 (1.4)	75 (5.5)
Switzerland	56 (4.2)	78 (3.5)	94 (1.6)	43 (4.7)	97 (1.1)	93 (1.8)	81 (3.2)

( ) Standard errors appear in parentheses.

Source: IEA Civic Education Study, Standard Population of 14-year-olds tested in 1999.

Table E.4 Teachers' Reports on Their Conceptualization of Civic Education

Country	Percentage of Students whose Teachers 'Agree' or 'Strongly Agree' that...			
	there is a broad consensus in our society as to what is worth learning	there cannot be agreement on what should be taught	teachers should teach according to curriculum standards	teachers should negotiate with students what is to be studied
Australia	46 (3.3)	21 (3.1)	82 (3.6)	49 (3.5)
Belgium (French)	33 (4.9)	18 (3.9)	61 (5.2)	79 (3.5)
Bulgaria	20 (3.0)	36 (3.7)	81 (3.1)	58 (4.7)
Chile	22 (2.3)	13 (2.2)	74 (2.8)	65 (3.4)
Cyprus	49 (3.2)	37 (3.2)	70 (3.1)	70 (3.2)
Czech Republic	51 (3.5)	13 (2.6)	93 (1.7)	29 (4.0)
Denmark	32 (2.7)	29 (2.8)	74 (2.5)	70 (3.3)
England	43 (2.5)	40 (3.1)	51 (2.9)	46 (2.8)
Estonia	26 (3.2)	27 (2.6)	81 (2.6)	72 (3.0)
Finland	50 (4.3)	18 (3.5)	81 (3.6)	59 (4.6)
Germany	31 (4.3)	18 (3.2)	79 (4.0)	39 (4.2)
Greece	60 (3.3)	38 (3.2)	62 (3.5)	45 (3.6)
Hong Kong (SAR)	41 (2.4)	75 (2.0)	64 (2.6)	86 (1.9)
Hungary	4 (1.7)	27 (3.8)	75 (3.9)	47 (4.3)
Italy	25 (2.8)	15 (2.6)	40 (3.1)	70 (2.9)
Latvia	12 (2.0)	35 (3.0)	85 (2.0)	54 (2.8)
Lithuania	32 (3.1)	23 (2.9)	83 (2.6)	69 (2.8)
Norway	36 (2.8)	18 (2.3)	76 (2.6)	89 (2.2)
Poland	14 (2.0)	15 (2.2)	66 (4.0)	82 (2.7)
Portugal	24 (2.6)	14 (2.0)	81 (2.0)	55 (2.8)
Romania	58 (3.4)	32 (3.6)	92 (1.4)	55 (3.6)
Russian Federation	36 (3.3)	17 (2.1)	91 (2.2)	60 (4.0)
Slovak Republic	68 (3.3)	17 (2.8)	94 (1.5)	22 (2.8)
Slovenia	20 (2.4)	46 (2.8)	83 (1.9)	50 (2.7)
Sweden	68 (6.2)	17 (3.9)	98 (2.0)	87 (3.3)
Switzerland	22 (3.0)	39 (3.7)	75 (3.7)	40 (3.8)

( ) Standard errors appear in parentheses.

Source: IEA Civic Education Study, Standard Population of 14-year-olds tested in 1999.

Table E.5 Teachers' Reports on What Students Learn in School

Country	Percent of Students whose Teachers 'Agree' or 'Strongly Agree' that Students Learn in School...						
	to understand people who have different ideas	to co-operate in groups with other students	to contribute to solve problems in the community	to be patriotic and loyal citizens of their country	how to act to protect the environment	to be concerned what happens in other countries	about importance of voting in national and local elections
Australia	86 (2.6)	95 (1.7)	68 (3.4)	37 (4.4)	90 (2.5)	79 (3.0)	65 (3.9)
Belgium (French)	91 (2.6)	85 (3.5)	69 (4.8)	33 (4.0)	79 (4.1)	79 (3.9)	56 (5.2)
Bulgaria	82 (2.7)	81 (3.5)	57 (4.4)	88 (3.0)	91 (1.9)	81 (3.1)	39 (3.6)
Chile	87 (1.8)	95 (1.6)	75 (2.7)	86 (2.1)	93 (1.6)	76 (2.6)	78 (2.9)
Cyprus	86 (1.8)	86 (1.8)	75 (2.3)	96 (1.1)	87 (2.3)	83 (2.2)	90 (2.1)
Czech Republic	89 (2.0)	91 (1.9)	87 (2.3)	88 (2.3)	99 (0.5)	97 (1.2)	89 (2.2)
Denmark	91 (1.9)	99 (0.6)	67 (2.9)	31 (2.9)	93 (1.4)	95 (1.5)	89 (1.9)
England	96 (1.1)	98 (0.7)	67 (2.8)	22 (2.7)	93 (1.4)	85 (2.3)	48 (2.9)
Estonia	83 (3.0)	93 (1.9)	59 (3.5)	83 (2.3)	91 (2.0)	88 (2.2)	79 (2.6)
Finland	81 (3.7)	95 (2.2)	41 (4.6)	80 (4.0)	90 (3.0)	85 (3.4)	93 (2.3)
Germany	83 (3.1)	80 (3.8)	50 (5.0)	25 (3.4)	91 (2.6)	87 (3.3)	84 (2.7)
Greece	79 (3.2)	79 (2.8)	76 (2.9)	83 (2.6)	86 (2.2)	71 (3.4)	82 (2.8)
Hong Kong (SAR)	65 (2.3)	89 (1.8)	37 (2.4)	29 (2.6)	72 (2.6)	39 (2.9)	71 (2.5)
Hungary	85 (3.2)	95 (1.8)	58 (4.2)	84 (3.0)	91 (2.5)	76 (3.4)	86 (2.9)
Italy	82 (2.4)	72 (2.7)	54 (3.5)	35 (3.4)	76 (2.7)	77 (2.6)	66 (3.2)
Latvia	85 (2.0)	93 (1.7)	61 (3.2)	79 (2.6)	90 (1.9)	92 (1.6)	76 (2.5)
Lithuania	93 (1.9)	94 (1.8)	79 (2.8)	89 (2.1)	94 (1.4)	92 (1.6)	72 (2.7)
Norway	97 (1.4)	95 (1.3)	48 (3.6)	50 (3.2)	88 (2.0)	95 (1.1)	90 (1.9)
Poland	97 (0.9)	97 (0.8)	65 (3.8)	97 (0.8)	98 (0.8)	89 (2.1)	89 (2.0)
Portugal	88 (1.8)	95 (1.1)	63 (2.6)	55 (2.8)	95 (1.0)	72 (2.4)	59 (2.7)
Romania	85 (2.3)	89 (1.9)	81 (2.5)	97 (0.9)	92 (1.6)	88 (1.8)	84 (2.0)
Russian Federation	96 (1.1)	94 (1.3)	62 (3.7)	98 (0.9)	95 (1.5)	98 (0.8)	89 (2.7)
Slovak Republic	86 (2.6)	90 (2.3)	92 (1.8)	94 (1.7)	99 (0.7)	96 (1.2)	93 (1.9)
Slovenia	94 (1.5)	94 (1.4)	89 (1.8)	66 (2.8)	95 (1.3)	86 (1.9)	41 (2.7)
Sweden	96 (1.7)	96 (1.6)	67 (5.6)	23 (4.4)	92 (3.6)	98 (0.7)	99 (0.6)
Switzerland	90 (2.1)	91 (2.5)	54 (4.1)	29 (4.2)	87 (2.9)	91 (2.5)	72 (4.1)

( ) Standard errors appear in parentheses.

Source: IEA Civic Education Study, Standard Population of 14-year-olds tested in 1999.

CITIZENSHIP AND EDUCATION IN TWENTY-EIGHT COUNTRIES

REFERENCES

Adler, M. A. (1996) Xenophobia and ethnoviolence in contemporary Germany. *Critical Sociology, 22*(1), 29-51.

Allerbeck, K. R., Jennings, M. K. and Rosenmayr, L. (1979) Generations and families: Political action. In S. H. Barnes, M. Kaase *et al.* (Eds.), *Political action: Mass participation in five Western democracies.* (pp.487–521) Beverly Hills: Sage Publications.

Anderson, C., Avery, P. G., Pederson, P. V., Smith, E. S. and Sullivan, J. L. (1997) Divergent perspectives on citizenship education: A Q-method study and survey of social studies teachers. *American Educational Research Journal, 34*(2), 333–64.

Angvik, M. and von Borries, B. (Eds.) (1997) *Youth and history: A comparative European survey on historical consciousness and political attitudes among adolescents* (Vol. A-B) Hamburg: Korber-Stiftung.

Barnes, S. H., Kaase, M. *et al.* (1979) *Political action: Mass participation in five Western democracies.* Beverly Hills: Sage Publications.

Barrett, M. (1996) English children's acquisition of a European identity. In G. M. Breakwell and E. Lyons (Eds.), *Changing European identities: Social psychological analyses of social change* (pp.349–70) Oxford: Butterworth-Heinemann: a division of Reed Educational and Professional Publishing Ltd.

Baughn, C. C. and Yaprak, A. (1996) Economic nationalism: Conceptual and empirical development. *Political Psychology, 17*(4), 759–78.

Beaton, A. E., Mullis, I. V. S., Martin, M. O., Gonzalez, E. J., Kelly, D. L. and Smith, T. A. (1996) *Mathematics achievement in the middle school years: IEA's Third International Mathematics and Science Study (TIMSS).* Chesnut Hill, MA: TIMSS International Study Center, Boston College.

Beetham, D. (1994) Key principles and indices for a democratic audit. In D. Beetham (Ed.), *Defining and measuring democracy* (pp.25–43). Bakersfield, CA: Sage Publications.

Bennett, S. E. (1998) Young Americans' indifference to media coverage of public affairs. *Political Science and Politics, 31*(3), 535–41.

Billiet, J. B. (1995) Church involvement, ethnocentrism and voting for a radical right-wing party: Diverging behavioral outcomes of equal attitudinal dispositions. *Sociology of Religion, 56*(3), 303–26.

Bronfenbrenner, U. (1988) Interacting systems in human development. In N. Bolger, C. Caspi, G. Downey and M. Moorehouse (Eds.), *Persons in context: Developmental processes* (pp.25–50). Cambridge, England: Cambridge University Press.

Buckingham, D. (1999) Young people, politics and news media: Beyond political socialization. *Oxford Review of Education, 25,* 171–84.

Campbell, A., Converse, P. E., Miller, W. E. and Stokes, D. E. (1964) *The American voter* (rev. ed.) New York: Wiley.

Chaffee, S., Morduchowicz, R. and Galperin, H. (1998) Education for democracy in Argentina: Effects of a newspapers in schools program. In O. Ichilov (Ed.), *Citizenship and citizenship education in a changing world* (pp.149–73) London: Woburn Press.

Chaffee, S. H., Ward, L. S. and Tipton, L. P. (1970) Mass communication and political socialization. *Journalism Quarterly, 47,* 447–59.

Chall, J. and Henry, D. (1991) Reading and civic literacy: Are we literate enough to meet our civic responsibilities. In S. Stotsky (Ed.), *Connecting civic education and language education.* New York: Teachers College Press.

Chryssochoou, X. (1996) How group membership is formed: Self-categorization or group beliefs? The construction of a European identity in France and Greece. In G. M. Breakwell and E. Lyons (Eds.), *Changing European identities: Social psychological analyses of social change* (pp.297–314) Oxford: Butterworth-Heinemann: A division of Reed Educational and Professional Publishing Ltd.

Cinnirella, M. (1997) Towards a European identity? Interactions between the national and European social identities manifested by university students in Britain and Italy. *British Journal of Social Psychology, 36,* 19–31.

Clark, T. N. and Hoffmann-Martinot, V. (1998) *The new political culture.* Boulder, CO: Westview Press.

Comstock, F. and Paik, H. (1991) *Television and the American child.* San Diego: Academic Press.

Connell, R. (1972) *The child's construction of politics.* Melbourne: Melbourne University Press.

Conover, P. J., Crewe, I. M. and Searing, D. D. (1991) The nature of citizenship in the United States and Great Britain: Empirical comments on theoretical themes. *Journal of Politics, 53*(3), 800–32.

Conover, P. J. and Searing, D. D. (2000) A political socialization perspective. In L. M. McDonnell, P. M. Timpane and R. Benjamin (Eds.), *Rediscovering the democratic purposes of education* (pp.91–124) Lawrence: University Press of Kansas.

Currie, C., Hurrelmann, K., Setterobutte, W., Smith, R. and Todd, J. (2000) *Health behavior of school-aged children: A WHO cross-national study (HBSC) international report.* Copenhagen, Denmark: World Health Organization Regional Office for Europe.

Dahl, R. (1998) *On democracy.* New Haven: Yale University Press.

Dalton, R. (1996) *Citizen politics.* Chatham: Chatham House Publication.

Dalton, R. (1999) Political support in advanced industrial democracies. In P. Norris (Ed.), *Critical citizens: Global support for democratic government* (pp.57–77) Oxford: Oxford University Press.

Dalton, R. (2000) Citizen attitudes and political behavior. *Comparative Political Studies, 33*(6/7), 912–30.

Damico, A. J., Damico, S. B. and Conway, M. M. (1998) The democratic education of women: High school and beyond. *Women and Politics, 19*(2), 1–31.

Davies, I., Gregory, I. and Riley, S. (1999) *Good citizenship and educational provision.* London: Falmer Press.

Deliyanni-Kouimtzi, K. and Ziogou, R. (1995) Gendered youth transitions in Northern Greece: Between tradition and modernity through education. In L. Chisholm, P. Buchner, H-H. Kruger and M. du Bois-Reymond (Eds.), *Growing up in Europe: Contemporary horizons in childhood and youth studies* (Vol. 2, pp.209–20) Berlin, New York: Walter de Gruyter.

Diamond, J. (1999) *Developing democracy: Toward consolidation.* Baltimore: Johns Hopkins University Press.

Diaz-Veizades, J., Widaman, K., Little, T. and Gibbs, K. (1995) The measurement and structure of human rights attitudes. *The Journal of Social Psychology, 135*(3), 313–28.

Doig, B., Piper, K., Mellor, S. and Masters, G. (1993-94) *Conceptual understanding in social education.* Melbourne, Australia: Australian Council for Educational Research.

Doise, W., Spini, D. and Clemence, A. (1999) Human rights studied as social representations in a cross-national context. *European Journal of Psychology, 29,* 1–29.

Dowse, R. E. and Hughes, J. A. (1971) Girls, boys and politics. *British Journal of Sociology, 22,* 53–67.

Elley, W. (1994) *The IEA study of reading literacy: Achievement and instruction in thirty-two school systems.* Oxford/New York/Tokyo: Pergamon.

Flanagan, C. (1999) *The role of values in youth political development: Evidence from cross-national work.* Unpublished manuscript, Pennsylvania State University.

Flanagan, C. A., Bowes, J. M., Jonsson, B., Csapo, B. and Sheblanova, E. (1998) Ties that bind: Correlates of adolescents' civic commitments in seven countries. *Journal of Social Issues, 54*(3), 457–75.

Flanagan, C. A., Jonsson, B., Botcheva, L., Csapo, B., Bowes, J., Macek, P., Averina, J. and Sheblanova, E. (1999) Adolescents and the 'social contract': Developmental roots of citizenship in seven countries. In M. Yates and J. Youniss (Eds.), *Roots of civic identity: International perspectives on community service and activism in youth* (pp.135–56) Cambridge: Cambridge University Press.

Flanagan, C. and Sherrod, L. (1998) Youth political development: An introduction. *Journal of Social Issues, 54*(3), 447–57.

Foy, P., Rust, K. and Schleicher, A. (1996) TIMSS sample design. In M. O. Martin and D. J. Kelly (Eds.), *Third International Mathematics and Science Study technical report* (Vol. 1) Chestnut Hill, MA: Boston College.

Frederiksen, N., Mislevy, R. and Bejar, I. (1993) *Test theory for a new generation of tests.* Hillsdale, NJ: Lawrence Erlbaum Associates.

Frindte, W., Funke, F. and Waldzus, S. (1996) Xenophobia and right-wing extremism in German youth groups—some evidence against unidimensional misinterpretations. *International Journal of Intercultural Relations, 20*(3–4), 463–78.

Fuchs, D. (1991) The normalization of the unconventional: New forms of political action and new social movements. In G. Meyer and F. Ryszka (Eds.), *Political participation and democracy in Poland and West Germany* (pp.148–69) Warsaw: Osrodek Batan Spolecznych.

Fuchs, D. (1999) The democratic culture of unified Germany. In P. Norris (Ed.), *Critical citizens: Global support for democratic government* (pp.123–45) Oxford: Oxford University Press.

Fuchs, D. and Klingemann, H.-D. (1995) Citizens and the state: A relationship transformed. In D. Fuchs and H.-D. Klingemann (Eds.), *Citizens and the state* (Vol. 1, pp.419–43) Oxford: Oxford University Press.

Furnham, A. and Gunter, B. (1989) *The anatomy of adolescence: Young people's social attitudes in Britain.* New York: Routledge.

Gabriel, O. W. and van Deth, J. W. (1995) Political interest. In J. W. van Deth and E. Scarbrough (Eds.), *The impact of values* (Vol. 4, pp.390–411) Oxford: Oxford University Press.

Galambos, N. L., Almeida, D. M. and Petersen, A. C. (1990) Masculinity, femininity and sex role attitudes in early adolescence: Exploring gender intensification. *Child Development, 61*(6), 1905–1914.

Gille, M. and Krüger, W. (Eds.) (2000) *Unzufriedene Demokraten. Politische Orientierung der 16–29 jahrigen im vereinigten Deutschland.* Opladen: Leske+Budrich.

Gillespie, D. and Spohn, C. (1987) Adolescents' attitudes toward women in politics: The effect of gender and race. *Gender and Society, 1*(2), 208–18.

Gillespie, D. and Spohn, C. (1990) Adolescents' attitudes toward women in politics: A follow-up study. *Women and Politics, 10*(1), 1–16.

Gordon, T., Holland, J. and Lahelma, E. (2000) *Making spaces: Citizenship and differences in schools.* New York: St. Martin's Press.

Gundelach, P. (1995) Grass-roots activity. In J. W. van Deth and E. Scarbrough (Eds.), *The impact of values* (Vol. 4, pp.412–41) Oxford: Oxford University Press.

Hahn, C. (1996) Gender and political learning. *Theory and Research in Social Education, 24*(1), 8–35.

Hahn, C. (1998) *Becoming political: Comparative perspectives on citizenship education.* Albany: State University of New York Press.

Hambleton, R. K., Swaminathan, H. and Rogers, H. J. (1991) *Fundamentals of item response theory.* Newbury Park, London, New Delhi: SAGE Publications.

Hart, D., Atkins, R. and Ford, D. (1998) Urban America as a context for the development of moral identity in adolescence. *Journal of Social Issues, 54*(3), 513–30.

Hayes, B. C. and Makkai, T. (1996) Politics and the mass media: The differential impact of gender. *Women and Politics, 16,* 45–74.

Held, D. (1996) *Models of democracy.* Stanford, CA: Stanford University Press.

Hess, R. D. and Torney, J. V. (1967) *The development of political attitudes in children.* Chicago: Aldine.

Hibbing, J. and Patterson, S. (1994) Public trust in the new parliaments of Central and Eastern Europe. *Political Studies, 62,* 570–92.

Hilton, D. J., Erb, H.-P. , Dermoit, M. and Molian, D. J. (1996) Social representations of history and attitudes to European unification in Britain, France and Germany. In G. M. Breakwell and E. Lyons (Eds.), *Changing European identities: Social psychological analyses of social change* (pp.275–96) Oxford: Butterworth-Heinemann: A division of Reed Educational and Professional Publishing Ltd.

Hofer, M. (1999) Community service and social cognitive development in German adolescents. In M. Yates and J. Youniss (Eds.), *Roots of civic identity: International perspectives on community service and activism in youth.* (pp.114–34) Cambridge: Cambridge University Press.

Huckfeldt, R. and Sprague, J. (1993) Citizens, contexts and politics. In A. W. Finifter (Ed.), *Political science: The state of the discipline II* (pp.281–303) Washington, D.C.: The American Science Association.

Ichilov, O. (1991) Political socialization and schooling effects among Israeli adolescents. *Comparative Education Review, 35*(3), 430–46.

Ichilov, O. and Nave, N. (1981) The 'good citizen' as viewed by Israeli adolescents. *Comparative Politics, 13*(3), 361–76.

Inglehart, R. (1997) *Modernization and postmodernization: Cultural, economic and political change in 43 societies.* Princeton: Princeton University Press.

Inglehart, R. and Baker, W. (2000) Modernization, cultural change and the persistence of traditional values. *American Sociological Review, 65,* 19–51.

Italiano, P. (1991) *L'identite culturelle des jeunes francophones.* University de Liege: Centre Liegeois d'Etude de l'Opinion.

Janoski, T. (1998) *Citizenship and civil society: A framework of rights and obligations in liberal, traditional and social democratic regimes.* Cambridge: Cambridge University Press.

Jennings, M. K. and van Deth, J. W. (1990) *Continuities in political action.* Berlin, New York: Walter de Gruyter.

Jonsson, B. and Flanagan, C. (2000) Young people's views on distributive justice, rights and obligations: A cross-cultural study. *International Social Science Journal, 52,* 195–208.

Jöreskog, K. G. (1990) New Developments in LISREL: Analysis of ordinal variables using polychronic correlations and weighted least squares. *Quality and Quantity, 24,* 387–404.

Kaase, M. (1984) The challenge of 'participatory revolution' in pluralistic democracies. *International Political Science Review, 5,* 299–318.

Kaase, M. (1989) Politische Einstellungen der Jugend. In M. Markewska and R. Nave-Herz (Eds.), *Handbuch der Familien-und Jugendforschung* (Vol. 2, pp.607–24) Neuwied: Luchterhand.

Kaase, M. (1990) Mass participation. In M. K. Jennings, J. W. van Deth *et al.* (Eds.), *Continuities in political action* (pp.23–67) Berlin, New York: Walter de Gruyter.

Kaase, M. (1999) Interpersonal trust, political trust and non-institutionalised political participation in Western Europe. *West European Politics, 22*(3), 1–21.

Kaase, M. and Newton, K. (1995) *Beliefs in government.* Oxford: Oxford University Press.

Klein-Allermann, E., Kracke, B., Noack, P. and Hofer, M. (1995) Micro and macrosocial conditions of adolescents' aggressiveness and antiforeigner attitudes. *New Directions for Child Development, 70,* 71–83.

Klingemann, H.-D. (1999) Mapping political support in advanced industrial democracies. In P. Norris (Ed.), *Critical citizens: Global support for democratic government* (pp.31–56) Oxford: Oxford University Press.

Knigge, P. (1997) *Send 'em all back? Anti-immigration sentiment in Western Europe.* Paper presented at the American Political Science Association, Washington, D.C.

Kosterman, R. and Feshbach, S. (1989) Toward a measure of patriotic and nationalistic attitudes. *Political Psychology, 10*(2), 257–74.

Kracke, B., Oepke, M., Wild, E. and Noack, P. (1998) Adolescents, families and German unification: The impact of social change on antiforeigner and antidemocratic attitudes. In J. Nurmi (Ed.), *Adolescents, cultures and conflicts: Growing up in contemporary Europe* (pp.149–70) New York: Garland Publishing, Inc.

Kuhn, H.-P. (2000) *Mediennutzung und politische sozialisation: Eine empirische studie zum Zusammenhang zwischen Mediennutzung und politischer Identitatsbildung im Jugendalter.* Opladen: Leske+Budrich.

Lahteenmaa, J. (1995) Youth culture in transition to post-modernity: Finland. In L. Chisholm, P. Buchner, H.-H. Kruger and M. du Bois-Reymond (Eds.), *Growing up in Europe: Contemporary horizons in childhood and youth studies* (Vol. 2, pp.229–36) Berlin, New York: Walter de Gruyter.

Lave, J. and Wenger, E. (1991) *Situated learning: Legitimate peripheral participation.* Cambridge: Cambridge University Press.

Lee, W. O. (1999) A comparative study of teachers' perceptions of good citizenship in three Chinese cities: Guangzhou, Hangzhou and Hong Kong. In J. Lu (Ed.), *Education of Chinese: The global prospect of national cultural tradition* (pp.270–93) Nanjing: Nanjing Normal University Press.

Legge, J. S. J. (1996) Antiforeign sentiment in Germany: Power theory versus symbolic explanations of prejudice. *The Journal of Politics, 58*(2), 516–27.

Lehmann, R., Schulz, W. *et al.* (forthcoming) *Technical report: IEA Civic Education Study.* Amsterdam: IEA.

Leung, S. (1997) *The making of an alienated generation: The political socialization of secondary school students in transitional Hong Kong.* Aldershot: Ashgate.

Lijphart, A. (1997) Unequal participation: Democracy's unresolved dilemma. *American Political Science Review, 91*(1), 1–14.

Linnenbrink, L. and Anderman, E. M. (1995, April) *Motivation and news-seeking behavior.* Paper presented at the annual meeting of the American Educational Research Association, San Francisco, CA.

Lutkus, A. D., Weiss, A. R., Campbell, J. R., Mazzeo, J. and Lazer, S. (1999) *The NAEP Civics Report Card for the Nation.* Washington, D.C.: National Center for Education Statistics.

Marta, E., Rossi, G. and Boccacin, L. (1999) Youth, solidarity and civic commitment in Italy: An analysis of the personal and social characteristics of volunteers and their organizations. In M. Yates and J. Youniss (Eds.), *Roots of civic identity: International perspectives on community service and activism in youth* (pp.73–96). Cambridge: Cambridge University Press.

McAllister, I. (1999) The economic performance of governments. In P. Norris (Ed.), *Critical citizens: global support for democratic governments* (pp.188–203) Oxford: Oxford University Press.

McAllister, I. and White, S. (1994) Political participation in postcommunist Russia: Voting, activism and the potential for mass protest. *Political Studies, 42,* 593–615.

McIntyre, B. (1993) Trust in media and government: A recursive model for natives of Hong Kong and Mainland China. *Communication Research Reports, 10*(2), 203–08.

Menezes, I. and Campos, B. (1997) The process of value-meaning construction: A cross section study. *European Journal of Social Psychology, 27,* 55–73.

Meyer, G. and Ryszka, F. (Eds.) (1991) *Political participation and democracy in Poland and West Germany.* Warsaw: Osrodek Batan Spolecznych.

Miller, W. L., Timpson, A. M. and Lessnoff, M. (1996) *Political culture in contemporary Britain: People and politicians, principles and practice.* Oxford: Clarendon Press.

Minulescu, M. (1995) Rumanian childhood and youth research and policy in transition. In L. Chisholm, P. Buchner, H.-H. Kruger and M. du Bois-Reymond (Eds.), *Growing up in Europe: Contemporary horizons in childhood and youth studies* (Vol. 2, pp.251–58) Berlin, New York: Walter de Gruyter.

Moodie, E., Markova, I. and Plichtova, J. (1995) Lay representations of democracy: A study in two cultures. *Culture and Psychology, 1,* 423–53.

Moscovici, S. (1998) Notes towards a description of social representations. *European Journal of Social Psychology, 18,* 211–50.

Muller-Peters, A. (1998) The significance of national pride and national identity to the attitude toward the single European currency: A Europe-wide comparison. *Journal of Economic Psychology, 19,* 701–19.

Newton, K. (1999) Social and political trust in established democracies. In P. Norris (Ed.), *Critical citizens: Global support for democratic government* (pp.169–87) Oxford: Oxford University Press.

Newton, K. and Norris, P. (2000) Confidence in public institutions: Faith, culture or performance? In S. J. Pharr and R. D. Putnam (Eds.), *Disaffecting democracies: What's troubling the trilateral countries?* (pp.52–73) Princeton: Princeton University Press.

Nie, N. H., Junn, J. and Stehlik-Barry, K. (1996) *Education and democratic citizenship in America.* Chicago: University of Chicago Press.

Niemi, R. and Hepburn, M. (1995) The rebirth of political socialization. *Perspectives in Political Science, 24,* 7–16.

Niemi, R. and Junn, J. (1998) *Civic education: What makes students learn?* New Haven: Yale University Press.

Norris, P. (1996) Does television erode social capital? A reply to Putnam. *Political Science and Politics, 24,* 474–80.

Norris, P. (1999) *Critical citizens: Global support for democratic government.* Oxford: Oxford University Press.

Norton, P. (1997) The United Kingdom: Restoring confidence? *Parliamentary Affairs, 50,* 357–72.

Oswald, H. (1999) Political socialization in the new states of Germany. In M. Yates and J. Youniss (Eds.), *Roots of civic identity: International perspectives on community service and activism in youth* (pp.97–114) Cambridge: Cambridge University Press.

Oswald, H. and Schmid, C. (1998) Political participation of young people in East Germany. *German Politics, 7,* 147–64.

Owen, D. and Dennis, J. (1992) Sex differences in politicization: The influence of mass media. *Women and Politics, 12*(4), 19–41.

Parry, G., Moyser, G. and Day, N. (1992) *Political participation and democracy in Britain.* Cambridge: Cambridge University Press.

Pettigrew, T. F. and Meertens, R. W. (1995) Subtle and blatant prejudice in Western Europe. *European Journal of Social Psychology, 25,* 57–75.

Pharr, S. J. and Putnam, R. D. (Eds.) (2000) *Disaffected democracies: What's troubling the trilateral countries?* Princeton: Princeton University Press.

Piaget, J. and Weil, A. (1951) The development in children of the idea of the homeland and of relations with other countries. *International Social Science Bulletin, 3,* 561–78.

Plasser, F., Ulram, P. and Waldrauch, H. (1998) *Democratic consolidation in East-Central Europe.* New York: St. Martins.

Player, K., Roker, D. and Coleman, J. (1998, April) *Challenging the image: Service learning among British adolescents.* Paper presented at the Annual Meeting of the American Educational Research Association, San Diego, CA.

Prior, W. (1999) What it means to be a 'good citizen' in Australia: Perceptions of teachers, students and parents. *Theory and Research in Social Education, 27*(2), 215–48.

Putnam, R. D. (1996) The strange disappearance of civic America. *The American Prospect, 24*, 34–48.

Putnam, R. D. (2000) *Bowling alone: The collapse and revival of American community.* New York: Simon and Schuster.

Putnam, R. D., Leonardi, R. and Nanetti, R. Y. (1993) *Making democracy work: Civic traditions in modern Italy.* Princeton: Princeton University Press.

Putnam, R. D., Pharr, S. J. and Dalton, R. J. (2000) Introduction: What's troubling the trilateral democracies? In S. J. Pharr and R. D. Putnam (Eds.), *Disaffected democracies: What's troubling the trilateral countries?* (pp. 3–30) Princeton: Princeton University Press.

Rahn, W. and Transue, J. (1998) Social trust and value change: The decline of social capital in American youth, 1976–1995. *Political Psychology, 19*(3), 545–66.

Rasinski, K. A. and Smith, T. W. (1994) Fairness motivations and tradeoffs underlying public support for government environmental spending in nine nations. *Journal of Social Issues, 50*(3), 179–97.

Robinson, J. P., Shaver, P. R. and Wrightsman, L. S. (1999) *Measures of political attitudes* (Vol. 2 of Measures of Social Psychological Attitudes) San Diego: Academic Press.

Roker, D., Player, K. and Coleman, J. (1999) Exploring adolescent altruism: British young people's involvement in voluntary work and campaigning. In M. Yates and J. Youniss (Eds.), *Roots of civic identity: International perspectives on community service and activism in youth* (pp. 56–72). Cambridge: Cambridge University Press.

Roller, E. (1994) Ideological basis of the market economy: Attitudes toward distribution principles and the role of government in Western and Eastern Germany. *European Sociological Review, 10*(2), 105–17.

Roller, E. (1995) The welfare state: The equality dimension. In O. Borre and E. Scarborough (Eds.), *The scope of government.* Oxford: Oxford University Press.

Roller, E. and Wessels, B. (1996) Contexts of political protest in western democracies: Political organization and modernity. In F. E. Weil (Ed.), *Extremism, protest, social movements and democracy* (Vol. III on Research on Democracy and Society, pp. 91–134) Greenwich, CT: JAI Press.

Rose, R., Mishler, W. and Haerpfer, C. (1998) *Democracy and its alternatives: Understanding post-Communist society.* Baltimore: Johns Hopkins University Press.

Sapiro, V. (1998) Democracy minus women is not democracy: Gender and world changes in citizenship. In O. Ichilov (Ed.), *Citizenship and citizenship education in a changing world* (pp. 174–90) London: Woburn Press.

Schwille, J. and Amadeo, J. (forthcoming) The paradoxical situation of civic education in school: Ubiquitous and yet elusive. In G. Steiner-Khamsi, J. Torney-Purta and J. Schwille (Eds.), *New paradigms and recurring paradoxes in education for citizenship*. Amsterdam: Elsevier Press.

Shapiro, R. Y. and Mahajan, H. (1986) Gender differences in policy preferences: A summary of trends from the 1960s to the 1980s. *Public Opinion Quarterly, 50*, 42–61.

Sigel, R. and Hoskin, M. (1981) *The political involvement of adolescents*. New Brunswick, NJ: Rutgers University Press.

Sinatra, G., Beck, I. and McKeown, M. (1992) A longitudinal characterization of young students' knowledge of their country's government. *American Educational Research Journal, 29*, 633–61.

Slater, J. (1995) *Teaching history in the new Europe*. London: Cassell.

Sniderman, P. M., Peri, P., de Figueiredo, R. J. P. J. and Piazza, T. (2000) *The outsider: Prejudice and politics in Italy*. Princeton: Princeton University Press.

Sousa, E. S. (1996) Components of social identity or the Achilles heel of the field in the case of European integration? In G. M. Breakwell and E. Lyons (Eds.), *Changing European identities: Social psychological analyses of social change* (pp.315–28) Oxford: Butterworth-Heinemann: A division of Reed Educational and Professional Publishing Ltd.

Steiner-Khamsi, G., Torney-Purta, J. and Schwille, J. (forthcoming) *New paradigms and recurring paradoxes in education for citizenship*. Amsterdam: Elsevier Press.

Stodolsky, S. (1988) *The subject matters: Classroom activity in mathematics and social studies*. Chicago: University of Chicago Press.

Theiss-Morse, E. (1993) Conceptualizations of good citizenship and political participation. *Political Behavior, 15*(4), 355–80.

Topalova, V. (1996) Changing social identities of the Bulgarians. In G. M. Breakwell and E. Lyons (Eds.), *Changing European identities: Social psychological analyses of social change* (pp.169-80) Oxford: Butterworth-Heinemann: A division of Reed Educational and Professional Publishing Ltd.

Topf, R. (1995) Beyond electoral participation. In H.-D. Klingemann and D. Fuchs (Eds.), *Citizens and the state* (pp.52–91) Oxford: Oxford University Press.

Torney, J. V., Oppenheim, A. N. and Farnen, R. F. (1975) *Civic education in ten countries: An empirical study*. New York: John Wiley and Sons.

Torney-Purta, J. (1983) The global awareness survey: Implications for teacher education. *Theory into Practice, 21*, 200–05.

Torney-Purta, J. (1984) Political socialization and policy: The U.S. in a cross-national context. In H. Stevenson and A. Siegel (Eds.), *Review of research in child development and social policy* (pp.471–523) Chicago: University of Chicago Press.

Torney-Purta, J. (2000) An international perspective on the NAEP Civics Report Card. *The Social Studies, 94*, 148–50.

Torney-Purta, J., Hahn, C. and Amadeo, J. (2001) Principles of subject-specific instruction in education for citizenship. In J. Brophy (Ed.), *Subject-specific instructional methods and activities* (pp.371–408) Greenwich, CT: JAI Press.

Torney-Purta, J., Schwille, J. and Amadeo, J. (1999) *Civic education across countries: Twenty-four national case studies from the IEA Civic Education Project.* Amsterdam and Washington, D.C.: IEA and National Council for Social Studies.

Toth, O. (1995) Political-moral attitudes amongst young people in post-communist Hungary. In L. Chisholm, P. Buchner, H.-H. Kruger and M. du Bois-Reymond (Eds.), *Growing up in Europe: Contemporary horizons in childhood and youth studies* (Vol. 2, pp.189–94) Berlin, New York: Walter de Gruyter.

Turner, J. C. (1987) *Rediscovering the social group: A self-categorization theory.* Oxford: Basil Blackwell.

Ule, M. (1995) Growing up and social change in Slovenia. In L. Chisholm, P. Buchner, H.-H. Kruger and M. du Bois-Reymond (Eds.), *Growing up in Europe: Contemporary horizons in childhood and youth studies* (Vol. 2, pp.161–72) Berlin, New York: Walter de Gruyter.

van Deth, J. W., Maraffi, M., Newton, K. and Whiteley, P. F. (1999) *Social capital and European democracy.* London, New York: Routledge.

Verba, S., Schlozman, K. L. and Brady, H. E. (1995) *Voice and equality: Civic voluntarism in American politics.* Cambridge: Harvard University Press.

Vontz, T. S., Metcalf, K. K. and Patrick, J. J. (2000) *Project Citizen and the civic development of adolescent students in Indiana, Latvia and Lithuania.* Bloomington, IN: The ERIC Clearinghouse for Social Studies/Social Science Education.

Walker, D. (1996) Young people, politics and the media. In H. Robert and D. Sachdev (Eds.), *Young people's social attitudes.* Ilford: Barnados.

Walt Whitman Center for the Culture and Politics of Democracy (1997) *The Measuring Citzenship Project: The final report.* New Brunswick, NJ: Rutgers University.

Watts, M. W. (1996) Political xenophobia in the transition from socialism: threat, racism and ideology among East German youth. *Political Psychology, 17*(1), 97–126.

Weiss, H. (1999) Youth in four post-communist countries: Political values and nationalist traditions. In S. Hubner-Funk and M. du Bois-Reymond (Eds.), *European yearbook on youth policy and research: Vol. 2 Intercultural reconstruction: Trends and challenges* (pp.13–31) New York: Walter de Gruyter.

Wenger, E. (1998) *Communities of practice: Learning, meaning and identity.* Cambridge: Cambridge University Press.

Westin, C. (1998) Immigration, xenophobia and youthful opinion. In J. Nurmi (Ed.), *Adolescents, cultures and conflicts: Growing up in contemporary Europe.* (pp.225–41) New York: Garland Publishing, Inc.

Yates, M. (1999) Community service and political-moral discussions among adolescents: A study of a mandatory school-based program in the United States. In M. Yates and J. Youniss (Eds.), *Roots of civic identity: International perspectives on community service and activism in youth* (pp.16–31). Cambridge: Cambridge University Press.

Yeich, S. and Levine, R. (1994) Political efficacy: Enhancing the construct and its relationship to mobilization of people. *Journal of Community Psychology, 22,* 259–69.

Youniss, J., McLellan, J. A. and Yates, M. (1997) What we know about engendering civic identity. *American Behavioral Scientist, 40,* 620–31.

ACKNOWLEDGMENTS

The IEA Civic Education Study began Phase 1 in 1994, transitioning in 1997 into Phase 2—the test and survey reported in this volume. The scholarly contributions of the members of the International Steering Committee have been extremely important to the substantive guidance of the study during both phases. The authors of this volume want to thank Barbara Fratczak-Rudnicka, Georgia Kontogiannopoulou-Polydorides, Bruno Losito, Barbara Malak-Minkiewicz, Ingrid Munck, John Schwille, Gita Steiner-Khamsi and Lee Wing On, who served as members of the committee during Phase 2, and Ray Adams, representing the IEA Technical Advisory Group. They have brought several disciplinary perspectives, as well as viewpoints from different parts of the world. The committee prepared the study's overall design in the proposal, wrote and reviewed items for the instruments, planned and interpreted data analysis, led groups at meetings, and reviewed this volume in detail. We are grateful for their thoughtful contributions and for the spirit of innovation with which they approached the study.

The commitment and competence of the National Research Coordinators over nearly seven years has made this collaborative effort both successful and enjoyable. They have participated in every part of Phase 2, from reviewing instruments, to sampling, testing and supervising data entry, and finally reviewing analysis and this volume. Their thoughtful comments at meetings and as reviewers have enriched all participants' understanding of this subject area and its cross-national variations. The names of the National Coordinators appear later in this section, with their addresses (so that readers can request information about their national reports).

Since 1998 the major funder for the international coordination of Phase 2 (reported in this volume) has been the Deutsche Forschungsgemeinschaft (DFG or German Science Association) through a grant to the Humboldt University of Berlin to support the International Coordinating Center. During 2000 and 2001 substantial additional funding for analysis and publication is being provided by the William T. Grant Foundation through a grant to the University of Maryland at College Park (Department of Human Development).

Other funding and support in Germany came from the Bundeszentrale für Politische Bildung (Federal Agency for Civic Education), and in the United States from the National Center for Education Statistics of the United States Department of Education (for quality control and scaling) and the Carnegie Corporation of New York (for instrument preparation during the transition from Phase 1 to Phase 2). The Pew Charitable Trusts of Philadelphia funded Phase 1 of the study, which provided the background for this volume and resulted in the volume, *Civic education across countries: Twenty-four national case studies from the IEA Civic Education Project* (IEA, 1999).

The IEA Secretariat in Amsterdam provided funds and support throughout both phases of the study, and managed matching funds from the participating countries. We are especially grateful to Barbara Malak-Minkiewicz, who was the liaison between the International Steering Committee and the Secretariat. Hans Wagemaker (Executive Director), Alejandro Tiana Ferrer (Chair), Tjeerd

Plomp (former Chair) and Leendert Dijkhuizen (Financial Officer) provided important support. Ray Adams, Chair of the IEA Technical Executive Group (TEG), gave excellent technical advice, educating us as he explained both what we should do and why. Pierre Foy, a member of TEG, and Ken Ross gave helpful advice on sampling and weighting. Richard Wolf, Chair of the IEA Publications Committee, reviewed the manuscript with his usual care. Michael Martin, Eugenio Gonzalez and Ina Mullis were generous with their help based on their experience with IEA TIMSS and TIMSS-R. Paula Wagemaker provided thoughtful editing that was always responsive to authors' concerns, and Becky Bliss designed the publication with skill.

Two institutions have made enormous contributions to the study in supporting research time for authors, computer and management services, and office space. The Humboldt University of Berlin, where the International Coordinator is a faculty member, and the University of Maryland at College Park (Department of Human Development and Graduate School), where the Chair of the International Steering Committee is a faculty member, deserve special thanks.

At Humboldt, Wolfram Schulz handled the multifaceted and essential tasks of the Associate International Coordinator of the study from mid-1998, taking over this role from Donald Gray. Vera Husfeld contributed professional expertise to the scaling and the production of figures, while Roumiana Nikolova produced various materials included in this volume.

In Maryland, Jo-Ann Amadeo began as the Associate International Coordinator of the study in 1997. Her skills in synthesizing material, guiding the graduate assistants and mobilizing information for decision-making have been essential to this volume's timely completion. Jo Peng's accounting expertise has been vital. Wendy Richardson and Stephen Tonks prepared the annotated bibliographies on which the reviews of literature are based and proofread the manuscript. Wendy also prepared the reference list, with the care that requires. John Behrens and Vladimir Pavlov helped with technical issues.

Heiko Sibberns and Ursula Itzlinger of the IEA Data Processing Center (DPC) in Hamburg were invaluable in working with the national coordinators on sampling as well as in performing the many activities involved in producing the analysis upon which the scales and figures are based. Kristin Habeck also worked on the analysis. The study has benefited enormously from the impressive skills of the DPC staff.

Bruno Losito and Heinrich Mintrop capably and creatively dealt with the analysis of the teacher and school instruments, and the preparation of Chapter 9 of this volume. The tables for Chapter 9 were produced by Annamaria D'Apice at the National Institute for the Evaluation of the Education System in Frascati, Italy. Christa Händle served as an advisor for the teacher instrument design.

The primary responsibility for the analysis found in the other chapters rests with the following: Chapter 2, Judith Torney-Purta and Wolfram Schulz; Chapter 3, Rainer Lehmann and Wolfram Schulz; Chapters 4, 5 and 7, Judith Torney-Purta; Chapter 6, Hans Oswald; Chapter 8, Wolfram Schulz, Judith Torney-Purta and Rainer Lehmann.

The authors want to express special thanks to all the members of the large IEA network, many of whom we have never met but whose professionalism and competence have been essential to this study. This includes the IEA General Assembly representatives, National Research Coordinators, staff members of their organizations, those who provided funds within countries, and appointees to National Expert Panels.

We would like to thank the nearly 90,000 students and their teachers who responded to the IEA Civic Education survey in 1999. Without the cooperation of school administrators, teachers and students we would not have been privileged to have this glimpse into the civic world of 14-year-olds across five continents.

Finally, we wish to thank our families who have given substantive as well as personal support to all of us throughout the study.

Judith Torney-Purta
Rainer Lehmann
Hans Oswald
Wolfram Schulz

Addresses of National Research Coordinators

AUSTRALIA
Kerry Kennedy
University of Canberra, University Drive
Bruce ACT 2616
Email: kerryk@adminserver.canberra.edu.au

BELGIUM (FRENCH)
Annette Lafontaine and Christiane Blondin
Service de Pedagogie Experimentale
5 Bld du Rectorat
B4000 Liege (Sart-Tilman)
[http://www.ulg.ac.be/pedaexpe/SPE98.html#A3.1]
Emails: a.lafontaine@ulg.ac.be
cblondin@ulg.ac.be

BULGARIA
Roumen Nikolov
Sofia University
Faculty of Math & Informatics
Department of Information Technology
5, James Bouchier St., Sofia 1126
Sofia 1126
[http://www-it.fmi.uni-sofia.bg/~roumen/]
Email: roumen@fmi.uni-sofia.bg

CHILE

Leonor Cariola
Ministerio de Educación
UCE
Alameda Bernardo O'Higgins # 1146, Sector B, Piso 8
Santiago
[http://www.mineduc.cl]
Email: lcariola@mineduc.cl

COLOMBIA

Carlos A. Pardo and Jose Guillermo Ortiz
SNP-ICFES
Calle 17 Nr. 3-40 piso 10
Bogotá
[http://www.icfes.co]
Emails: cpardo@hemeroteca.icfes.gov.co
profab400@acuario.icfes.gov

CYPRUS

Constantinos Papanastasiou and Mary Koutselini
University of Cyprus
Department of Education
P.O. Box 20537
CY-1678 Nicosia
[http://www.ucy.ac.cy/faculty/cp/]
Emails: edpapan@ucy.ac.cy
edmaryk@ucy.ac.cy

CZECH REPUBLIC

Jana Strakova and Ivana Krizova
UIV/IIE
Senovazne nam.26
P.O. BOX c.1
11006 Praha 1
[http://www.uiv.cz/]
Emails: janastr@alfa.uiv.cz
ivana@alfa.uiv.cz

DENMARK

Lars-Henrik Schmidt
Danmarks Pædagogiske Universitet
Emdrupvej 101
DK-2400 København NV
Email: schmidt@dpu.dk

ENGLAND

David Kerr
National Foundation for Educational Research (NFER)
The Mere
Upton Park, Slough, Berkshire, SLI 2DQ
[http://www.nfer.ac.uk/risheets/iec.htm]
Email: d.Kerr@nfer.ac.uk

ESTONIA
Anu Toots
Tallin University of Educational Sciences
Department of Government
Narva mnt. 25
10120 Tallinn
[http://www.tpu.ee/]
Email: anuto@tpu.ee

FINLAND
Sakari Suutarinen
University of Jyväskylä
Institute for Education Research
P.O. Box 35, 40351
Jyväskylä
[http://www.jyu.fi/ktl/civics.htm]
Email: suutarin@piaget.edu.jyu.fi

GERMANY
Jürgen Baumert and Detlef Oesterreich
Max-Planck-Institut für Bildungsforschung
Lentzeallee 94
D-14195 Berlin
[http://www.mpib-berlin.mpg.de/EuB/program/areas/projectI-4.htm]
Emails: sekbaumert@mpib-berlin.mpg.de
        Oest@mpib-berlin.mpg.de

GREECE
Georgia Kontogiannopoulou-Polydorides
University of Athens
Department of Pre-school Education, Neo Chimio 3rd Floor
13 A Navarinou St.
Athens 10680
[http://www.cc.uoa.gr/]
Email: gpol@cc.uoa.gr

HONG KONG (SAR)
Lee Wing On
Hong Kong Institute of Education
Centre for Citizenship Education
10 Lo Ping Road, Tai Po, New Territories
[http://www.ied.edu.hk/sfe/cce/eindex.htm]
Email: WOLEE@ied.edu.hk

HUNGARY
Zsuzsa Matrai
National Institute of Public Education
Center for Evaluation Studies
Dorottya u. 8
1051 Budapest
[http://www.oki.hu/1e.htm]
Email: matraiz@mail.matav.hu

ITALY
Bruno Losito
National Center for the Evaluation of the Education System (CEDE)
Villa Falconieri
I-00044 Frascati (Roma)
[http://www.cede.it/cede/default.htm]
Email: blosito@cede.it

LATVIA
Andris Kangro
University of Latvia
Faculty of Education and Psychology
Jurmalas gatve 74/76
Riga LV-1083
[http://www.eduinf.lu.lv]
Email: kangro@eduinf.lu.lv

LITHUANIA
Irena Zaleskiene
Institute of Pedagogy
Department of Social Sciences
M. Katkaus 44
2600 Vilnius
[http://www.elnet.lt/pi/e-about.htm]
Email: zaleskiene@pi.elnet.lt

NORWAY
Rolf Mikkelsen
University of Oslo
Institute for Teacher Education and School Development
PO Box 1099 Blindern
0316 Oslo
[http://www.ils.uio.no/civic/]
Email: rolf.mikkelsen@ils.uio.no

POLAND
Adam Fraczek
University of Warsaw
Faculty of Education
Mokotowska Str.16/20
00-561 Warsaw
[http://www.iss.uw.edu.pl/]
Email: adamfra@samba.iss.uw.edu.pl

PORTUGAL
Isabel Menezes
Inst. De Inovacao Educacional
Tr. Das Terras de Sant 'Ana 15
1250 Lisboa Codex
[http://www.iie.min-edu.pt/eng/iieproj.htm]
Email: imenezes@psi.up.pt

ROMANIA

Gheorghe Bunescu
Institute for Education Sciences
Str. Stirbei Voda, nr. 37
70732 Bucharest
Email: ise@acc.usis.ro

RUSSIAN FEDERATION

Galina Kovalyova
Russian Academy of Education
Center for Evaluating the Quality of Education
Institute for General Secondary Education
Pogodinskay st. 8, rooms 201, 202, 204
119905 Moscow
Emails: gkovalev@aha.ru
         centeroko@ioso.iip.net

SLOVAK REPUBLIC

Maria Capova
SPU-National Institute for Education
Pluhova 8
SK - 830 +Bratislava
Email: spu@spu.sanet.sk

SLOVENIA

Marjan Simenc
Educational Research Institute, Pedagoski Institut
Gerbiceva 62, p.p. 76
61111 Ljubljana
Email: marjan.simenc@guest.arnes.si

SWEDEN

Sverker Hard and Kersti Blidberg
Swedish National Agency for Education
Skolverket
SE-106 20 Stockholm
[http://www.skolverket.se/]
Emails: sverker.hard@skolverket.se
         Kersti.blidberg@skolverket.se

SWITZERLAND

Fritz Oser
University of Fribourg
Department of Education
Rue Faucigny 2
CH-17+Fribourg
[http://www.unifr.ch/pedg/]
Email: Fritz.Oser@unifr.ch

UNITED STATES OF AMERICA
Carole Hahn
Emory University
Division of Educational Studies
1784 Decatur Road, Suite 240
Atlanta, GA 30322
[http://nces.ed.gov/surveys/cived/]
Email: chahn@emory.edu

Addresses of International Steering Committee Members and Consultant

(who are not also NRCs or authors; see full listing opposite the title page)

Ray Adams (*ex-officio*)
ACER – The Australian Council for Educational Research
Private Bag 55
Camberwell VIC 3124
AUSTRALIA

Barbara Fratczak-Rudnicka
DEMOSKOP
ul. Dubois 9
00-182 Warsaw
POLAND

Barbara Malak-Minkiewicz
IEA Secretariat
Herengracht 487
1017 BT Amsterdam
THE NETHERLANDS

Heinrich Mintrop (*consultant*)
Graduate School of Education and Information Sciences
3335 Moore Hall, Box 951521
UCLA
Los Angeles, CA 90095
UNITED STATES OF AMERICA

John Schwille
Michigan State University
College of Education, 518 Erickson Hall
East Lansing, MI 48824-1034
UNITED STATES OF AMERICA

Gita Steiner-Khamsi
Teachers College, Columbia University
International and Comparative Education
Box 55, 525 West 120th Street
New York, NY 10027
UNITED STATES OF AMERICA

Ingrid Munck
Statskontoret
Box 2280
SE-103 17 Stockholm
SWEDEN

Addresses of Authors

Rainer Lehmann, *International Coordinator*
Wolfram Schulz, *Associate International Coordinator*
Humboldt University of Berlin
Philosophische Fakultät IV
Abteilung Empirische Bildungsforschung
Unter den Linden 6
10099 Berlin
GERMANY
[http://www2.hu-berlin.de/empir_bf/iea_e.html]
Emails: rainer.lehmann@educat.hu-berlin.de
wolfram.schulz@rz.hu-berlin.de

Hans Oswald
Potsdam University
Institut für Pädagogik
PO Box 60 15 53
14415 Potsdam
GERMANY
Email: oswald@rz.uni-potsdam.de

Judith Torney-Purta, *International Steering Committee Chair*
Department of Human Development
College of Education
Benjamin Building 3304
University of Maryland
College Park, MD 20742
UNITED STATES OF AMERICA
[http://www.wam.umd.edu/~iea/]
Email: jt22@umail.umd.edu